THE
SECRET
ARMY

·THE·
SECRET
ARMY

DAVID J. BERCUSON

STEIN AND DAY/*Publishers*/New York

This book is dedicated to the memory of
Leonard Fitchett, Stanley Andrews, and
Dov Sugarman, and to all those who served.

First published in the United States of America in 1984
First published in Canada in 1983 by Lester & Orpen Dennys Limited
Copyright © 1983 by David J. Bercuson
All rights reserved, Stein and Day, Incorporated
Printed in the United States of America
STEIN AND DAY/*Publishers*
Scarborough House
Briarcliff Manor, N.Y. 10510

This book has been published with the help of a grant from the Social
Science Federation of Canada, using funds provided by the Social Sciences
and Humanities Research Council of Canada.

Library of Congress Cataloging in Publication Data

Bercuson, David Jay.
    The secret army.

    Bibliography: p.
    Includes index.
    1. Israel-Arab War, 1948-1949—Participation, Foreign.
2. Israel-Arab War, 1948-1949. I. Title.
DS126.9.B47   1984   956 .042   84-40238
ISBN 0-8128-2984-0

"...every one of your fighting men shall
go across armed in the van of your
kinsmen. And you shall assist them
until the Lord has given your kinsmen
a haven, such as you have."

Joshua 1.14-15

Contents

Illustrations

Israel's first Spitfire being assembled
Irvin Schindler's B-17 at Royal Canadian Air Force station in Nova
    Scotia
Lionel Drucker from Canada
Syd Cohen from South Africa
Len Fritchett from Canada
False identity card of volunteer Murray Cappell
Cappell in Seventh Brigade armored car
Pilots of 101 Fighter Squadron
The *Altalena* beached and gutted off Tel Aviv
The first homemade Spitfire
Czech supplied Avia S-199
Harvards used as dive bombers by 35 Squadron
Norseman aircraft
101 Squadron Spitfires readied for takeoff
Bill Katz of the U.S., commander of 69 Squadron, with squadron
    personnel, in front of a B-17
Palmach troops ready to climb aboard a C-46 during Operation Dust

Acknowledgments

This book could not have been completed without the generous help and co-operation of many people and institutions. My principal research assistant in Canada was Susan Kooyman, a diligent worker who needed little guidance and produced excellent results. I also drew upon the services of Suzette Lewin and Monique Gywnn. Doreen Nordquist typed the transcripts of my interviews, while Norma Milton typed the manuscript and gave me valuable advice on style, continuity, and organization. In London I received help from Lieutenant Commander Charles McDermott Stuart, a former Royal Navy officer now doing contract research. He saved me many hours of work at the Public Records Office at Kew. In Israel, Jacob Markovitzky was both research assistant and translator and turned up many key documents I might not have been aware of otherwise. Janet Hamilton's thoughtful critique of an earlier version of this work helped me to make this a better and more readable book.

I am grateful to the staffs at the Public Archives of Canada (particularly Lawrence Tapper and Barbara Wilson), the Canada Department of External Affairs, Historical Division (where Ann Trowel Hillmer gave much assistance), the Canadian Jewish Congress Archives in Montreal (especially David Rome), the Jewish Historical Society of Western Canada, and the Ottawa Jewish Historical Society. In the United States I was well served by the excellent and knowledgeable staff at the National Archives in both the Military and Diplomatic Archives branches, the staffs at the Harry S. Truman Library, the United Nations Archives, and the Jewish Agency Archives and Library. In Israel I was given much needed guidance and assistance by Haim Sarid, archivist of the Israel Defence Forces Archives, and by Micha

Kaufman. Dr. Michael Heymann, archivist of the Central Zionist Archives, helped me greatly, as did the staff of the Israel State Archives in the Prime Minister's office, Jerusalem.

A great many people contributed suggestions, information, advice, names, guidance, and support that helped ease the monumental research job. I am grateful to the following: in Israel—David Eschel, Elly Eyal, Arye Hashavia, Gershon Rivlin, Elkanan Oren, Shula Harris, Arthur Goldberg, Lieutenant Colonel Yossi Aboudi, Eddy Kaplansky, Yosef Bodinsky; in Canada—Harold Kates, Shel Silverman, Elly Silverman, Ben Ocopnik, Shirley Berman, Brereton Greenhous, Brian Nolan, Joseph N. Frank, Jack Macleod, Peter Gold, Jack Hurtig, Ayala Zacks-Abramov, Dr. George Liban; in the United States—Syd Rabinovitch, Harry Eisner, Murray Rubenstein, Henry Katzew; in South Africa—Marcus Arkin and the South African Zionist Federation; in Italy—Luca Codignola. It would take a book to list all the ways these people generously shared their time. I hope each of them knows how grateful I am. I am certain each will see a small part of his or her handiwork in this volume.

I am indebted to colleagues who encouraged me to undertake this work. This includes several good friends—Robert Bothwell, Michael Bliss, Craig Brown, Irving Abella, and Jack Granatstein. Bob and Jack also read most of the manuscript in an earlier draft. My research over three years was generously supported by the University of Calgary, the Social Sciences and Humanities Research Council of Canada, and the Killam Resident Fellowship program at the University of Calgary. I could not have completed the project without this support. I am grateful to the veterans and other participants in the events retold here who gave generously of their time for interviews—I would have liked to include a small piece of every story in the book. I also received the help and co-operation of the American Veterans of Israel and the Israel Defence Forces.

Cheryl, Michael, and Sharon uprooted themselves from home and hearth to follow my wanderings half way around the globe in pursuit of a wild dream, and for this I am deeply grateful.

Despite all the help and co-operation I received, the final product is my responsibility and I alone am to blame for mistakes and omissions.

David Jay Bercuson

Preface

This is a history of the Arab-Israeli war of 1948—the Israeli War of
Independence. It is different from other books on that war, however,
because it is the story of the *mahal*—the more than 5000 foreign
volunteers who served with the Israeli forces—and of Israel's efforts to
obtain the modern military equipment necessary to win the war and
establish itself as a newly independent country. The 1948 war is the key
event in the history of the Arab-Israeli conflict because Israel was born
out of its victory in that war, and the face of the Middle East was
unalterably changed by that birth. All the elements of the Arab-Zionist
conflict from the late 1880s to 1948 can be found in the causes of that
war and all the roots of the current political and military troubles in
that area can be traced to the war's results. If Israel had lost that war,
the new state would have died a quick death.

Much has already been written about the 1948 war, but a key part of
the story—the roles played by foreign volunteers in the fighting and by
many Jews outside Palestine in providing much-needed military supplies—has been all but ignored, even in Israel. It is, however, necessary
to understand this factor in order to comprehend more fully why and
how Israel won, and what that victory represented. It is often alleged
today, for example, that Israel was created by the United Nations, by
the Great Powers, by "world imperialism". The allegation is based on
the assumption that Israeli independence was established with the
active diplomatic and military support of Great Britain and the United
States, and was backed up by the United Nations, which resolved, in
November 1947, to partition Palestine into two independent states,
one Jewish and the other Arab. It is claimed by some observers that
Israel was created by this resolution and thrust into the middle of the

Arab world, which totally rejected it. That rejection was, and is, real enough, but the concurrent notion that Israel was established by the United Nations and sustained during the 1947-49 war by the Great Powers is totally false. It was the Jewish people themselves, as represented by the Zionist movement, who created the foundations of the Jewish state in Palestine. It was also the Jews themselves, with the limited help of four or five small countries, who won the war. If the time comes when that is more fully grasped by Israel's enemies and allies alike, Israel will no longer be thought of as a mere "client", as a front for something else, and will be viewed as a nation in its own right, created and sustained by its own people for their own purposes.

The roots of modern Israel were planted by the Zionist pioneers who began to settle in Palestine, then part of the Ottoman Empire, in the 1880s. These pioneers were neither sent nor brought to Palestine by any country to serve its own national interest; they went to help build the foundations of a modern Jewish homeland and to lead the Jews of the world back to normalcy and national sovereignty. In 1917, the British, acting in their own interest as a major combatant in World War I, issued the Balfour Declaration, which promised support for "the establishment in Palestine of a national home for the Jewish people" and pledged "to facilitate the achievement of this object". In the thirty years that followed, Britain brought modern laws and government to Palestine and helped establish the infrastructure upon which a "national home" could be based. The British built roads, laid railway lines, and created a modern telegraph, telephone, and postal system. At times, British troops also defended Jewish settlements against Arab attack, especially during the Arab revolt of 1936-39. But Britain did not bring a single Jew to Palestine; did not buy a single square centimetre of land for Jewish settlement; did not establish Jewish towns, villages, or farms; and did not underwrite the creation, within the Jewish community, of a network of educational and social services. All this was done by the Jews of Palestine, aided by Jews in the Diaspora, out of a conviction that they needed a homeland of their own in Palestine, and that Jews alone were responsible for building and settling it.

This same Jewish self-reliance was largely responsible for the Israeli victory in the War of Independence. The U.N. partition resolution of November 1947 prompted Britain to decide upon a quick exit from Palestine and gave the Jewish community there, the Yishuv, its opportunity to declare the independence of Israel as of May 15, 1948. But the United Nations sent not one soldier, provided not a single gun, and imposed no sanctions to deter the Arab League countries from launching an invasion of Israel in the first moments of its nationhood. In the face of implacable Arab hostility, the U.N. partition resolution was worth nothing more than the paper it was written on if it was not backed up by armed force, and this support the United Nations was unwilling to provide. The U.N. resolution, therefore, did not create Israel; the Israeli armed forces created Israel, by backing the U.N. resolution with military power and winning a victory.

When Palestine began to slide towards war in 1945, the Yishuv already had a well-organized underground fighting force, the Haganah, with a command system, an officer corps, some light arms, a training program, and a mobile field force. However, it was used almost exclusively as a covert defence force to protect Jewish settlements and to organize and carry out the illegal immigration program that brought thousands of Jewish refugees to Palestine in defiance of British law. Most Haganah officers had never served in a regular army and had no experience commanding large groups of soldiers in conventional warfare. Few Haganah personnel had any training in the use or maintenance of heavy equipment, planes, tanks, armoured cars, artillery, and mortars; and few knew how to operate an effective surveillance and communications network. There was no air force to speak of. There were no planes and few pilots. Although more than 30,000 Palestine Jews had served in the British army during World War II, the British were very careful to keep the vast majority out of combat units and deny them specialized training. For the most part, Jewish soldiers drove trucks, operated supply depots, and directed traffic because the British suspected that one day the same Jewish troops might be fighting the British army. The Haganah was good at what it did. It may have been one of the best underground forces in the world in 1945; but it was not able to meet the threat of full-scale invasion by conventional armies supported by air power and naval units. Many leaders of the Yishuv realized that the struggle to establish a Jewish state would likely result in a war between the small Jewish community of Palestine and the surrounding Arab countries. They soon saw that the Haganah had to be quickly transformed into a conventional army with the arms and expertise necessary to match Arab fire power and to defeat a potential invasion. To accomplish this, they turned for help to the Jews of the

Diaspora, who became Israel's most important allies in the War of Independence.

In its struggle for survival, Israel did have both active and passive support from some foreign countries. Czechoslovakia, with the quiet approval of the Soviet Union, supplied Israel with vital arms and equipment; but all transactions were carried out on a cash-and-carry basis. France, Italy, Holland, Panama, and Yugoslavia looked the other way when their soil was used for transshipment of supplies or the dispatch of volunteers. But Israel's most important allies were Jews from abroad who, along with a handful of non-Jews, provided much of the military expertise and a large part of the arms needed for victory. Hundreds of thousands of Jews had served in the armed services of the Allied countries during World War II at every level of command and in all capacities. They had learned the skills needed for modern warfare. They provided an obvious force to operate—and to train Israelis in the operation of—the major weapons of war that would enable the Haganah to defeat a much better equipped Arab invasion force. The weapons, however, were not available to the Israelis at the start of the war. Britain had done its best during the last months of the British Mandate in Palestine to ensure that the Jews had as little weaponry as possible; and there was no place in Palestine to hide such equipment. The Israelis were hard-pressed to stockpile even all the light weapons they required. When war broke out British and U.S. policy hindered Israeli efforts to acquire modern weapons to match Arab arms. Both countries refused to sell any military equipment to Israel, despite its material disadvantages compared to the Arab League countries, and despite continuing British delivery of military equipment to Egypt, Iraq, and Jordan, until two weeks *after* the Arab invasion of Israel had started. Not only was there no help, there was no even-handedness.

Almost everything Israel needed had to be collected abroad and brought into the country. To do this the Israelis turned to Jews in the Diaspora to give millions of dollars, send thousands of tons of medical supplies, clothing, and other non-military equipment, and smuggle the necessary weapons. They also recruited veterans, who volunteered by the thousands, to serve with the Israeli forces. The arms smuggled to Israel supplemented those sold to them by the Czechs. Transport planes brought thousands of tons of supplies and equipment—including guns and disassembled fighter planes—to Israel from Czechoslovakia and other points in Europe, America, and South Africa. These planes were used to distribute weapons, food, and medical supplies to beleaguered Jewish settlements in the first weeks of the Arab invasion. The volunteers flew the planes, manned the tanks and armoured cars, fired the artillery, operated the radios and radar, and kept the equipment—much of it old and already worn out—in good operating order. They taught the Israelis much about organizing a conventional army, establishing army medical facilities, and employing heavy weapons.

Until now no book has presented the whole story of the volunteers: how and why they were recruited, why they volunteered, their contribution to the Israeli victory, and their eventual fate. And no book has told the whole story of the gathering of arms for the Israeli war effort, though there have been other books which have covered parts of this story. Benjamin Kagan's *The Secret Battle for Israel*, for example, concentrated mainly on the Israeli Air Force from Kagan's own viewpoint as a participant in the war. Kagan was, at the time, the Israeli Air Force representative in Prague, Czechoslovakia, which was the chief supply source of Israeli fighter planes and other weapons during the war. Leonard Slater's *The Pledge* concentrated on Israeli arms-gathering in the United States and on the role American Jews played in helping to acquire military equipment and smuggle it out of the country in defiance of a government arms embargo. Slater's detective work—he depended mainly on personal interviews—was impressive, but he wrote little of the arms-gathering in other countries and almost nothing about foreign volunteers (Americans and others) in combat. Other books and articles have contained something of the *mahal* story, but most have been either fictionalized accounts or personal memoirs, like Benjamin Dunkelman's *Dual Allegiance*.

It was not previously possible to verify details of how a worldwide recruiting network was established by the Israelis in a few short months in early 1948, of how volunteers were recruited, often in defiance of local laws banning foreign enlistment, and of the important role those volunteers played in the War of Independence. Now many of those records are open. *The Secret Army* is based primarily on extensive research in government and military archives in Israel, the United States, Great Britain, and Canada. I also interviewed a great many volunteer veterans of this war and each interview added something to my knowledge of what was happening and gave me additional "feel" for the subject. Most will not find their names here, however, though all interviews have been listed in my bibliography.

The Israelis, for the most part, did not keep units of volunteers together as the Spanish Republicans did in the Spanish Civil War. Instead, they deliberately scattered them throughout the Israeli forces and deployed them where they were most needed, usually within Israeli units and alongside Israeli troops. In recruiting volunteers from abroad, the Israelis were not looking for more bodies; they had plenty of those. They sought experts—pilots, radar and radio operators and technicians, airframe mechanics, tank drivers, mortar and artillery men, and others—to create a modern army out of the Haganah.

There were concentrations of volunteers in the air force, which was, for all intents and purposes, an all-volunteer force. Such units as the Seventh Brigade and the tank companies of the Eighth Brigade also had a heavy volunteer component. It is doubtful, however, if these units accounted for even half of the total number of volunteers in the Israeli forces. Many volunteers served alone in all-Israeli units, and a large number preferred this, as it enabled them to learn more about Israel, the Israeli people, and the Hebrew language. It was, therefore, an impossible job to try to write the story of every volunteer in every unit, or to follow individual volunteers from their countries of origin as they made their way to Israel. I judged it better to concentrate on the units that had large numbers of volunteers, pointing out their important contributions to the war effort, and to cover the rest by way of illustration and example.

Throughout this book I have concentrated almost exclusively on the activities of the Haganah in the collection and shipment of clandestine arms and the raising of foreign volunteers. The military arm of Revisionist Zionism—the Irgun—engaged in the same practices. The most spectacular result of its activities was the tragedy of the *Altalena*, which is recounted here. I have, for the most part, ignored the Revisionists, however, because I believe their efforts to gather arms and recruit foreign volunteers were much more restricted in scope than those of the Haganah and much less important to the outcome of the war. A recent volume, *Terror Out of Zion: The Shock Troops of Israeli Independence* by J. Bowyer Bell provides good coverage of the Revisionist and Irgun activities.

No one can claim, and I certainly do not, that Israel defeated the Arabs in the 1948 war without any help at all from other countries. It is clear that some help was given. But the time has surely arrived when all who purport to try to understand the Middle East conflict must finally realize that Israel was not created by other countries to compensate the Jews for the Holocaust, that it was not established by the Great Powers as a "tool" of western imperialism, and that it was not guided, guarded, or protected during its most difficult birth by the United Nations. When the Arab League armies invaded Israel in the early hours of May 15, 1948, Israel stood alone, aided primarily by those Diaspora Jews who were determined to do all in their power to ensure its birth and survival. If this book can help people to grasp that very basic fact, it will have contributed a great deal both to Israel's knowledge of itself and to a more general understanding of the Arab-Israeli conflict by Israel's friends and enemies alike.

1

"We Shall Drink Jewish Blood"

The ancient stones of the holy city of Jerusalem rang to the cries of street hawkers and pedlars in the Arab market. Children played in the narrow streets under the bright sun of a glorious spring day in Palestine. It was April 4, 1920. As Jews prepared for the Passover festival due to begin the next day and Christians began to gather for the Easter pilgrimage, Moslems poured into the city for the celebration of the Feast of the Prophet Moses. The Moslem religious authorities had requested and received permission from the British military government to hold a parade through the streets of the ancient walled city. As a British military band led the procession, the Military Governor watched with interest from a balcony. The parade ended at the golden dome of the Mosque of Omar on the temple mount. There an Arab nationalist leader gave a violent harangue against the Jews. Suddenly a mob, wielding knives and screaming "we shall drink Jewish blood", broke from the crowd and ran through the streets to the Jewish quarter where it swept down on startled and unsuspecting Jews. Within minutes Jewish dead and wounded lay in the streets, and Jewish homes and shops were looted and set ablaze. Three days of rioting had begun.

Members of a small Jewish self-defence group that had suspected trouble had posted themselves around and outside the old city walls, some on rooftops where they could see into the Jewish quarter. When they saw the riot break out, they tried to get into the city, but were stopped by British troops. The British sealed off the entrances to the city, arrested the group and their leader, Vladimir "Zeev" Jabotinsky, and charged them, under the old Ottoman penal code, with banditry, inciting the people to "mutual hatred", pillage, rape, devastation, and

1

murder. Finally, when the Arab mob had been running out of control for most of three days, the government sent the army into the Jewish quarter and declared martial law. Jabotinsky and his followers were tried by a British military court and sentenced to long prison terms.[1]

The blood was soon washed from the cobblestone streets of Jerusalem, but the massacre was not as easily wiped from the memory of the Yishuv. Arabs had attacked Jews before in Palestine, but those incidents were almost certainly perpetrated by bandits with little thought of politics, nationalism, or even religion. Weak victims had always invited attack in the chaos that had been Ottoman Palestine. However, the Jerusalem massacre of April 1920 was different because it was religiously and politically motivated. The riot reflected a growing Arab desire to rid Palestine of Jews. Arabs had been angered by the promises made to the Zionists by the British in the Balfour Declaration of 1917, fearing the promises would deny Arabs eventual statehood. The attack also showed that the British, whatever their promises to the Zionists, could not be counted upon to protect Jewish lives.

I

The Arab hate that exploded into murderous fury in Jerusalem in 1920 was directed at Zionism, an ideology that had as its central idea the re-creation of a Jewish homeland in Palestine two thousand years after the last Jewish state had been destroyed by the Roman Empire. It was clear almost from the start that this re-creation would be done against the wishes of the vast majority of the inhabitants of Palestine—the Arabs.

Modern political Zionism, as distinct from the centuries-old religious yearnings of Jews for a return to the promised land led by God's Messiah, developed in the 1880s and 1890s. It had its roots in small, idealistic movements, based primarily in Russia, under the messiah-like leadership of Theodor Herzl. Herzl, an assimilated Hungarian-born Jew, was Paris correspondent for a Vienna paper. He had long pondered the solution to the "Jewish question" and had once thought the only answer to be mass conversion of all the world's Jews, except for a token handful, in a solemn ceremony at the Vatican.

Herzl was living in Paris during the treason trial of French army captain Alfred Dreyfus. Dreyfus, a Jew, was accused of passing military secrets to Germany and was tried, sentenced, and imprisoned on Devil's Island in 1894. Though he was later exonerated, his trial sparked anti-semitic outrages in France. Herzl became convinced that Jews needed their own state in their ancient homeland if they were to escape the mounting ravages of anti-semitism. In 1897 he organized the first Zionist Congress at Basle, Switzerland. Delegates came from most of the world's Jewish communities and adopted Herzl's vision as their political aim.

Herzl spent the last years of his life—he died in 1904—trying to negotiate with the Turks, the Germans, and the British to gain support for the re-establishment of a Jewish state. The Turks ruled Palestine as part of the Ottoman Empire. Twice, in 1896 and 1901, Herzl made the long, arduous journey to Constantinople to woo Sultan Abdul Hamid II. Herzl promised Jewish financial aid to retire the massive Turkish debt in return for a charter for Jewish settlement in Palestine.[2] He failed to gain such a charter, but small groups of Zionist pioneers, mainly from Russia, took up Herzl's vision and began to trickle into Palestine. They joined a small and ancient community of religious Jews who lived mainly inside the walls of Jerusalem, and a newer group of Jewish farmers who had settled, in the 1880s, on lands belonging to the French baron Edmond James de Rothschild.

By the outbreak of World War I, 85,000 Jews lived in Palestine. They suffered intense hardships during the war and were terrorized by the Turkish authorities; thousands were starved or exiled. When the war ended in 1918 fewer than 55,000 were left compared to about 600,000 Arabs.

Ironically, however, World War I brought a boost to Zionism when, in November 1917, the British cabinet swung its full weight behind the Zionist movement with the Balfour Declaration. This was part of a letter written by British Foreign Secretary Arthur Balfour to Lord Rothschild in which Balfour declared that British policy aimed at "the establishment in Palestine of a national home for the Jewish people". This support was given with the qualification that nothing would be done to "prejudice the civil and religious rights of existing non-Jewish communities in Palestine, or the rights and political status enjoyed by Jews in any other country".[3]

The declaration was timely because British forces, led by General Allenby, were at that very moment beginning their conquest of Palestine from the Turks. In fact, the Balfour Declaration prompted the raising of a Jewish Legion, recruited from Jews in Palestine and western countries, to fight under Allenby's command in the liberation of Palestine. In future years there would be much disagreement over the exact meaning of the declaration, but there was no doubt it was a tremendous stimulus to Zionist efforts.

The Balfour Declaration resulted from a complex mix of motives inside the British cabinet. British Prime Minister David Lloyd George, and Balfour were personally sympathetic to Zionism. Lloyd George was also influenced by his own religious background, the support of South African Defence Minister Jan Christiaan Smuts, and a growing friendship with Dr. Chaim Weizmann, who had contributed significantly to the war effort through his work on explosives. (Weizmann, a Russian-born chemist and ardent Zionist, ironically held no executive position in the Zionist movement at the time. He was first elected president of the World Zionist Organization in 1920, and first president of the State of Israel in 1948.) The cabinet's main motive, however, was undoubtedly a desire to attract world-wide Jewish support in the war against the Central Powers. This desire was the result of an overestimation of Jewry's political importance in other countries, particularly the United States.

The Balfour Declaration appeared to the Arabs to run directly counter to British promises made to them in the fall of 1915 in a series of letters between the Sharif Husain of Mecca and Sir Henry McMahon, British High Commissioner in Egypt.[4] McMahon, acting for the British government, had tried to persuade Husain to lead his Arab followers in a revolt against the Turks. Husain had been willing as long as Britain guaranteed independence to the Arabs after the Turks had been defeated. Husain had been influenced by Arab nationalists, whose roots stretched back to the 1860s, and who proclaimed Arab unity, demanded Arab independence, and pledged themselves to the maintenance of Arabic culture. Husain was willing to risk all in a revolt, if that revolt would achieve Arab independence. He sought British guarantees and they were given.

"Great Britain is prepared to recognize and uphold the independence of the Arabs in all the regions lying within the frontiers proposed by the Sharif of Mecca," McMahon's October 24, 1915, letter to Husain promised. McMahon excluded certain areas from his pledge: "The districts of Mersin and Alexandretta, and portions of Syria lying to the west of the Districts of Damascus, Homs, Hama and Aleppo" were not "purely Arab" and were therefore "excepted from the proposed delineation".[5] Did McMahon thereby specifically exclude Palestine from the area promised to Husain? It is unlikely, because he was undoubtedly referring to the Lebanon and those other areas lying to the west of Syria that were inhabited by large numbers of Christians. In 1916 this territory was allotted to the French in a secret agreement between Britain and France (the Sykes-Picot Agreement). This agreement virtually divided up the Turkish Empire into colonial possessions, which were to be either directly controlled by the two powers, or at least under their influence after the war. This too was a violation of the McMahon promises.

After World War I Britain was given responsibility for governing Palestine as a mandated territory of the League of Nations. Britain was charged by the League with responsibility for creating the national home for the Jewish people promised by Balfour in 1917, but it was not an easy task. Britain was caught between, on the one hand, the rising ambitions and expectations of the Zionists, who claimed Palestine as theirs by historical right and British promise, and, on the other, the Arabs of Palestine and Syria, who claimed Palestine by right of possession and another British promise. Two rival peoples; two rival nationalisms.

Chaim Weizmann and the Emir Faisal, Husain's son, tried to work out a compromise in 1919, but the effort was stillborn[6] because each demanded concessions the other was unwilling to give. It is doubtful, however, if Faisal represented the mainstream of Arab nationalism; most Arab leaders saw the Zionists as an illegitimate group, representing yet another effort of British and French imperialism to keep the Arabs in a colonial status. The Syrian General Congress, meeting in Damascus in July 1919, proclaimed:

> We reject the claims of the Zionists for the establishment of a Jewish commonwealth in that part of southern Syria which is known as Palestine and we are opposed to Jewish immigration into any part of the country. We do not acknowledge that they have a title, and we regard their claims as a grave menace to our national, political and economic life.[7]

This conviction was deeply rooted. Moreover, the Palestine Arabs believed that they alone of all Arabs would be denied national independence because of the promises to the Zionists contained in the Balfour Declaration. Given these two factors, the outbreak of politically and religiously inspired violence in April 1920 was a foregone conclusion.

5

There had been sporadic efforts to organize Jewish self-defence groups in Palestine before 1920, but the Arab attack spurred the leaders of the Yishuv to think more seriously about defence. They created an underground organization known as the Haganah, the Hebrew word for defence. However, when peace appeared to settle over Palestine once again in the early 1920s under a benign and efficient British Mandatory administration, little effort was put into preparing the Haganah for action. For the most part it existed only on paper, with few weapons and almost no skilled leadership. In 1929, when Arab violence again exploded in Jerusalem, Hebron, and other communities across Palestine, the Jews were ill-prepared to defend themselves and 133 were killed by Arab rioters. It was not until the outbreak of full-scale revolt by the Arabs of Palestine in 1936 that leaders of the Yishuv began to build the Haganah into a real fighting force.

The Arab revolt of 1936, led by the Mufti of Jerusalem, Haj Amin el Husseini, aimed to rid Palestine both of Jews and of the British and to establish an independent Arab state in place of the Mandate. In the 1930s, Arab nationalists grew increasingly angry as they watched the Jewish population swell with the arrival of German Jews fleeing the Nazi terror. Husseini appointed Fauzi al-Kaukji, an Iraqi officer trained by the Turks, as supreme commander of the Arab forces. The fighting was most intense in 1936, but raged sporadically until 1939, with the brunt borne by the British. The Arabs controlled most of the road network and isolated many Jewish settlements and British positions, but the British increased their forces in Palestine to about 30,000 troops and eventually secured the roads to major towns and villages of the country.[8]

The revolt ended in 1939 when Britain caved in to Arab pressure and issued a White Paper that severely restricted Jewish immigration to, and land ownership in, Palestine. British commitment to the Balfour Declaration was clearly abandoned; and British responsibility to the League of Nations to establish a Jewish national home was abrogated. The British rejected this interpretation, however. They claimed that a national home had already been established, since more than 300,000 Jews were living in Palestine, and that they had thereby carried out their pledge. The White Paper came after a cold, hard appraisal of British Middle East policy in light of the looming conflict with Nazi Germany. British policymakers like Colonial Secretary Malcolm Mac-

Donald, once a strong backer of Zionism, concluded that Arab support should be sought at the expense of earlier commitments to the Zionists: Jewish support was simply not in doubt.[9] The Yishuv was outraged by the White Paper. They viewed it as a callous surrender to the Mufti and feared that the new policy meant Yishuv growth would soon end and that the Jews would be a permanent minority in Palestine. Worse, the White Paper barred the gates of Palestine to thousands of European Jewish refugees trying to flee Nazi persecution.

III

The Arab revolt of 1936 brought a virtual rebirth of the Haganah. Traditional Haganah doctrine was based on a policy of restraint: the Haganah's task was purely defence of Jewish settlements and no reprisals or offensive operations were carried out. "Innocents" were to be spared at all costs.[10] After 1936, two men changed this policy. Yitzhak Sadeh was a former Soviet Army officer who led the Jewish Settlement Police, a force authorized by the British and charged with the defence of Jewish settlements during the Arab revolt. Sadeh rejected the concept of restraint, trained the Jewish Settlement Police to be more offensively minded, and led his force in ambushing Arab bands close to their own villages. In 1938 his doctrines were reinforced by the arrival, in Palestine, of an extraordinary man—Captain Orde Wingate, a British army officer schooled in the Bible and with a strong emotional attachment to the Jewish people and Zionism. He was somewhat eccentric and Jews avoided him at first, but he managed to convince mistrustful Jewish leaders that he was interested in their cause. With the approval of his superiors—the British needed all the help they could get in putting down the Arab revolt—Wingate formed the Special Night Squads, most of whose members were also members of the Haganah. Their purpose was to launch raids and set ambushes under cover of darkness. The Haganah men not only received training in night action but were also taught how to handle small groups of men in the field.[11] Wingate's ideas, combined with those of Sadeh, left an indelible mark on Jewish military tactics in Palestine. When the Arab revolt ended in 1939 Wingate was tranferred out of Palestine because his superiors were uneasy about his close relationship to the Jewish community. Wingate later led the "Chindits" in Burma during World War II and was promoted to Major General before being killed in action.

In 1940 the Haganah was reorganized and placed on a more permanent footing, although it was still an underground army. Sadeh was put in command of a small, permanent field force and a general staff, and general staff headquarters were set up. Yaacov Dori was appointed Chief of Staff and a number of paid staff officers were placed under him. The new field formations were to be co-ordinated by a central command. They were kept distinct from the home guard units, which were composed of older men and women and charged with the defence of towns and settlements.[12]

Palestine Jews participated in World War II in large numbers. Even before British Prime Minister Winston Churchill ordered establishment of a distinct Jewish Brigade in November 1944, thousands of Palestine Jews had flocked to the British forces. By the war's end 32,000 men and women had served. Though still technically illegal, the Haganah worked with the British to prepare for a possible German invasion of Palestine. Haganah members fought against Vichy forces in Syria and prepared for a possible last-ditch stand in Judea and Samaria, in the event that British defences in Egypt collapsed. (Judea and Samaria are the ancient names, in continuous use since Roman times, for the mountainous regions of central Palestine. Judea lies to the west of the Dead Sea; Samaria is north of Jerusalem.)

The British worked with the Palestine Jews—they had little choice—but they did not fully trust them and were reluctant to establish a separate Jewish fighting unit. Some Jews received training in communications, artillery, and commando units, and there were a handful in the air force; but most served as support troops, driving trucks or motorcycles.[13] Very few were trained as air crew, in tank fighting, artillery, or mortars, or in the hundreds of specialized jobs that were so much a part of modern warfare. Few rose to high command positions that gave experience in handling large numbers of troops in combat operations. The skills that were learned were invaluable to the Haganah; but the Haganah remained an underground army primarily trained for night commando operations.

This characteristic was strengthened in 1941 with the establishment by the Haganah of an elite commando group known as the Palmach. Sadeh was appointed first commander and brought his doctrine of quick offensive strikes to the job. The Palmach was composed of young men and women trained in commando tactics, especially for night attacks. They travelled extensively around Palestine familiarizing themselves with every important geographical feature and acquainting themselves with key towns and villages. There was little discipline in the Palmach, which was egalitarian and socialist in political doctrine. The style was loose and free-wheeling; but this allowed individual initiative and courage to come to the fore.[14]

For most of World War II an informal truce existed between the Haganah and the British. It was a marriage of necessity only, because British restrictions on Jewish immigration continued and untold thousands of European Jews, who might have found refuge in Palestine, were condemned to death in Nazi death camps. The Yishuv and the Jewish Agency (the political body responsible for negotiating the Zionist position in Palestine) supported Britain, but were determined to destroy the 1939 White Paper. As the war dragged on and prospects of Nazi triumph diminished, restiveness increased in the Yishuv. The first shots in the war between the British and the Yishuv were fired in 1944, not by the Haganah, but by the Irgun and the Lehi.

The Irgun was established in 1931 by Vladimir Jabotinsky, whose earlier disagreement with the socialist orientation of the Jewish Agency had led him to found the Revisionist movement in 1924. The military arm of Revisionism was named Irgun Zvai Leumi in Hebrew—or National Military Organization. The Irgun, like the Haganah, languished during the thirties but grew stronger in arms and members after 1940 when leadership passed to Menachem Begin. The Irgun opposed Jewish Agency and Haganah policies during the war, and at one point the Haganah actually helped the British hunt down Irgun leaders. Irgun tactics were hit-and-run; Irgun specialties were the bomb and the revolver. Members received almost no formal military training. It was not unlike the Irish Republican Army. The Lehi, or Stern Gang, named after founder Avraham Yair Stern, was an extremist breakaway group from the Irgun. Assassination was its chief tactic. Both the Irgun and the Lehi launched attacks on the British military in 1944. The Lehi assassinated Lord Moyne, the British Minister Resident in Cairo, in November 1944. Moyne's killing brought little benefit to the Zionist cause because Churchill, a close personal friend of Moyne, was sickened by his death and lost considerable sympathy for Zionism.[15]

IV

By the end of World War II the Haganah had developed a sophisticated structure with branches that reached into Europe and North America. In fact, it reflected the increasingly sophisticated and broadly based nature of the people it was founded to protect and from which it drew its strength. From a community of about 55,000 at the end of World War I the Yishuv had grown to more than half a million by 1945. Jewish agricultural settlements, the collectivist *kibbutzim* and the co-operative *moshavim*, had been established as far north as the upper Galilee, in the finger of Palestine between Syria and Lebanon, and as far south as the northern Negev. The largest concentration of Jewish population lived in the city of Tel Aviv, established in 1909 in the sand dunes by the sea to the north of Jaffa. There were other large Jewish communities in Jerusalem, Haifa, Tiberias, and Safed. Many of Palestine's Jews were industrial workers labouring in small industries first founded in the 1920s or set up by German refugees in the 1930s. Only about 6 per cent were farmers.

There was a thriving cultural life, with a symphony orchestra and a large variety of newspapers and periodicals and theatres. Political life literally bubbled, with parties of the left, centre, and right vying for the allegiance of a highly politically conscious electorate. There was an active trade-union movement based upon the Histadrut—the central labour federation. And there were a number of health-insurance funds, sports clubs, financial institutions, and both a religious and a secular Hebrew school system funded by taxes levied on the Jewish community. There was even an unofficial governmental structure which operated within the over-all limits of the British Mandate. This consisted of a national council or Vaad Leumi, elected by universal suffrage, and the Jewish Agency Executive, led by David Ben Gurion. The latter functioned as an unofficial cabinet representing the people of the Yishuv and the World Zionist Organization, which itself was led, during most of this period, by Chaim Weizmann. Weizmann was unable to visit the Yishuv during the war; but when he travelled to Palestine in 1945 he was overwhelmed by the growth and development that had taken place there during his absence. He later recorded his feelings:

> ...the great war effort had given the Jews of Palestine a heightened self-reliance, a justified sense of merit and achievement...and a high degree of technical development....The National Home was in fact here—unrecognized, and by that lack of recognition frustrated in the fulfillment of its task.[16]

Few Jews had taken any interest in Zionism when it first developed as a political movement in the 1880s. The very idea of a national Jewish revival seemed at best mad, at worst likely to provoke anti-semitic reaction. In the turmoil that was eastern-European Jewish life in the last decades of the nineteenth century and the years leading up to World War I, Zionists vied with Jewish socialists, assimilationists, and the religiously orthodox for the allegiance of the Jewish masses. The Zionists usually came out a poor second. In western Europe, Britain, and the United States, the established Jewish communities feared that Zionists would provoke Christian majorities to stop and even reverse the tentative acceptance granted Jews over time since the French Revolution. Even in the 1920s and 1930s, after the promises of the Balfour Declaration, the establishment of the Yishuv, and the dramatic revelation of Hitler's persecution of the Jews, Zionism in the Diaspora grew only slowly. Although many Jewish homes contained the little blue box of the Jewish National Fund, used to collect pennies for the purchase of land in Palestine, few Jews were active in the Zionist movement and fewer still thought of their destiny as linked in any way with the Jews of Palestine. World War II and the Holocaust were to change all that.

Six million European Jews were murdered during the war. They were killed by Nazis who believed that Jews were *untermenschen*— subhuman—a vermin that scourged the human race and had to be eradicated. This policy was an extension of the racial anti-semitism espoused in some French and German circles since the late nineteenth century. By the outbreak of World War II, this anti-semitism had worked its way into the politics of several European countries. The genocide practised by the Nazis against the Jews was new, however, in its total ruthlessness; the Nazis aimed to exterminate the Jews and to destroy all traces of their existence. When World War II ended, only a remnant of east-European Jewry had survived and the Polish Jews—the heart and soul of east-European Jewry—had been practically wiped out.

News of the murder of European Jewry had been leaking out of Hitler's Europe from mid-1941. By 1943 there was no doubt in Allied capitals that the Nazis were engaged in the systematic, deliberate killing of all Jews under their control. Despite this knowledge nothing was done to save those destined for the gas chambers whether by bombing the rail lines to Auschwitz, threatening the Germans with retaliation, or attempting to ransom those Jews who were still alive. There was also little effort to admit Jewish refugees living in neutral countries or countries allied with Germany to Great Britain, the United States, Canada, or other western countries. Moreover, the British, ever worried about inflaming Arab opinion, continued to bar the gates to Palestine. Although Jewish and Zionist leaders in Palestine and elsewhere also became aware of the horrible truth before the war ended, all efforts to convince Allied governments to take specific action to save Jews failed; the saving of Jews was not a war priority of the Allied powers.[17]

When the full truth about the Holocaust became known to Jews during the last months of the war—the Russians liberated Auschwitz in January 1945—support for Zionism grew by leaps and bounds. The two largest mainstream Zionist organizations in the United States had contained only 110,000 members in 1939, but their ranks swelled to 280,000 by 1945 and to 500,000 by 1948.[18] The destruction of European Jewry had taken place because the Jews in Europe, in Palestine, and elsewhere, lacking national sovereignty, had been powerless to affect events and to save or offer refuge to their own people. The rapid growth of Zionism and the outpouring from Diaspora Jews of financial and material help for the Jewish refugees and for the Yishuv signalled a growing awareness among Jews that the remnant had to be saved and that the gates of Palestine had to be opened. If the British were not prepared to allow the Jewish refugees of Europe to find a haven in Palestine, Jewish independence had to be won, whatever the cost. As the curtain rang down on centuries of Jewish life in eastern Europe, the attention of world Jewry shifted to Palestine where the next drama of the Jewish struggle for survival was about to be enacted.

2

"Go to Buy Arms"

On November 30, 1947, a bus crowded with Jewish passengers trundled over the two-lane road on its way from Netanya to Jerusalem in Palestine. The small knot of Arabs in *keffiyahs*, standing by the road, was not an unusual sight, and the driver probably paid no heed to them. As the bus drew alongside the group, however, the Arabs shouldered rifles and opened fire at close range. The driver quickly shifted gears and kicked the accelerator down as screams of panic mingled with cries of pain and the blood of dead and wounded passengers collected in pools on the rough wooden floor.

This attack was only one of many violent outbreaks that took place in Palestine on November 30 and over the next few days. The Arab Higher Committee, which functioned as the unofficial government of the Palestine Arabs, called a three-day general strike. On the second day of the strike an Arab mob poured into the heart of the old Jewish commercial district in Jerusalem and attacked Jewish stores and their owners; the attackers stabbed, looted, burned, and stoned without interference from British police officers. In Haifa, gunfire broke out between Jews in the Hadar Hacarmel section of the city and Arabs in the downtown Arab quarter, and the Arabs attempted to take control of a bridge linking the Jewish part of town with the predominantly Jewish suburbs. Within days fighting had spread to the southern outskirts of Tel Aviv and the northern Negev. Arabs also mounted an attack on a Jewish convoy carrying supplies south from Jerusalem to the Etzion Bloc of settlements on the road to Hebron.[1] The warfare between Palestine Arab and Palestine Jew that had flared up several times since the spring of 1920 had now exploded into a full-scale civil conflict for control of Palestine.

The Palestine civil war broke out the day after the United Nations General Assembly voted to recommend that the solution to the festering problem of Palestine was to end the British Mandate and partition the country into a Jewish state, an Arab state, and a U.N.-controlled enclave that would include Jerusalem and its immediate environment. The two states were to be tied together by an economic union and the United Nations was to oversee the partition and emergence of the two states through the U.N. Palestine Commission. This vote was the culmination of more than two years of mounting diplomatic crisis between Britain and the United States over Palestine and the future of the European Jewish refugees. During the same period the Haganah, the Irgun, and the Stern Gang had struggled continuously against the British Mandate.

In the months following the end of World War II, the Jewish community in Palestine had turned increasingly to active resistance and open revolt. The Haganah was charged with the task of organizing a European network to smuggle displaced persons to Palestine. Month after month refugees sailed for the Promised Land aboard crowded, rusty ships purchased by the Haganah and manned both by volunteer crews from abroad and by Haganah veterans. The Royal Navy mounted a blockade to stop this "illegal" immigration, as the British termed it, while the world watched the spectacle of British troops herding the refugees of Hitler's Holocaust into detention camps in Palestine and Cyprus and sending them back behind the barbed wire of the displaced persons camps in Europe.

While the Haganah concentrated on defying the White Paper, the Irgun and the Lehi intensified their military operations against the British in Palestine. The British eventually stationed 100,000 troops there to counter the mounting campaign of assassinations, ambushes, bombings, kidnappings, and attacks against air bases, trains, officers' clubs, and army bases. In January 1946 the Irgun penetrated Aqir air base to steal arms. In February they destroyed three bombers and damaged eight others at Qastina air base. In April they destroyed five railway bridges, while the Lehi killed seven British soldiers. In June £100,000 of damage was done to the Palestine railway network and six British officers were kidnapped. In July the anti-British terror appeared to peak with the Irgun bombing of the Mandate offices in the King David Hotel in Jerusalem. Ninety-one persons—British, Jewish, and Arab—were killed and forty-five were injured in the explosion.

The British responded with wholesale arrests, floggings, curfews, roadblocks, constant searches, martial law, and hangings. By late 1946 there was one British soldier or policeman for every five Jews in Palestine. Even so, the anti-British terror persisted and the immigrant ships continued to sail from Europe. British attempts to end the Palestine crisis by conciliating both Arabs and Jews were a miserable failure; Jews demanded the right to bring refugees to Palestine from Europe while Arabs insisted they be kept out. Britain was reluctant to leave Palestine for strategic reasons but found it increasingly costly to stay. World War II had drained the British treasury, and the British people wanted an end to the sacrifice of their sons and daughters in Palestine.[2]

Britain had made efforts to find a solution for Palestine during World War II, and at one point London was actively considering the imposition of partition in Palestine after the war. When Lord Moyne was assassinated in 1944 these efforts came to a halt and Palestine was put on a back burner until the war ended. By the autumn of 1945, with a new Labour government in power in London and tension mounting in Palestine, it was apparent that some solution had to be found.

Britain's answer was to convince the United States to participate in the Anglo-American Committee of Inquiry. This committee, which was composed of three official representatives from each country, held hearings in New York, London, and Palestine. The committee heard many witnesses from both sides before issuing its report on May 1, 1946. The report recommended the immediate admission of 100,000 Jewish refugees to Palestine and the continuation of the British Mandate for the foreseeable future.

Other recommendations were not so clear: Palestine should not become a Jewish state or an Arab state; future Jewish immigration, after the 100,000 had been admitted, should not be subject to an Arab veto; Jewish immigration should not continue indefinitely until the Arabs became a minority in the country. Although the recommendations were unanimous, none were instituted by the British. One month later a second, smaller commission examined the report of the Anglo-American Committee to see how it might be implemented, but again nothing resulted.

In September 1946, and again in February 1947, Britain made further efforts to bring Arabs and Jews together at a series of conferences in London, but the two sides would not compromise on basic principles. The Zionists wanted the White Paper restrictions of 1939 to be lifted or they wanted statehood, even if only in part of Palestine. The Arabs refused to agree to any further Jewish immigration, demanded immediate statehood for Palestine with its Arab majority, and refused to consider any partition scheme no matter how small the Jewish state that might result from it. The British decided to ask the United Nations for help.[3]

In late February of 1947 Britain placed the Palestine problem before the United Nations. At a special session of the General Assembly starting on April 28, 1947, the Special Committee on Palestine (UNSCOP) was appointed with instructions to report to the General Assembly by the end of August. The Special Committee, whose members were from eleven countries with no apparent connection to Palestine, toured Palestine and heard submissions from government officials and the Jewish Agency. In Beirut, Lebanon, they met with representatives of the Arab countries and then flew to Geneva to prepare their report. In Europe, several committee members visited refugee camps and interviewed the homeless Jews there. On August 31, 1947, the committee issued its findings. The majority recommended that Palestine should be granted immediate independence and divided into Jewish and Arab states joined in an economic union. Jerusalem was to be administered directly by the United Nations. The Arabs strongly opposed these recommendations, but both the United States and the Soviet Union supported them.[4]

When the U.N. General Assembly convened in New York in September 1947, Palestine was clearly one of the most important and dramatic items on the agenda. While delegations busied themselves studying the UNSCOP report and trying to decide how it might be implemented, Arabs and Jews lobbied furiously to line up support for the final vote. The UNSCOP recommendations projected two truncated states, wound in tight embrace; but it provided no blueprint for their establishment or for the maintenance of peace and order in Palestine while partition was taking place. This was most important in light of the violent history of Arab-Jewish relations and the deeply felt passions on both sides.

After many weeks of discussion, a General Assembly committee worked out a compromise that was acceptable to both the United States and the Soviet Union: law and order within each state would be maintained by local armed militias and the Security Council would be asked to assume its obligations under the U.N. charter in the event of a "threat to the peace".[5] This weak solution was totally unrealistic given the nature of the problem, but it was generally accepted by those who supported partition. Perhaps some delegates thought that Britain or the United States would use their armed forces to police partition. Others may have believed that, once approved by the United Nations, the partition would be accepted, albeit reluctantly, by the Arabs as a *fait accompli*. Both assumptions were tragically wrong. When partition was approved by a two-thirds majority in the General Assembly on November 29, it sparked the outbreak of civil war the very next day.

II

Fauzi al-Kaukji, commander of the Arab forces during the 1936-39 revolt, was ready to fight for Palestine even before the General Assembly voted on partition. At a mass rally in Kornayel, Lebanon, on October 5, 1947, he called upon Arabs in Palestine and elsewhere to join his new Arab Liberation Army to wage a holy war—a *jihad*—to free the holy places. "If the Zionists, the Americans and others league themselves against us," he warned, "we Arabs will know how to defend our honour and inflict crushing defeats against our enemies." The United States Legation in Beirut reported that Kaukji attracted large delegations from Syria and Lebanon and that prevailing opinion in the Lebanese capital was that both Syria and Lebanon would "close their eyes" to the formation of volunteer armies on their territory. Kaukji, in fact, was a "great friend" of Riad Solh, the Lebanese Prime Minister, and could "certainly count on [his] support".[6] Kaukji's call to arms was heard all over the Arab world. Thousands of young men began to gather in southern Syria, lured by the promise of the glory to be gained in the battle to save Jerusalem or attracted by the prospect of plunder. There was even a handful of British Army deserters and ex-German prisoners of war among them.[7]

Kaukji's growing force was soon joined by a large contingent of Syrian troops and gendarmes that began to encamp along the northern border of Palestine in mid-October. A shortage of fuel and trucks slowed the build-up, but by October 15 at least 3000 troops were observed in the Kuneitra area, about thirteen kilometres from the Palestine frontier. The Syrian Defence Minister forecast that 7000 men would eventually be stationed there, though he claimed they would be used "only to fill [the] vacuum expected [in] Arab Palestine after British withdrawal". Until that occurred, he said, manoeuvres would be held.[8]

The Arab irregulars who gathered on the northern borders of Palestine in the fall of 1947 intended to operate in conjunction with the Palestine Arab forces already in place within Palestine's borders. Many of them had taken part in guerrilla operations during the 1936-39 fighting and about 6000 had served in the British Army during World War II, although most had been confined to garrison duty. Some had received training in basic tactics and light weapons, and a large number were employed as full-time or auxiliary police. Some 1700 served in the Transjordan Frontier Force. (The Emirate of Transjordan, a British protectorate, was formed by Britain in 1921 from that part of the Palestine Mandate east of the Jordan River. In 1946 it was granted independence as the Kingdom of Transjordan. It is now known as the Hashemite Kingdom of Jordan.) Local defence and guerrilla operations in Arab Palestine were based on a village system whereby the *mukhtar*, or mayor, called the male population to action. This was effective enough in the villages; it made every village into a well-defended position and allowed village fighters to cover local road junctions and passes. However, it did not allow large-scale mobilization of fighting units that could be sent into action far from home.[9]

The Holy Land had known war for thousands of years. The Arabs, like the Jews before them, built their villages atop hills overlooking the passes through which commerce flowed and invading armies marched. From these vantage points they could pour withering fire down on enemies who tried to pass below. In the mountainous Galilee, and in the hills and mountains of Judea and Samaria, Arab villages dominated the routes that linked Jewish settlements. Once war began, the Arabs easily cut those settlements off from more heavily populated Jewish areas on the coastal plain and in Jerusalem.

The Palestine Arab forces were disorganized and poorly armed in mid-1947, but the armies of the surrounding Arab countries were in much better condition. The most formidable, though by no means the largest, was the Arab Legion of the Kingdom of Transjordan. By early 1947 the Legion consisted of about 8000 troops commanded by thirty-seven British officers under Commander-in-Chief Captain John Glubb, who was known to the Arabs as Glubb Pasha. He was a thrice-wounded veteran of World War I. He had joined the Arab Legion under contract in 1930 and in 1939 was made commander. He built the Legion from a small desert cavalry unit that depended heavily on camels into a mobile striking force equipped with armoured cars and artillery, twenty-five pounders, and mountain howitzers. Under British leadership and training, the Legion moulded Bedouins, Druse, Palestine Arabs, and others into an effective, disciplined force.

The Egyptian Army was 55,000 strong on paper, but it was inexperienced, badly organized, and poorly led. Some Egyptians had been trained in anti-aircraft defence in World War II, but most were new to uniform. The Egyptians, none the less, possessed armoured cars, tanks, and artillery, and boasted an air force with a motley collection of World War II-vintage British and Italian aircraft. As the Palestine crisis developed in 1947, the Egyptians were already launched on a major program to equip their forces with newer British weapons. They could also fall back on the 1936 Anglo-Egyptian Treaty, which afforded them British protection in case of attack.

The Syrian Army consisted of about 8000 troops backed by a small number of French-built tanks and a small air force. It was even worse-trained than the Egyptian Army, and most officers and men were new recruits. The Syrian Army was only slightly better equipped than the Lebanese, which numbered less than 4000 men and possessed a number of light tanks and armoured cars. The Iraqis, perhaps the best-equipped of all the Arab forces, boasted about one hundred planes, artillery, armoured cars, and anti-tank and anti-aircraft guns. Their army numbered approximately 21,000 men. But the Iraqis, too, suffered from lack of training and experience.[10]

In the initial stages of the war the Palestine Arabs, acting in village units or with the irregulars of the Arab Liberation Army, fought alone against the Jews. Indeed, the Mufti had insisted at an Arab League council meeting in October 1947 that it was the task of the Palestine Arabs alone to defeat the Jews and that Arab League aid should be limited to training, financial support, and arms supplies.[11] The Palestine Arab aim was, through control of the roads, to cut off Jewish settlements one by one, starve them to the point where they could no longer defend themselves, and then wipe them out. There seems to have been no thought given to acquiring heavy weapons, and there is no evidence that Arab League countries intended to supply such equipment to any Palestine Arab group. Given the Palestine Arabs' good strategic positions, from which they could control the roads of

Palestine, it may not have seemed necessary.

The Mufti wanted to lead the forthcoming battle against the Zionists. In the autumn of 1947 it appeared that he would have his way, and that Arab League support would be limited to the supply of light weapons and the granting of sanctuaries along the Palestine borders for the massing of Arab irregulars. Most leaders of the Yishuv and the Haganah thought it would end there, and that there would never be full-scale war between the Yishuv and the surrounding Arab countries. The one notable dissenter from this opinion was the man who was responsible for organizing the defence of the Yishuv, David Ben Gurion.

III

The sun-bleached buildings of Tel Aviv simmered in the heat of an August 1947 afternoon as the council of the Mapai (Labour) party met to consider the defence problems the Yishuv was likely to face in the coming months. David Ben Gurion, party leader, Chairman of the Jewish Agency Executive, and unofficial minister of defence, was the centre of attention. With his bushy, unkempt hair and forceful personality, he was already a legendary figure in Palestine. He was a *bona fide* pioneer of the Zionist movement, having walked to Palestine from his native Russia at the age of twenty. He had founded the Mapai party. He headed the Histadrut and had served as Chairman of the Jewish Agency Executive since 1935. He had believed for some time that there was little chance a Jewish state could be established in Palestine without war. Eventually, he was convinced, the Yishuv would be plunged into armed conflict not only with the Arabs of Palestine but with the surrounding Arab countries. He knew that the Haganah was not ready for such a fight.

When the council meeting began, Ben Gurion reviewed the military situation and asked hard, rhetorical questions about the Haganah's abilities to defend the Yishuv. Jewish military inferiority was a threat to the continued existence of the Yishuv, he claimed. He warned that, with survival at stake, "it would be a grave, or perhaps fatal error to refuse to understand the situation and prepare to meet it with all our strength. . . ." The Haganah must be prepared to confront the face of real war. It had to "obtain heavy arms: tanks, artillery, halftracks and heavy mortars for [the] ground units, fighter planes for the foundation of an air force, torpedo boats and even submarines for the navy."[12] Ben Gurion believed that the Haganah lacked the necessary equipment and expertise to fight conventional Arab armies. Even the elite Palmach commandos lacked trained officers, experience, an adequate budget, and a clear sense of military direction.

Ben Gurion was virtually alone in his belief that the Yishuv faced a full invasion from the armies of the surrounding Arab countries.[13] Many other leaders of the Yishuv and the Haganah were confident that the forthcoming battle would pit the Palestine Arabs and the Palestine Jews against each other in a civil war. In such a fight, the Haganah would be the equal of anything the Palestine Arabs could throw against it. The Haganah was not undermanned and could count on approximately 43,000 men and women—32,000 in the home guard and 8000 in the field corps. And it was not untrained: members of the field corps spent a few weeks each year and several days every month training with their units, while the Palmach, with 3100 men and women and 1000 reservists, was a full-time force[14]. But the Haganah was poorly equipped. In April 1947 it possessed about 12,000 rifles and submachine guns, 630 light and medium machine guns, and 760 two- and three-inch mortars.

There was no navy or air force as such, although the nucleus for future services existed. Several Palmach members had served as frogmen or naval commandos with the Royal Navy. Others had worked on immigrant ships or had manned small speedboats to bring immigrants ashore from blockade-running ships.[15] A handful of Palestine Jews had served in the Royal Air Force and the United States Army Air Force, and there were a number of Jewish flying and gliding clubs and a small Jewish-owned airline, Aviron. The aircraft were mostly obsolete light planes or small, twin-engine, wooden passenger planes obtained from a variety of sources.[16]

By August 1947, Ben Gurion had already been working on the weaponry problem for two years. At that time, on a visit to the United States, he had met with a group of men in New York called together by Rudolph Sonneborn, an American Jewish philanthrophist, and had made a special plea for help—for funds, facilities, whatever was needed—to build up Jewish strength in Palestine.[17] Ben Gurion had been particularly interested in getting machinery to manufacture ammunition and light weapons in Palestine under British noses.

This was part of the Haganah effort to secure weapons and explosives in Europe and the United States that had begun in the liberated areas of Europe in 1944 and that continued after the war ended. Haganah agents, some with the Jewish Brigade in Italy, worked with other members of the brigade and with sympathetic soldiers in Allied armies to beg, buy, and steal small arms, ammunition, and explosives. They took weapons from arms dumps and supply trains, or from Allied troops who sold or gave away souvenir German arms. Everything was needed; anything was taken. The arms were transported in clandestine truck convoys (that sometimes also carried Jewish refugees) to secret caches in France or Italy. From there the weapons were sent to Palestine by ship, smuggled inside mislabelled crates or camouflaged as used machinery.[18]

After Ben Gurion's visit to the United States in 1945 the Haganah extended its arms collecting to North America. Yaacov Dori, Haganah Chief of Staff, co-ordinated these activities for a time from New York City. Dori was later replaced by Shlomo Shamir, a former intelligence officer in the British Army.

Haim Slavin, who was in charge of underground arms manufacturing in Palestine for the Haganah, was also sent to the United States to work with a handful of American volunteers to buy and ship surplus arms-manufacturing machinery. The machinery, carefully broken down and labelled for easy reassembly, was disguised and shipped to Palestine along with explosives and small arms donated by American Jewish war veterans.[19] By the beginning of 1947 the machinery for making arms, as well as shipments of pistols, rifles, machine guns, ammunition, and explosives were being regularly smuggled into Palestine from Europe and the United States. But it was a slow process and it could not re-equip the Haganah to meet real armies in open battle.

In the latter part of 1947 Ben Gurion stepped up his efforts to find and acquire heavy weaponry for the Haganah by sending abroad two experienced Haganah undercover agents with reputations for performing the impossible.

The first to go was Yehuda Arazi, a long-time Haganah agent with extensive underground experience, who was sent to New York in late August or early September. Arazi could have been a hero for a spy novel. Under Haganah orders, he had joined the Palestine Police in the 1930s and had risen through the ranks to become an inspector in the Counter-Intelligence Division in Jerusalem. Later, before World War II, he purchased arms for the Haganah in eastern Europe, returning to

Palestine to work with British Intelligence when the fighting broke out. Before the end of the war he was back in Europe, this time in Italy, helping members of the Jewish Brigade smuggle arms and refugees to Palestine.[20]

Ehud Avriel was sent two months later. He had been a key Haganah agent in Europe, organizing the transit of illegal immigrants from refugee camps in eastern Europe to Palestine. He had returned from Europe to work on his kibbutz, but one afternoon he was summoned to the Jewish Agency in Jerusalem for a meeting with Ben Gurion. Avriel listened quietly while Ben Gurion told him of the grave danger the Yishuv faced because of the forthcoming U.N. vote. "Much as I regret to break you away from your family and your kibbutz so soon after your return," Ben Gurion told him, "you must go to Europe again. On a short mission this time—to buy arms." Ben Gurion handed Avriel a list of the Haganah's immediate requirements and the next morning, with a borrowed shirt, a Bible, and a copy of *Faust*, Avriel boarded a Swissair flight to Europe.[21]

While Arazi and Avriel began their search for arms, a motley collection of private aircraft and obsolete passenger planes owned by different air clubs, airlines, and private citizens was formed into a Haganah-controlled air service in Palestine. The guiding spirit behind the Sherut Avir, as it was called in Hebrew, was Aharon Remez. Remez had been a sergeant pilot in the Royal Air Force and was on a Zionist mission to the United States when war broke out in 1939. When the Battle of Britain began, he volunteered for service with the RAF and was eventually sent to Canada where he was given flight training in the British Commonwealth Air Training Plan. He was later transferred to Britain to fly fighters and eventually ended up chasing German V-1 buzz bombs in fast, stripped-down Tempest fighters. After the Normandy landings, Remez flew fighter-bomber missions in Europe.

Remez—one of the very few Palestine Jews with air-combat experience—returned to Palestine after the war determined to put his knowledge to use. In May of 1947, he and Heyman Shamir, a veteran of the United States Army Air Force, were given the official go-ahead by the Haganah high command to set up a consolidated air service. On November 10, 1947, the Sherut Avir was created. Remez was named chief of operations and Shamir was put in charge of pilot training. Alex Ziloni, an engineer with little flying experience, was nominated chief of staff, and Isaac Eshel, head of the small airline Aviron, became, in

Remez's words, "a political overseer". (Remez soon replaced Ziloni as chief of staff.)[22] The Air Service was a start towards an air force, but only a start: its total strength was eleven light planes of different types and in varying stages of obsolescence.[23]

IV

On a cold dawn in January 1948, the sentries at the Royal Air Force base at Aqir, south of Tel Aviv, waved the convoy of twenty canvas-covered trucks out of the gates. With a clashing of gears the trucks quickly picked up speed and disappeared down the highway. They carried twenty-one disassembled Auster single-engine light planes that had just been purchased from the British for the alleged use of Aviron.

Several days earlier, Remez, Ziloni, and others in the Sherut Avir had learned that the planes, which were surplus and in terrible condition, were for sale. Ziloni had driven to Aqir to look them over. Despite their condition, he immediately recognized how valuable they could be, and when public tenders were called for, Aviron submitted a bid. When the officer in charge of sales at Aqir demanded financial guarantees, Ziloni was forced to make a trip to Jerusalem to get the necessary documents. When he returned to Aqir, Ziloni convinced the officer that, because of the Austers' condition, Aviron's bid would probably be the only one tendered, and a deal was soon completed.

Within hours the trucks arrived at the base and the Austers were disassembled and loaded. The Haganah men worked through the night and, the Austers safely aboard, the convoy departed at dawn.[24] The aircraft were spirited away and reassembled into a smaller number of usable planes. Each was given the same Palestine registration number so that the British and Arabs would not know how many were flying. Occasionally a Jewish pilot would land at an airport and find himself staring at an identical Auster sporting the same registration. At times like those a quick turnaround and takeoff saved many embarrassing questions from British authorities. When the Foreign Office in London learned of the sale there was an immediate and angry reaction: Britain had broken its own embargo on the shipment and sale of weapons and military supplies to anyone in Palestine.[25]

Britain's Middle East arms policy had first been outlined to the House of Commons in the fall of 1947. The embargo was a curious one as such bans go: no arms would be sold or shipped to Palestine, but existing agreements to supply weapons to Egypt, Iraq, and Transjordan would be fulfilled.[26] The policy was outlined to the Americans in December 1947: an embargo on all weapons to Palestine; no new agreements to sell arms to the Middle East; a continuation of shipments of arms already contracted for, as long as there was no evidence that those weapons were being misused.[27]

This remained the British approach until the end of May 1948, and it was a most unfair policy. The Jews of Palestine were not allowed to purchase arms from Britain or bring weapons into Palestine; but Egypt, Iraq, Transjordan, and other countries with whom Britain had arms-supply contracts would receive modern, up-to-date weaponry in preparation for the conflict to come. Britain's motives were simple. Because Arab friendship was commercially and militarily important to Britain, it was imperative to maintain good relations with the Arab countries—particularly with the military of those countries.[28]

In the early months of 1948 Britain shipped millions of dollars worth of military equipment to the Middle East. Iraq received armoured cars, machine guns, artillery, fighter planes, anti-tank guns, scout cars, and armoured personnel carriers. Egypt acquired more than 11,000 rounds of high-explosive and anti-tank shells. The Transjordan Arab Legion was subsidized by London and received "normal maintenance for a force of 7000" on a daily basis from the British Middle East command in Cairo. In addition, Transjordan had the loan of several British artillery pieces and anti-tank guns for "training purposes".[29] At the very time that Arab irregulars were massing on Palestine's northern border, Lebanon and Syria received rifles, machine guns, and ammunition already contracted for. This happened in spite of warnings from General Sir Alan Cunningham, the British High Commissioner in Palestine, that the Arab states were providing and would continue to provide arms to Palestine Arabs.[30]

American arms policy was far more even-handed in conception and execution. Shortly after the U.N. partition was voted on, the U.S. State Department announced on December 5, 1947 a total embargo on arms shipments to the Middle East.[31] This policy was scrupulously followed with all the enforcement power that the federal government could muster. It was fair in that it was even-handed; but it was unfair when placed in the larger context of British arms supplies to Arab countries. It blocked any chance the Yishuv or its American supporters may have had of openly buying weapons from the vast stocks of war-surplus equipment rusting away in scrap yards and airplane parks all over the United States. That unfairness was soon apparent to American Zionists and their supporters, and they began to place tremendous pressure on Washington to lift its embargo as long as Britain continued to ship weapons to the Arabs.

V

On January 15, 1948, U.S. Undersecretary of State Robert Lovett was enjoying a quiet Sunday at his Washington home when his rest was broken by the visit of three influential members of the U.S. Senate. Arthur Vanderberg of Michigan, Alec Smith of New Jersey,and Irving M. Ives of New York were not known for pro-Zionist positions, but all were worried by increasing public concern over the embargo issue. The three asked Lovett if it were true that British arms were still being shipped to the Arabs. They also told him that some statement that British arms were not being supplied to the Arabs was necessary. Otherwise it would be very difficult to withstand the pressures being brought to bear on Congress by "organized groups" to force the lifting of the U.S. embargo. The next morning Lovett asked Lord Inverchapel, the British Ambassador to the United States, to come to an urgent meeting at the State Department. Lovett was clearly upset and wanted London to know that he was under great pressure to lift the embargo. He told Inverchapel of his Sunday meeting, showed him sheaves of full-page newspaper advertisements calling for an end to the U.S. embargo, and declared that Jews were bombarding Congress with letters and telegrams that were having a "devastating...effect". The senators were willing to withstand the pressure provided there "was not a shred [of] evidence upon which the Jews could base a claim that an injustice was being done to them. . . ." Inverchapel told Lovett all he knew about current British policy, but there was nothing new in what he said. Lovett warned that the present situation was "full of dynamite" and urged the British to suspend arms exports for the time being. He did not want to remove the U.S. embargo or embarrass London. He hoped, therefore, that some way could be found to suspend British arms exports. He "begged for a very early decision."[32]

In London the next evening, British Prime Minister Clement Attlee met with Minister of Defence A.V. Alexander, Colonial Secretary Arthur Creech-Jones, and two officials of the Foreign Office to discuss

Lovett's concerns. They were worried about events in the United States, but they had problems of their own. One Foreign Office official thought that if Britain had to choose between maintaining its arms supply to the Arabs or having the U.S. embargo lifted, the former was the "less bad" course. The Foreign Office was convinced that if Britain stopped delivering military supplies to Iraq, the Iraqi Army would turn against Britain, and the new treaty between the two countries would not be ratified. The impact on Britain's position in the Middle East would be "so serious that it must be avoided at all costs".[33] The arms shipments were to continue despite American pressure.

The Jewish Agency was fully aware that British and American arms policy, taken together, could lead to military disaster. It continued to try, at several levels, to get the United States to lift or modify its ban. Chaim Weizmann wrote to President Harry S. Truman that the Jews of Palestine were deficient in "the equipment necessary for their defence". It was, he said, a paradox that the Jews were "the only people in the Near East threatened by aggression . . . who have not been able to provide freely for their own defence".[34]

In Washington, Moshe Shertok, unofficial foreign minister of the Jewish Agency, met twice with State Department officials to ask for U.S. aid in procuring arms. The officials were evasive, however, and told Shertok that the State Department would be willing to go into the issue only after considerable discussion. He was informed that the U.N. Palestine Commission, which had been established to implement the partition scheme, was "the competent organ to deal with the matter". Shertok also met with two Defense Department officials who gave him little reason for hope, repeated State Department views about the importance of the United Nations, and pointed out that arms to Jews could also mean arms to Arabs.[35]

These constant references to the United Nations were peculiar. The Palestine Commission was not empowered to authorize military action to defend partition. No troops had been offered by any country to the United Nations to support the commission's recommendations and the British, in fact, had refused to co-operate with the commission. The fighting had begun in Palestine. People were dying. But the United Nations could not, and apparently would not, act to end the bloodshed. Only the Jews would, or could, defend the U.N. decision by force of arms. There was, therefore, a real basis for Shertok's view that the Jews were only asking for help "in implementing a U.N.

decision and in protecting themselves against those who defy it".

While Jewish Agency leaders lobbied the State Department and the administration, Zionists and their supporters put heavy pressure on representatives of both political parties. They sent telegrams and letters, held public and private meetings, organized rallies, and placed advertisements in newspapers and magazines. After months of news-reels and headlines showing British troops intercepting refugee ships off the coast of Palestine and herding displaced persons into detention camps on Cyprus and elsewhere, the public was well primed for this public-relations barrage. There was no doubt in the minds of many senators and congressmen that there would come a day of political reckoning if the United States continued to deny arms to the Palestine Jews. But there would also be more than a political reckoning; there would be defiance of U.S. law. In mid-January 1948, Washington Senator Warren G. Magnuson wrote to Secretary of State George C. Marshall attacking the U.S. embargo and claiming that, since the end of World War II, the United States had transferred over 37 million dollars worth of war-surplus property to the Arab League states. Magnuson pointed out that the British had announced that arms shipments to Arab League countries would continue. He quoted London sources confirming that 25 million dollars worth of military stores were being supplied to Egypt, Iraq, and Transjordan. He claimed, in view of this evidence, that American policy would only "spur the aggressors in their incendiary course", and warned that "certain well-intentioned Americans" would break the law to defy the arms embargo because "American citizens are drawn by tradition to every struggle for freedom and justice". Magnuson claimed that the Jews of Palestine were capable of defending themselves provided they were not "cut off from all sources of supply. . .".[36]

Despite Magnuson's urgings, the State Department held firm. It defended the embargo as necessary to "prevent any action likely to increase bloodshed or to make a peaceful settlement more difficult". It further claimed that the general problem of maintaining internal order in Palestine was the reponsibility of the U.N. Palestine Commission and would undoubtedly be one of the first items on the commission's agenda for study. It was the State Department's "hope" that the peoples of Palestine would "co-operate in the peaceful implementation of the General Assembly's resolution".[37]

This "hope" was ridiculous in the light of the bloody reality. By mid-

January 1948 at least twenty Arabs and Jews were being killed in Palestine every day, and there was no realistic prospect of outside intervention to end the fighting. Shortly after the partition vote, the British had announced their intention to leave Palestine by May 15, 1948. They were making every effort to expedite that withdrawal. They did nothing to maintain general order in Palestine and intervened in the fighting only when it was absolutely necessary to do so, usually to save British lives.

American Zionists, Jewish Agency officials, and politicians like Magnuson who were sympathetic to the cause of the Palestine Jews could not move the State Department or the administration from their course. Lifting the embargo might do irreparable damage to American interests in the Arab world. George Kennan, head of the Policy Planning Staff in the State Department and one of Washington's most respected diplomats, took the view that the violence in Palestine was the "main responsibility [of] the Jewish leaders and organizations who . . . pushed so persistently for the pursuit of objectives which could scarcely fail to lead to violent results".[38]

The United States had supported Jewish statehood when it voted for partition in the U.N. General Assembly, but U.S. support stopped there. No arms would be available with which Jews could defend themselves or defend the establishment of the state that the United Nations had recommended they should have. Meanwhile, the Arabs would continue to receive the best of almost everything from their British mentors. Magnuson's forecast that Jews and other sympathetic Americans would view this as extremely unfair was correct; so were his fears that they would break the law to set this injustice right.

3

"A Matter of
Great Importance"

Ehud Avriel was a frustrated man. In November 1947, David Ben Gurion had sent him to Europe to buy arms. Instead, Avriel had spent several weeks in Paris making no connections and buying no arms. Every lead had turned out to be false. It was easy enough for Ben Gurion to demand results. It was much harder to make illicit purchases, in quantity, of the type of equipment the Haganah needed so badly. And, in the meantime, Paris newspapers carried daily accounts of the fighting in Palestine, of the growing number of Jewish settlements under siege, and of the almost complete blockade of Jewish Jerusalem. Avriel seemed to be wasting his time while the Yishuv went up in flames. It was enough to cause an active man like Avriel to sink into despair.

One afternoon in early 1948 Avriel waited in his hotel room for a visit from Robert Adam Abromovici, a Rumanian-born Jew living in Paris who was alleged to have connections with the Czechoslovak arms industry. A colleague had suggested the meeting and Avriel had agreed. He had no great expectations, though. He had already met countless confidence men, fly-by-night operators, and outright crooks. But what was there to lose? To Avriel's surprise, however, Abromovici was able to show him full catalogues from the best-known Czech arms manufacturers and to give quotes on prices and delivery dates. He also produced two airline tickets: "I expected you to be interested," he told Avriel, "so I took the liberty of purchasing the tickets for our flight to Prague tomorrow morning."[1]

Within days after his arrival in Prague, and with the help of Abromovici and Dr. Otto Felix, a Czech-born Jew who had settled in Palestine after the Munich crisis in 1938, Avriel concluded an agreement with the Czechs for a cash purchase of 10,000 rifles, 4500 heavy machine guns, and three million rounds of ammunition. The agreement was ostensibly made with Avriel as representative of the government of Ethiopia (Avriel carried a supply of stolen letterheads). The Czechs must have known quite well who the customer was; in any case, Foreign Minister Jan Masaryk and his deputy, Vladimir Clementis, helped smooth out the legal technicalities and bureaucratic obstacles. It was made clear to Avriel that other sales could follow, and broad hints were dropped that fighters—Messerschmitts, Spitfires, and Mosquitoes—and perhaps other heavy weapons would be available for sale in the near future.[2]

There were many reasons why the Czechs decided to sell weapons to the Palestine Jews.[3] A straight need for cash, particularly dollars, cannot be discounted. For many years the Czechs had sold arms to anyone who could pay, sometimes sending weapons to both sides of a conflict at the same time.[4] In fact, the Czechs had concluded an agreement to sell rifles to Syria shortly before their first contract was signed with Avriel. But the rifles to Syria were a one-time-only affair, while the equipment sold to Avriel was the first batch of many. Even after the Communist Party took control of the Czech government in February 1948, the arms flow to the Jews continued.

The Czech need for hard currency may have been a major factor, but it was certainly not the only one. The arms sales also fell in with the then current Soviet policy of supporting the emergence of an independent Jewish state in Palestine. The Soviet Union had supported the UNSCOP partition proposals in autumn 1947. It continued to pursue a pro-partition policy throughout 1948. This may have been designed to keep the United States and Britain off balance in the Middle East. It may also have aimed at creating a pro-Soviet Jewish state in an area dominated by conservative Arab regimes tied to Great Britain. The U.S.S.R. may also have hoped that an Arab-Jewish war would give Moscow an opportunity to intervene militarily in the area.

Soviet motives cannot be known with certainty, but the results of Soviet actions are clear enough. The Soviet Bloc voted for partition at the United Nations in November 1947 and Czechs sold arms to the Jews. Although Czechoslovakia was still nominally independent up to the Communist takeover in February 1948, its foreign policy had been designed with a sharp eye to Soviet interests because the Czech mouse was anxious to please the Soviet elephant.

Without a means of transporting the Czech weapons to Palestine, Avriel's success meant little. Czechoslovakia is totally landlocked. This made transport through or over other countries a necessity. Negotiations with Poland produced no results. The Hungarian government, however, which was fully aware of the real nature and destination of the cargoes, allowed the arms to be shipped from Bratislava, Czechoslovakia, via the Danube River to Vukovar in Yugoslavia.

Permission then had to be gained to ship through Yugoslavia to an Adriatic port. To obtain it, Avriel went to Belgrade where he looked up old acquaintances who had fought with Tito partisans during the war. Alexsander Rankovic, Yugoslav Minister of the Interior, was one old friend who allowed the Czech weapons to be shipped by rail from Vukovar to the port of Sibenik on the Adriatic.

Next, Avriel and Munya Mardor, another Haganah agent, went to Italy to secure a vessel to carry the weapons to Palestine. There, with the help of an Italian-Jewish businessman, they chartered the 500-ton *Nora*. The arms were hidden beneath a load of Italian onions and shipped from Yugoslavia to Palestine on March 28.[5]

I

The sound of truck engines floated up through the dark to Arab guerrillas crouched behind rocks and pine trees above the Tel Aviv-Jerusalem road. The fighters were about to attack yet another supply convoy bringing food, medicine, and other supplies to beleaguered Jewish Jerusalem.

The trucks were soon revealed in the dim light of dawn. As the lead truck, which had been specially reinforced to break through road blocks, approached the crude barrier that lay across the road, firing broke out. Suddenly the truck hit a mine and blew up, blocking any forward progress. In the confusion of the convoy's sudden halt, trucks in the rear continued to press forward, ignoring the order of the convoy commander to keep well apart so as not to present a compact target for the Arab riflemen. Moving quickly and keeping under cover as much as possible, the Arabs began to approach the stalled convoy, all the time pouring withering fire on the trucks below. The trucks were mostly home-made "sandwich" armoured trucks fashioned in Haganah workshops using sheet steel and plywood to cover standard truck chassis. Inside, Jewish defenders bathed in sweat squinted out of firing slats and peep holes searching for targets. One by one the Arabs disabled the trucks and killed the defenders. More than fourteen burned-out wrecks littered the highway before the remainder of the convoy managed to back down the road and beat a retreat to the assembly point at Hulda. It was March 24, 1948.[6]

Since the beginning of the year the fighting in Palestine had intensified daily. The sporadic and unorganized violence of December had given way to Arab Liberation Army attacks on Jewish settlements in the Galilee, the Hebron hills, and the northern Negev. The Etzion Bloc of settlements south of Jerusalem had been completely cut off. A relief force of thirty-five Haganah fighters sent from Jerusalem had been annihilated. The Arab Liberation Army had failed to capture any settlements in the first months of fighting, however, and by early March it had turned its attention to the Palestine road system.

By the end of March, Jewish settlements in the Negev had been cut off, the links from Haifa to the Jewish farms in the western Galilee were severed, the siege of the Etzion Bloc had been tightened, and the blockade of Jewish Jerusalem had produced acute shortages of food, medicine, and ammunition. Until March 24 a few supply trucks had always managed to push through; the March 24 convoy was the first to be stopped completely. Casualties were mounting by the hour, and it was clear that the Yishuv's battle for survival was not going well.[7]

Zionist troubles in Palestine had been compounded by a dramatic turn of events at the United Nations in New York. On March 19, Senator Warren Austin, U.S. ambassador to the U.N., told a meeting of the permanent members of the Security Council that the United States now wanted, above all, to stop the fighting. It believed that partition should be suspended and that Palestine should be placed under U.N. trusteeship. Senator Austin requested the Security Council to put these recommendations before a special session of the General Assembly and to order the U.N. Palestine Commission to "suspend its efforts to implement the proposed partition plan".[8] If Austin's recommendations were carried out, it would be a major body blow to the hopes for Jewish statehood.

This U.S. abandonment of support for partition was caused by a mix of factors. The United States feared Soviet intervention and the State Department was concerned over the loss of U.S. influence in Arab capitals. But the about-face had been triggered by the fighting in Palestine. Arab arms had achieved a significant diplomatic victory.

II

Adolph W. Schwimmer, "Al" to his friends, was concerned about the fate of the Jewish refugees in Europe. By the autumn of 1947 Schwimmer, who was thirty and single, had completed a tour of duty with the United States Army Air Force in World War II and had flown on at least 280 trans-Atlantic crossings as a flight engineer with Trans World Air Lines. At one point, Schwimmer had approached Shlomo Shamir, the Haganah representative in New York, to suggest using planes to smuggle refugees from Europe to Palestine but Shamir had not appeared to be receptive to the idea. One day in September 1947, however, Schwimmer received a long-distance telephone call at his parents' home in Bridgeport, Connecticut, from a Mr. Albert Miller in New York. Miller told Schwimmer that he wanted to talk to him "on a matter of great importance", and arranged a meeting on the sidewalk in front of Grand Central Station in Manhattan. Schwimmer agreed to go, met Miller, and was taken to the offices of the Pratt Steamship Company on East 42nd Street.

In reality, "Miller" was Yehuda Arazi, in New York to buy arms. Arazi told Schwimmer that he was a representative of the Jewish Agency sent to start an airline in anticipation of future air service to Palestine. He needed Schwimmer's help. Schwimmer agreed, as long as he was not asked to break the law. Arazi then asked about the possible purchase of long-range aircraft and gave Schwimmer a large amount of cash for expenses. Schwimmer said that they could find planes in California, where many of the major aircraft factories in the United States were located and where there were several large air bases that were used as depots for surplus transports. He suggested that the Lockheed Constellation or the Douglas C-54, both large four-engine planes, would fit the bill.[9]

By the end of World War II the United States had become the world's largest storehouse of war-surplus weapons and military equipment and was home to over five million Jews. These factors made the United States a prime target for Haganah arms-procurement programs.

From 1945 on, the Haganah had maintained an active presence in the United States, primarily in the greater New York City area, which had some two million Jewish residents. At Ben Gurion's direction, the Haganah and the Jewish Agency sent some of their ablest representatives to the United States to spearhead and help organize American operations and to co-ordinate U.S. activities with the needs of the Yishuv. Yaacov Dori, Shlomo Shamir, and others—among them Haim Slavin and Yehuda Arazi—found themselves pounding the sidewalks of New York in defence of the Jews of Palestine. By late 1947 the organization they helped build, with headquarters at the Hotel Fourteen in Manhattan, had swung into action.

In early 1948, the leadership passed from Shlomo Shamir to a representative with less military experience than any of his predecessors, a farmer from the Galilee, Teddy Kollek. The organization Kollek inherited from Shamir included a steadily growing number of American volunteer workers and a handful of Jewish Palestinian undercover operators such as Yehuda Arazi. Kollek simply took over the reins. He ran the operation with a loose but steady hand, paying the minimum of attention to small details, and specializing, instead, in strengthening personal contacts with those who could help the cause in some way.

This style was probably best suited to the type of organization the Haganah was forced to run in the United States after the announcement of the arms embargo made most of what it was doing illegal. To avoid government harassment and to lessen the possibility that a slip-up on one phase of the work would lead to the uncovering of all Haganah activities, the different operations were kept separate.[10] One unit, under the direction of Jewish Palestinians Danny Shind and Davidka Nameri, dealt with the purchase, manning, and outfitting of immigrant ships. Another unit handled the publication of *Haganah Speaks*, a small newspaper purportedly published by the American Friends of Haganah. *Haganah Speaks* was designed to act as a balance to the publicity being given in the United States to the Irgun. The Irgun was backed by the American League for a Free Palestine, and its spectacular blows against the British in Palestine were played up by vocal American supporters like Ben Hecht, a Hollywood screenwriter. Pro-Irgun rallies always brought impassioned speeches, large donations, and columns of newspaper coverage. *Haganah Speaks* was a less-flamboyant effort to bring the activities of the Haganah to the attention of the American Jewish public.

Kollek later described his job as that of a "traffic cop" bringing "the various experts, and specialists into contact with their potential co-workers, advisors, and suppliers".[11] He remained in regular touch with Rabbi Abba Hillel Silver, head of the Jewish Agency in the United States, and with the Sonneborn Institute, the loosely organized group of businessmen first brought together by Rudolph Sonneborn to meet Ben Gurion in the summer of 1945. Kollek also co-ordinated the branch operations that channelled volunteers, equipment, and aircraft to Palestine. The network was complex and consisted of dummy companies, semi-legal agencies, and legitimate businesses that hid illicit activities beneath a cloak of respectability. For electronics there was Radio Communications Engineering, under the direction of Danny Fliderblum, a young New Yorker. For recruitment of Haganah volunteers there was Land and Labor for Palestine, headed by Major Wellesley Aron, a former officer in the Jewish Brigade. For aircraft there was Service Airways, nominally led by ex-army pilot Irvin "Swifty" Schindler, but also under the close supervision of Nahum Bernstein. Bernstein was a New York lawyer who had served with the Office of Strategic Services (forerunner to the Central Intelligence Agency) during World War II.[12]

New York was the headquarters, but the network was far-flung. It extended to the west coast of the United States, to Canada, and to every major city in the United States with a large Jewish population. It was built on informal contact; recruiting was done by word of mouth. Mutual trust and dedication to a single cause—the defence of the Yishuv in Palestine—cemented the network.

The organization itself was financed on a shoestring, but millions of dollars were funnelled through it for the purchase of everything from bandages to bombers. Although some cash came from overseas, most was locally raised at small private meetings. Donors contributed directly to the Jewish Agency. No questions were asked; no receipts were given. This fund-raising was done without any direct contact with either established Zionist or non-Zionist Jewish organizations or such Jewish charitable institutions as the United Palestine Appeal. The method of fund-raising produced tremendous wastes of money, but it also brought results.[13]

The Sonneborn Institute operated for two and a half years before its activities were formalized with the creation of Materials for Palestine in January 1948.[14] Institute members met at least once a week over lunch, usually on Thursday afternoons. Sonneborn presided. Important guests from Palestine—Haganah officials or men like Abba Eban or Moshe Shertok from the Jewish Agency political department—often attended and brought the businessmen up to date on the current situation in Palestine or at the United Nations.

36

Institute members raised funds, located supplies, and established contact with individuals across the country who could help with some particular job or other. In this period little attention was paid to the nature of the goods handled—some were "white" (medical supplies, farm implements, clothing); others were "black" (explosives, arms, aircraft parts, machinery for manufacturing weapons). When Materials for Palestine was founded these functions were divided. Exports prohibited by the arms embargo were handled by one or more of the dummy corporations—Foundry Associates, Oved Trading Corporation, Radio Communications Engineering, or, in Canada, Victory Equipment & Supply Company Limited. Materials for Palestine (called Aid to Palestine in Canada) collected and exported non-military equipment and launched large drives across the United States and Canada to collect anything—apart from money—that the Palestine Jewish community would need. Fund-raising was left to the established Jewish charities.

Of all the items that were in short supply in Palestine, airplanes were the most desperately needed. For Ben Gurion's strategy to work, some way had to be found to get arms already stockpiled in Europe or North America into the hands of the Haganah well in advance of the British departure from Palestine. Air transport was the obvious answer. In addition to transports, fighters and bombers would eventually be needed to defend the Yishuv against air attack and to blunt the spearheads of the expected Arab invasion. The challenging task of setting up an American network to supply this need had been given to Yehuda Arazi.

Arazi had extensive underground experience that would be useful on such a mission. He was also a loner, capable of the single-mindedness to act as if he had *carte blanche* to go wherever, spend whatever, and deal with whomever necessary to accomplish his objectives. Thus, although he operated under the nominal direction of Haganah headquarters at the Hotel Fourteen, in many respects he ran his own show.

At the end of World War II, the United States had possessed the world's largest air force. Thousands of U.S. Army fighters, bombers, transports, trainers, and auxiliary aircraft were based all over the world and thousands more were still in the United States, some brand new, others ready for the scrap heap. When the war against Japan ended on September 2, 1945, much of this air force became instantly surplus to the peacetime needs of the country. Aircraft of every shape and type were transferred for disposal to the Reconstruction Finance Corporation, a federal government agency, or to the War Assets Administration in Washington. They were sold off at a fraction of their cost, most for scrap, some to ex-army pilots who hoped to make it big in the post-war world of civil air transport. For a few thousand dollars a man could buy a Curtis C-46 or a Douglas C-47 (the military version of the DC-3, referred to by Commonwealth forces as the "Dakota") with which he could start a freight business hauling dynamite in the Andes of South America, refugees in South East Asia, contraband cigarettes in the Middle East, or guns in North Africa. A fortune could be made on a single planeload of smuggled goods. Lives were lost when poorly serviced engines quit on takeoff, or when overloaded transports failed to lift from too-short runways. Denied access to the modern airplane factories of the United States and Great Britain, this was the world to which the Haganah—and Yehuda Arazi—were forced to turn.

Shortly after Arazi met Al Schwimmer in Manhattan, Schwimmer quit his job with TWA and flew to California. He was accompanied by Reynold Selk, a friend and former Air Corps mechanic. At the Lockheed Air Terminal in Burbank, California, the two men inspected six Constellations that had been used by the U.S. Army as transports, before being turned over to War Assets at the end of the war. Schwimmer and Selk decided these were the perfect aircraft for their needs. The Constellation could carry up to sixty passengers over a range of almost 5000 kilometres. In late 1947, it was considered to be a first-class aircraft. The Constellations at Lockheed Air Terminal could be had for only $15,000 each. This would not be the total cost, however. Money would have to be spent to bring the planes up to civilian standards before the Civil Aviation Administration (CAA) would certify them for flight operations.[15]

While Selk remained in California, Schwimmer returned to New York, reported to Arazi and Nahum Bernstein, and was given a cheque which he used to purchase three planes from the War Assets Administration in Washington.[16] (He was allowed to choose the best three.) Schwimmer returned immediately to Burbank and established his own company, Schwimmer Aviation, to do the conversion work on the Constellations using space rented from Lockheed. With a constant flow of funds from Bernstein—between December 1947 and March 1948 $164,000 was deposited in Schwimmer's account at the Hollywood branch of the Bank of America—Schwimmer and Selk hired

38

crews from Lockheed to prepare the aircraft for their mission. Schwimmer also purchased five old C-46 transports from the Reconstruction Finance Corporation at Ontario, California, and had them flown to Burbank for overhaul.[17]

While the aircraft were being prepared in California, Arazi's airline was being readied in New York. It was owned by Irvin Schindler, a U.S. Army Air Force veteran who had dreamed of getting into civil aviation after the war. Schindler and his wife, Edythe, who was also a pilot, had founded Service Airways in New York State in September 1944 with total assets of one four-passenger Beechcraft. Service Airways survived for a time by running charter flights out of a small airport in Andover, New Jersey, but business was slow and the money soon dried up. Schindler was then forced to take a job as a co-pilot on a non-scheduled airline that flew between New York and Miami (which was Schindler's home town), with occasional hops across the Atlantic. Schindler dreamed of bigger things and his dissatisfaction came to the attention of Nahum Bernstein, who offered him the chance to head a revived Service Airways. Schindler was to lease the three Constellations and five C-46s from Schwimmer and to keep the line operating until its real purpose became clear. Schindler jumped at the chance and soon Service Airways had headquarters on West 57th Street and $50,000 in an account at the Chase National Bank.[18]

Schwimmer's choice for chief pilot was Sam Lewis, a man with considerable experience of flying Constellations for TWA. Lewis and Schwimmer had got to know each other while flying for the U.S. Army's Air Transport Command during the war, and they had often shared a cockpit in TWA after both left the service. Lewis was no Zionist, but he had become disenchanted with TWA during a strike at the airline in late 1947, and he was interested in using his skills to help spirit Jewish refugees into Palestine. When Schwimmer telephoned Lewis to ask if he would like to fly planes to Palestine, Lewis not only agreed to help[19] but also persuaded Leo Gardner, another pilot, to join him.

On January 26, 1948, with Lewis as pilot, Gardner as co-pilot, and Schwimmer as flight engineer, the first of the Constellations was flown from Burbank to Millville Airport near Millville, New Jersey. (The CAA had issued a temporary registration for the ferry flight.) Millville's runways were long enough to accommodate the Constellations and C-46s, and the airport was close enough to New York City to be convenient and far enough away to be inconspicuous. The plan was to collect the entire Service Airways fleet at Millville while awaiting permanent certification from the CAA.

But certification did not come. Schwimmer's "homemade" modifications at Burbank—including installations of toilets, galleys, carpeting, seats, and all the other necessities of commercial aviation—were not enough for the CAA.[20] It required extensive changes to the fuel system of the engines involving the installation of expensive fuel-injection equipment to replace the carburetors that had been used for military operations. Schindler and the others considered the CAA requirements "extremely expensive, inadvisable, and unnecessary from [a] safety standpoint",[21] and it began to look as if Service Airways would not get off the ground.

By the end of January, U.S. government authorities, including the Federal Bureau of Investigation, were beginning to close in on the Haganah's other operations in the United States. On January 3 a case of explosives labelled "used industrial machinery" was being loaded aboard a freighter at a dock in Jersey City, New Jersey. The case broke open and several wooden crates of TNT tumbled out. On closer inspection, dock officials found seventy-six identical cases filled with explosives, some already aboard the freighter, but most still on the dock. Since the crates were being shipped to Palestine it was easy enough to guess who was shipping them and why. The newspapers had a field day, and the FBI was called in to investigate.[22]

The incident caused acute embarrassment for the United States in the Middle East. Cairo's *Al Misri* newspaper printed photographs of the scene under a headline that read: "The ammunition and weapons of the American Army are smuggled to the Jews of Palestine." Other Cairo papers complained that the United States was showing open favouritism to the Zionist cause and "doing the same thing in Palestine as Russia is doing in Greece and Rumania". Representatives of the Palestine Arabs and of several Arab governments protested to Washington.[23] This undoubtedly increased pressure on the State Department and the FBI to clamp down on the Haganah's activities.

With the CAA blocking Service Airways' operations and the whole Haganah network in danger of being uncovered by the FBI,[24] it was time to get Service Airways out of the country. The solution came in the form of an idea hatched in the mind of Martin B. Bellefond. Bellefond, an ex-Air Force major, wanted to start an airline in Panama, using the Panamanian flag as a "flag of convenience", as many shipping companies did. Bellefond knew Gilberto Arias, nephew to the Panamanian president and a prominent Panama attorney. When Bellefond told Arias of his plans, Arias was enthusiastic. Panama had an ideal spot to base the new airline in the form of a large 8 million dollar white elephant of an air terminal at Tocuman. Lineas Aereas de Panama, S.A.—LAPSA for short—was formed in Panama. Bellefond had no airplanes, however, so a chance meeting with Schindler proved fortunate for both; the new Panamanian airline would provide perfect cover for Service Airways[25] because once Service Airways' aircraft were leased to LAPSA they would carry foreign registration and would no longer be bound by CAA rules. The Tocuman field would also be far from the prying eyes of the FBI.

The contract between LAPSA and Service Airways, by which Service leased its aircraft to LAPSA, was signed February 15, 1948. Two days later, the Republic of Panama's Department of Aviation issued a certificate of registration for one Lockheed Constellation—the aircraft parked at Millville, New Jersey. The temporary registration numbers issued to Service Airways by the CAA to allow the plane to be flown from Burbank were taken off and RX 121 was painted on. LAPSA had a flagship.[26]

III

While Arazi, Schwimmer, Bernstein, and the others were putting the Jewish Agency's secret airline together in the United States, former South African Air Force fighter pilot Boris Senior was trying to buy airplanes in South Africa. One day in March 1948, Senior flew to the Kimberly airport to look over a collection of surplus P-40 fighters that were about to be sold at auction. A large number of scrap dealers had gathered at Kimberly to inspect the planes, and it quickly became apparent to Senior that most of the dealers were Jewish. The dealers, in turn, soon realized that Senior had a more than ordinary interest in the fighters. As the bidding began, one of the dealers approached Senior and asked quietly if he was interested in buying the planes. When Senior admitted that he was, the pattern of bidding quickly changed and the lot was soon hammered over to Senior at a little more than ten dollars each. Senior had purchased most of a fighter squadron, in excellent condition, for virtual pin money.

Owning the fighters was one thing; smuggling them into Palestine under British noses was another. Senior tried to arrange to have the planes sent through the Suez Canal by ship, but the project fell through. He then conjured up the idea of dismantling the fighters and flying them into Palestine in large transport aircraft, but the transport planes he needed were not available. He was soon forced to abandon the P-40s, sell them for scrap, and begin buying planes—including Dakotas—that could be flown to Palestine from South Africa.[27]

The search for weapons in South Africa was eased by the unabashedly pro-Zionist attitude of the government of Prime Minister Jan Christiaan Smuts and the strong Zionist sympathies of South Africa's approximately 110,000 Jews. Most of them had come from Lithuania where Zionism had strong roots; in addition, many undoubtedly felt the pressures of being members of a small community unsure of its position in South African society. There was unease over South Africa's race problems and perhaps also a feeling that South Africa could never be more than a temporary homeland for Jews because of these difficulties.[28]

There had been more than a streak of anti-semitism in the majority Boer community for many years. The leader of the National Party, the Opposition in the South African parliament, Dr. D. F. Malan, was against further Jewish immigration to South Africa. In an interview published in Die Burgher, his main party newspaper, only a few weeks before the Palestine partition vote at the United Nations, Malan was quoted as saying:

> I almost want to ask if there can be anyone today who still questions whether [a Jewish problem] exists. . . . The fact is that the Jewish people have no national home and as soon as their numbers in any land exceed a certain percentage it creates a race problem there. Anti-Semitism exists.[29]

By early December 1947, the South African Zionist Federation had started keeping records of those who volunteered for service in Palestine. At a mass rally in Coronation Hall in Johannesburg, forms were handed out asking volunteers for their names and addresses, and for particulars of their war service. In January 1948, Major Michael Comay, a South-African-born veteran and an important figure in the Political Department of the Jewish Agency, visited South Africa to tell the Jews of South Africa what was happening in Palestine. His unofficial duty was to make contact with local Zionists to help them organize a recruiting operation.[30]

In February, more emissaries arrived from Palestine. Among them were Yoel Palgi and Boris Senior. Palgi and Senior had extensive connections in South Africa. Both had served in World War II.

Palgi had been dropped behind German lines in eastern Europe in 1943, and had served with Tito's partisans in Yugoslavia. He had crossed into Hungary, where he was captured, imprisoned, and tortured. He managed to escape and spent the rest of the war harassing the Hungarian police and the Nazis in a number of daring escapades. Eventually he had joined the Haganah underground to help smuggle immigrants out of Europe.[31]

Senior was a veteran of the South African Air Force. He had attended the London School of Economics after the war, had joined the Irgun, and had become involved in an Irgun plot to assassinate Lieutenant General Evelyn Barker. Barker had served as General Officer commanding the British forces in Palestine. His stern measures against the Irgun and Lehi earned him their undying hatred. Senior and a fellow-student at the LSE, Ezer Weizman (Weizman had been a Palestinian fighter pilot in the Royal Air Force), were assigned the task of flying an assassin from France to England, and then back to the continent after the deed. The plan went awry, however, and British Intelligence closed in. Senior and Weizman had quickly left England, Weizman returning to Palestine, and Senior to South Africa. Immediately after the partition vote in November 1947, Senior sent Weizman a telegram to say he was coming, bought a ticket, and flew to Lydda airport in Palestine. Soon he had joined the Haganah Air Service along with Weizman and several other Palestinian-born pilots.[32]

When Senior was despatched to South Africa by Aharon Remez and Alex Ziloni he carried a letter from the "General Council of Jewish Aviation" in Palestine empowering him to recruit air crew and mechanics and to buy planes. He and Palgi worked closely together at the offices of the South African Zionist Federation, poring over lists of volunteers and interviewing those who looked most promising. Palgi was primarily responsible for recruiting, Senior for acquiring aircraft.

After his failure to smuggle the P-40s out of South Africa, Senior turned his attention to the purchase of civilian aircraft. These would be much easier to bring into Palestine using a variety of cover stories, different owners' names, and foreign registrations. Eventually, Senior purchased, for from ten to twelve thousand pounds each, a small fleet of single- and twin-engine light planes in first-class condition.[33] All that was now needed was to recruit crews and prepare for the airlift to Palestine.

IV

On a cold, snowy evening in Montreal, in early 1948, a party in a third-floor restaurant was interrupted by the ringing of the downstairs pay phone. Someone trudged up the stairs and called Joe Frank to the phone. Frank, a vice-president of the Zionist Organization of Canada, was worried. He had left instructions with his wife that he was not to be disturbed, and he knew that while he and the others were celebrating, a group of young men in a warehouse across the city were preparing a shipment of arms for Palestine. Something must be wrong. As Frank took the phone, he heard the voice of the local Haganah representative; the men had been discovered and the shipment had been seized. Frank listened, horrified thoughts of possible consequences racing through his mind. Who would be caught? How much did the government know? When would they come for him? He was more frightened than he had ever been before.[34] (Frank's fears were groundless. Neither he nor any other Zionist leader was ever charged with the illegal export of arms.)

Canada, like the United States, had been a major supplier of arms for the Allies during World War II. When the fighting ended, it became a dumping ground for huge amounts of surplus weaponry. It was a natural target for Haganah arms-collection activities. Canadian war equipment was not easy pickings, however. Canadian arms-export policies were co-ordinated with those of the United States and the United Kingdom,[35] and the Canadian government was anxious to help the British and the Americans keep a tight control on the flow of arms to the Middle East. Nevertheless, although Ottawa's attitude posed an obstacle for Canadian Jews determined to aid the Haganah, it did not stop them.

The Canadian supporters of the Haganah were a varied group. One of the men who had gathered in Sonneborn's office to meet Ben Gurion in the summer of 1945, and who was involved in the running of Aid to Palestine, the Canadian version of Materials for Palestine, was Samuel J. Zacks, a prominent Toronto businessman and Zionist leader.

Several Toronto Jews had also been involved in early attempts to assemble and test a prototype submachine gun designed in the United States for the Haganah by Carl Ekdahl.[36] The major Canadian effort to ship arms, aircraft, and other military equipment to Palestine was chanelled through the Victory Equipment & Supply Company Limited, a shoestring operation run with one telephone out of a small, dusty office at 422 McGill Street in Montreal.

Victory Equipment had been established by several prominent Canadian Zionists including Samuel Schwisberg and Joe Frank.[37] It worked side by side with Aid to Palestine (which collected non-military goods in Canada) and with the United Zionist Purchasing Commission, headed by Montreal lawyer Leon D. Crestohl.

The Purchasing Commission had been established by the United Zionist Council, the umbrella organization of Canadian Zionism. It was the ultimate source of funds for all purchases in Canada of both "white" and "black" supplies. It was vital, therefore, that there be a discreet connection between the Purchasing Commission and Victory Equipment. Walter Loewenson, secretary of the Purchasing Commission and secretary-treasurer of Victory Equipment, was the link.

Because Victory Equipment was ultimately responsible to Teddy Kollek's operation in New York, Loewenson laid down guidelines for Canadian purchasing and supply operations in consultation with Haganah headquarters at the Hotel Fourteen. Loewenson wanted Aid to Palestine to gather linen, food, clothing, and medical supplies; but what Loewenson referred to as "technical supplies and equipment" were to be reserved for the Purchasing Commission. He put the reason somewhat cryptically in a message to New York: "...this will give me better opportunities of mixing in, along with very harmless items, some things which it may be more difficult to get approval for, and for which we may not get [export] permits...."[38] What he did not add, because New York was no doubt already aware of it, was that Victory Equipment, not the Purchasing Commission, ultimately handled those "hot" items.

In the summer of 1948, Loewenson's place was taken by Joe Baumholz, an engineering student from McGill. Baumholz was a fast talker and good at making connections. He had volunteered to fight in Palestine, but his considerable organizational talents made him more valuable in Montreal. He too was the man in the central position—secretary-treasurer and sole employee of Victory Equipment and secretary to Crestohl's Purchasing Commission. Building on the foundation established by Loewenson, Baumholz worked out a foolproof method for financing Victory Equipment's purchases. The Purchasing Commission raised its funds openly from various Zionist organizations. However, Canadian currency-control regulations did not allow funds collected in Canada to be sent abroad,[39] so with the funds Baumholz then bought supplies directly from different dealers and distributors. (Baumholz never dealt directly with the Canadian War Assets Corporation, which was responsible for selling war surplus equipment. He always bought through private dealers.)

Victory Equipment was one of the many companies the Purchasing Commission dealt with but it was a company with a vital difference. When Baumholz, acting for Victory Equipment, bought bandages or blankets from legitimate suppliers he did it with the sole purpose of selling those supplies to the Purchasing Commission. When he billed the Purchasing Commission, he inflated the invoices. In this way Baumholz covered his costs and had money left to buy whatever military equipment he came across. Like Loewenson, he kept in constant touch with the New York headquarters. From headquarters he got lists of specific requirements; in addition he continually checked with New York to see if the radio sets, radar equipment, flame throwers, and Link trainers he had come across were needed and if the asking price was right.[40]

The Canadian Zionists were lucky to have a key friend in the government. Alex "Sandy" Skelton was the son of the late Dr. Oscar Douglas Skelton. O. D. Skelton had been Deputy Minister of the Department of External Affairs and a senior foreign policy advisor to Prime Minister William Lyon Mackenzie King. His son, Alex, a brilliant economist who had studied at Queen's University in the mid-1920s, had served on the Wartime Prices and Trade Board, and in other government agencies, during World War II. In the spring of 1947 he was appointed Acting Director General of Research in the Department of Reconstruction and Supply. In the summer of 1948 he joined the Department of Trade and Commerce as an Assistant Deputy Minister. Skelton—a hard drinker who could outswear any army sergeant—was also well connected in Ottawa's political and bureaucratic circles.

Skelton's father, who had died in 1941, had never shown any particular interest in or sympathy towards Zionism. Apart from some anti-British feeling no doubt inherited from his father, Alex himself betrayed few political sentiments. However, he was a close personal friend of Sam Zacks, whom he had met at Queen's, and of Moe Appel, who was one of the few men in Ottawa who could match Skelton drink for drink. The friendship with Skelton was important because, particularly after Skelton went to Trade and Commerce, he was able to arrange export permits for all sorts of questionable items. As Zacks wrote of him in October 1948: "...we have few better friends or more generous liberals than Alex Skelton."[41]

Moe Appel was another genuine character. He had worked as a newspaperman with the Ottawa *Citizen*. In 1942, he had left a city editor's job to join the Reuters News Agency as a war correspondent in Europe. After the war he was editor of Reuters' North American bureau in New York City. He left Reuters in 1946 to serve a brief stint with the American Jewish Congress, and then returned to Ottawa as Public Relations Director with the Zionist Organization of Canada. Appel was a short man with a rough manner of speech who easily saw behind facade and pretension. He had earned much respect in the newspaper business and had formed many valuable friendships in his numerous days—and nights—in Ottawa's favourite press haunts. He knew most of the key newspapermen, politicians, and top-level bureaucrats in the Canadian government. And, of course, he knew Alex Skelton.[42]

When Baumholz needed an export permit for a particularly difficult cargo, he called a special number in Ottawa and relayed his request to a Jewish lawyer who worked closely with Appel and Skelton. One such cargo (which was eventually shipped in the summer of 1948) was a number of Harvard trainers purchased by an Ontario scrap dealer.[43] These were single-engine monoplanes, built for a crew of two, that were easily convertible to military uses. The aircraft in question had been used to train pilots during the war. In autumn 1946, they had been routinely transferred from the Royal Canadian Air Force to the War Assets Corporation to be sold for scrap.[44] Baumholz needed a way to get them out of the country and a call went out to Ottawa.

When Appel learned of the problem he set up a meeting with the lawyer and Skelton. The three met at night at Appel's office at 46 Elgin Street. Appel had just moved in and there were, as he put it, "just enough chairs and a desk for whiskey". They began to drink and had soon consumed the best part of a large bottle. Skelton said little; Appel and the lawyer did most of the talking. The lawyer, normally not a drinking man, was soon sick to his stomach. Skelton was "doodling and doodling and doodling", Appel remembered. In the midst of his doodling, Skelton suddenly exclaimed: "I've got it, goddamnit." He looked up: "Do you guys have a spring fair in Tel Aviv?" "No," Appel said, "but we can create one." Skelton seemed satisfied. "You draw a plan. We'll dismantle the goddamned things, put them in crates, and send them to the Tel Aviv Spring Fair." Not long after, several large crates painted red, white, and blue and addressed to the Tel Aviv Spring Fair left Canada.[45] In Israel the contents of the crates were put back together, equipped with bomb racks, and pressed into service as dive bombers.

In Montreal, Baumholz was usually responsible for arranging warehousing, packing, and shipping of both legal and illegal goods. His favourite work place was Rappaport's Bottle and Supply Company on St. Lawrence Boulevard. There students, usually volunteers from Zionist youth groups, worked hard to crate the supplies and stencil destinations on the boxes. Only the military goods were mislabelled. "Technical equipment", "wire", "ingots", and so on were stencilled on crates containing radios, radar, and other military goods. Flame throwers became "insecticide sprayers".

From the warehouse the goods moved by rail or truck to the port—to Montreal harbour, if the St. Lawrence River was still ice-free; in the winter, to Halifax, Nova Scotia, St. John, New Brunswick, or even Portland, Maine. When the shipment was ready, Baumholz called New York. Elie Shalit, the man on Kollek's staff who co-ordinated shipping from North America, would then arrange to have a freighter pick up the cargo.[46]

By the summer of 1948 a steady stream of supplies was leaving Baumholz's warehouses in Montreal. There were clothes and blankets and canned pears and canned meat. There were also machine guns, flame throwers, and thousands of Mark 19 radio sets that had been built in Canada for Canadian and Allied use during the war. Some, built for the Soviet Union, were shipped to Palestine with Russian markings and instructions still on them. Canadian Jews may have contributed only a handful of planes and guns to the Jewish war effort, but Canadian radio sets and other radio equipment became the backbone of Israel's military communications network.

Baumholz and Victory Equipment were only one small part of a

48

world-wide Haganah operation. Similar activities were taking place from Brazil to Czechoslovakia, and from Burbank to Johannesburg. Some of the network's machinery had been set up in the closing years of World War II, some after Ben Gurion's visit with the Sonneborn group in 1945. But most of the operation had been hastily established in reaction to an obvious need in the months following the partition vote in the United Nations. In almost all countries where the Haganah sought help, the local Jewish communities responded selflessly. They had to. In Palestine the Haganah and the Yishuv were more hard pressed with each passing day.

Although arms from abroad were urgently needed for the battle to open the roads of Palestine, there were other equally vital requirements. Trained men with prior military experience, officers who had served with conventional armies, technical experts, army medical personnel, and maintenance specialists were also essential. The Haganah's war with the Palestine Arabs was only the beginning. When the British withdrew from Palestine leaving the way clear for an Arab League invasion, larger battles would follow. Thus, at Ben Gurion's urging, the Haganah had also embarked on a campaign to recruit foreign volunteers, mostly from among the hundreds of thousands of Jewish war veterans in the Allied countries, but also from among non-Jews who were willing to risk their lives to help the Jews of Palestine.

4

"I Am Going to Visit My Uncle"

Jules Cuburnek handed his birth certificate to the U.S. government passport officer in New York City. The official examined it closely for a few moments and then looked up: "I can't give you a passport," he said. Cuburnek was taken aback: "Why not, what do you mean?" "You don't have any first name," the officer replied as he handed the document back to Cuburnek for a look. Cuburnek stared at it for a moment. He had never really looked at it, never noticed its now embarrassing flaw. "What's your name?" the passport officer asked. "Jules," answered the now nervous Cuburnek. "Can you prove it? Is there anyone in the city who can swear to it?" Without thinking, Cuburnek said "no". The officer was adamant: "Look, you've got to have a mother or a father or a close relative." Cuburnek was from Chicago, but his sister lived in New York. He had not admitted this because he had been told to be careful and discreet. Now he was trapped. If he changed his mind and admitted that he had a sister living in the city the officer might become suspicious. If he did not, he would not get his passport and would not be allowed to leave the United States on the first leg of his secret journey to Palestine. "Oh, wait a minute, yes, yes," Cuburnek said. "My sister is coming in to New York at three o'clock today. She's coming in from Chicago." The passport officer looked at him for a moment: "All right, bring her in, she'll swear what your name is." Cuburnek's quick thinking had got him out of a tight spot.

In the early spring of 1948 Jules Cuburnek was thirty years old, a veteran of twenty-five missions over Europe in a U.S. Army Air Force B-17 during World War II. In the autumn of 1945 he was discharged from the army with the rank of captain and went into the drugstore business with his brothers and one sister in Chicago. He had rarely taken any interest in Jewish affairs before the war, but the anti-semitism he had met in the army awakened his interest in his Jewish background. While attending to his business in Chicago, he followed events in Palestine in the newspapers and avidly read books pleading the Zionist cause.

One day Cuburnek was drinking at the apartment of a fellow veteran when an argument broke out about whether or not Jews had kept "cushy" jobs for themselves in the army during the war. Cuburnek protested: "You guys are full of shit. I didn't have any cushy job. I went into the air force. In fact, I'll tell you the truth, there's no challenge in the world today. I wish there was something like the Spanish Civil War going on again where a guy could volunteer and do something for the world and change the world around." "You've got such a big mouth," one of the others shot back, "why don't you go to Palestine and fly for the Jews?" They had no air force, Cuburnek protested, but the other man pulled out a newspaper and showed him a story under the headline "Palestinian Air Force Bombs the Arabs". He was trapped. "Okay, all right, I'm going to get over there." Two weeks later he showed up at an office on Dearborn Street in Chicago. From there he was sent to New York where he was interviewed, and told to get his affairs in order prior to leaving for Palestine and to get a passport.[1] Jules Cuburnek had joined the Jewish air force in Palestine— an air force that still had virtually no planes, no bases, and very few pilots or air crew.

I

Since the end of the war, the Haganah had used foreign volunteers— mostly Americans, and a handful of Canadians—to help man the refugee ships that plied the Mediterranean bringing "illegal" immigrants to Palestine. By the spring of 1947, however, Ben Gurion made it clear that he wanted foreign volunteers for an even more important job—to help convert the Haganah into a conventional army. Ben Gurion was convinced that trained officers—either Palestinian Jews who had served with the British Army or foreign volunteeers, Jewish or not—were crucial to the defence of the Yishuv.[2]

This touched a raw nerve in the Haganah establishment, where a struggle for influence and position was going on between those officers who had gained their experience largely within Haganah ranks and those who had held commissions with the British forces. Ben Gurion wanted the Jewish forces in Palestine to be run along the lines of a regular army. He was particularly insistent that the British pattern be followed, even though the Haganah commanders, especially Israel Galili and Yigael Yadin, did not agree.[3] They and others like them who had come up through the ranks of the underground may have felt threatened by the prospect of reorganization that would put the skills of their British-trained colleagues at a premium. At one time Ben Gurion had even considered setting up an army command structure to parallel that of the Haganah using former British Army officers like Haim Laskov (Laskov had commanded a machine-gun platoon with the Jewish Brigade in Italy) and Shlomo Shamir.[4] He did not press this idea, however, since resistance to it was too strong.

Ben Gurion's search for foreign volunteers to aid the Haganah began in the United States in December 1947. At that time, Moshe Shertok, head of the Jewish Agency's Political Department and unofficial foreign minister, approached General John Hilldring, Assistant Secretary of State. Shertok was looking for help in obtaining military equipment and in enlisting the services of "two or three competent American officers who would be prepared to proceed to Palestine and advise on defence arrangements".[5] Shertok was looking for advisors, not volunteers. He wanted expert opinions on how best to prepare the Haganah and improve Yishuv defences. Hilldring had a reputation for being friendly to the Jews. He had been sympathetic to the Jewish refugees in Europe when he was in charge of occupied territories for the State Department.[6] He told Shertok that he would have to go "to the very top" on both requests and that it would probably be easier to get military advice than arms.[7] He did, however, know someone who might help—former U.S. Army Colonel David "Mickey" Marcus.

Marcus was a West Point graduate who had served with distinction in the U.S. Army in World War II. He had been Judge Advocate of the 27th Infantry Division in Hawaii, had served with the Civil Affairs Division at army headquarters in Washington, and had parachuted into France with the 101st Airborne Division during the Normandy campaign. As the war drew to a close his chief responsibility was helping to plan the post-war Allied occupation of Germany. In this capacity his commanding officer had been General John Hilldring.

By December 1947, Marcus had returned to civilian life and a private law practice in New York. He was soon approached by Shlomo Shamir. Shamir asked Marcus to help him find a high-ranking officer who would be willing to advise the Jewish Agency on a contract basis. Marcus and Shamir approached Major General Ralph C. Smith. Although Smith was interested, he demurred for fear that he would lose his army pension. It soon became obvious that Marcus himself was the only man available for the job. In early January 1948 he took leave from his law firm and prepared to go to Palestine with Shamir. There he was to examine the military situation and give his advice on the state of the Haganah's fighting ability.[8]

Marcus's agreement to help coincided with the establishment in Jerusalem, by the Jewish Agency Executive, of the Committee for Overseas Mobilization. The committee hurriedly drew up recruitment guidelines for Zionist groups throughout the world who were signing up volunteers for service in Palestine.

The guidelines, which were adopted by the Jewish Agency Executive at the end of January, called for two years of voluntary service, although in special cases recruitment committees could authorize a one-year term. The guidelines also specified that volunteers should be in their twenties, single or at least without children or other obligation to their families, and in good physical condition.

Volunteers would be kept in units with others who spoke the same language. Their immediate needs such as money, housing, food, and religious services would be provided for. The agency promised to try to provide life insurance for volunteers and pledged to return volunteers to their countries of origin when their service was completed. Those who chose to stay would be integrated into Palestinian society.

The agency also laid down strict lines of authority. Recruiting would be conducted in the United States, Canada, Latin America, and the British Isles. In all these countries, Zionist federations existed to organize the activities. The Zionist Executive in each country was the only institution authorized to carry out the mobilization; the Zionist emergency councils in the different countries would be under the supervision of and were to act on instructions from the Jewish Agency Executive in Jerusalem.[9]

II

Late in January, Marcus and Shamir flew from New York to Palestine. According to the contract Marcus had signed with the Jewish Agency he was to act as a consultant from January 15 to May 15 at $750 per month plus expenses. He travelled under the alias "Michael Stone".[10] He was tearing himself away from a potentially lucrative law practice; the funds provided partial compensation.

Marcus had wide military experience although he was not of the general officer rank that Ben Gurion had desired. Marcus was one of three former U.S. Army officers to visit Palestine for the Jewish Agency in the months leading up to the establishment of the State of Israel. The other two, Colonels Henschel and Krulevich, were both members of a Jewish War Veterans organization and both reported to "government and army" circles in Washington after their return from Palestine.[11] They were apparently playing two roles—consulting for the Jewish Agency on military matters and keeping the Pentagon informed of the state of Jewish forces in Palestine.

Marcus was in Palestine for about three months. During that time, he visited Haganah forces on almost every battle front. He examined training methods, officers' leadership qualities, and the troops' technical skills, and reported to Ben Gurion that he had discovered "less than he expected, more than he had hoped". Marcus had not found a single complete regiment that could be moved about and sent into combat. This was partly because of poor equipment—there was, he reported, a total lack of communications and transport facilities—but it was primarily caused by a dearth of trained leadership. There were men aplenty who could command small units, but none who could move and command the larger formations. Marcus suggested that regimental commanders be brought from the United States and that a one-month course in organizational skills for regimental and staff officers be established.[12] The course would be taught by regular army veterans such as himself and Shlomo Shamir.

Despite Marcus's judgment on the Jewish forces, Ben Gurion was delighted. The day after he received the report, Ben Gurion wrote Moshe Shertok in the United States that "the expert who came here with Shlomo completed his examination of our units; his report is very brilliant and he understands well our special situation." He asked Shertok to send "at least ten like Marcus".[13]

III

Major Wellesley Aron, formerly of the British Army and the Haganah, had been somewhat reluctant to make the long flight from the west coast to New York City. He was constantly shuffling back and forth between San Diego and Portland, Oregon, giving newspaper interviews, addressing audiences, and working with the B'nai B'rith Anti-Defamation League to counter anti-Zionist propaganda. The unexpected trip to New York would be tiring and was an unscheduled expense, but Teddy Kollek had insisted that the Haganah wanted him for an important job and such requests had to be taken seriously.

Shortly after his arrival in New York, Aron met Kollek, Rabbi Abba Hillel Silver, and other members of the Zionist Organization of America Executive. They asked him to take over an organization known as Land and Labor for Palestine and run it as a Haganah recruiting operation.

"How urgent is it?" Aron asked.

"It's absolutely vital," Kollek replied. "You must do it."

Aron was reluctant. "I left my family in a state of limbo in Los Angeles," he pointed out. "I'm becoming a shuttlecock here. It's not a way of life after six years away in the army, you know. . . . But, if it's so important, I'll do it." He said he would need a lot of help, since it was illegal to recruit American nationals for a foreign army. Kollek and others promised him all he would need. He also asked to be installed in "a low down area where [there was] a lot of coming and going" and Kollek found him a suite at the Hotel Breslin in Manhattan.[14]

Born in London, England, in 1901, Aron had been brought up as an upper-middle-class assimilated Jew with a Cambridge University education. At the age of twenty-five he was suddenly struck by a desire to seek his identity, to "either be a Jew or assimilated like the rest of my family", as he later recalled. He decided to settle in Palestine, where he married and started a family. Aron seemed almost like an archetype of the colonial Englishman, and despite his hard work and dedication to Zionism it took the Jews in Palestine a long time to accept him. Aron served with the British Army during World War II. He had been sent to the U.S. west coast by the Jewish Agency after the war to act as an unofficial roving ambassador to the Jewish community there.[15]

Aron's new charge, Land and Labor for Palestine, had been founded earlier as a recruiting agency for young men and women eager to work on agricultural settlements in Palestine; but as the crisis in Palestine intensified, it had become almost totally inactive. Land and Labor's work would be a good cover for Aron's recruiting operation.

Aron was not operating in a vacuum; he was responsible to Kollek, and his work was funded by the Jewish Agency. He met often with Rabbi Silver and co-ordinated his recruiting efforts with Schindler and others at Service Airways.

In its new role, Land and Labor was responsible for infantry specialists—experts in armour, artillery, mortars, communications, or any other types of military experience. Service Airways was responsible for air crew and aircraft-maintenance experts. Most of the money to recruit, train, and transport the volunteers was raised by the local Jewish community.[16]

Aron established branch offices in every major city in the United States that had a large Jewish population. The branch offices were staffed by volunteers. Their job was to contact Jewish veterans who might be willing to go to Palestine and who possessed the required skills. Contacts were made in a variety of ways. In some cities speakers addressed gatherings in synagogues or Jewish community halls. Their talks concentrated on the need for manpower in Palestine, but only hinted at the use that would be made of this manpower. Those interested in hearing more were told to wait until after the meeting and then, behind closed doors, the real purpose of Land and Labor was revealed and information about the qualifications and skills of the prospective volunteers was gathered. Interested persons were given an address or telephone number to contact.

Land and Labor volunteers also worked with Jewish branches of veterans' organizations or with the leaders of the smaller Jewish communities to identify Jewish war veterans who were then approached personally. Sometimes an entire list of Jewish war veterans was obtained, and cryptic letters were sent mentioning Palestine and manpower needs and giving a local telephone number to call. At other times an interested veteran sought information on his own and approached a local Zionist organization, Jewish charity, or branch office of Materials for Palestine.

Because caution was essential, inquiries were often met with blank stares and outright, sometimes hostile, denials. But if the prospective volunteer was persistent, if something in his manner or bearing overcame recruiters' suspicions, then a name was taken and a telephone number or address was given and contact with the local Land and Labor office was soon established.

In February, Heyman Shamir arrived in New York to co-ordinate the recruiting of air crews and to establish air routes to Palestine. Shamir was sent by Sherut Avir leaders who had decided, at a meeting in late January 1948, to work towards closer co-operation between themselves and the people like Schwimmer who were already buying aircraft abroad.[17]

Although Shamir operated as part of Kollek's team, he had considerable freedom of action.[18] He brought maps with routes to Palestine, lists of navigation aids, and sketches of the landing strips that the Haganah hoped to use. He also had a good idea of the types of people to recruit and worked closely with Lewis, Schindler, and others in recruiting and checking out volunteers from the greater New York area. Using lists of air force veterans obtained from a variety of sources, the recruiter made telephone calls to men with names that appeared Jewish and gave hints during the conversation that would allow the prospective recruit to guess what the caller had in mind. Each veteran who appeared interested was eventually interviewed by one of the Service Airways principals, while some were taken to Millville to be checked out by Lewis.[19]

It was all done as quietly as possible. U.S. law had severe penalties for American citizens serving with foreign armies against countries at peace with the United States. Section 10 of the United States Criminal Code prohibited "Enlisting or entering into the service of any foreign prince, state, colony, district, or people as a soldier, or as a marine, or seaman on board of any ship of war, letter of marque, or privateer." It also prohibited recruiting other persons for foreign military service.[20] But did Land and Labor recruit or merely supply information? Were the volunteers joining a foreign army or were they signing up for the two years of agricultural work stipulated in their agreements with Land and Labor? It was best for all concerned not to have the questions answered in the courts, with the possibility of fines or imprisonment.[21]

Despite all the precautions, it was inevitable that word would leak out. On more than one occasion Aron found himself face to face with the FBI. Once it was two special agents, a Protestant and an Irish Catholic. Aron "converted" the Catholic: "You know that what I'm doing, if I'm doing it, is simply what you people would like to do. Get the British out and get Ireland independent." But this did not work for the partner who kept on the case with dogged tenaciousness, eventually forcing Aron to close up shop and cart the files away to a vacant lot in Queens, where they were burned.[22]

Aron worked with a committee of former high-ranking American Jewish officers who helped formulate priorities, establish training and transportation procedures, interview the volunteers, and secure lists of former Jewish servicemen. When men began to arrive from Los Angeles or St. Louis or Chicago, they went to the Hotel Breslin for an appointment. There they were closely questioned about their former army service, their health, and their family status. They were told in no uncertain terms what they were getting themselves into, and they were asked ceaselessly about how they had arrived at the decision to go, and why. The work was similar to that being carried out at Service Airways just a few blocks away.

All American volunteers eventually passed through New York. Medical examinations were arranged—some at night at the Mount Sinai Hospital. Interviews were set up with psychiatrists, and passports were obtained for those without them. Here roadblocks were frequently encountered because, by early February 1948, the government was well aware that American citizens already in Palestine were finding their way into the Jewish forces. Each U.S. passport issued since 1937 contained the warning that it was "not valid for travel to or in any foreign state for the purpose of enlisting or serving in the armed forces of such a state".[23] Even though Palestine was not a state, the State Department viewed it as such for purposes of withdrawing passports from Americans serving in the Haganah. It was obvious, therefore, that volunteers applying for passports could not disclose their true destination or the purpose of their travel. Every possible ruse was tried. European destinations were given on passport applications. Holidays or education travel were put down as the purpose of the trip. Jewish businessmen were lined up to provide letters proving that the applicant was going to Europe on legitimate business.[24] Even so, the sudden flood of passport applications from Jewish males of military age raised immediate suspicions at the Passport Bureau. One particular official seemed to make it a personal crusade to ferret out the real purpose behind the applications and frequently asked if the applicant had any connection with Land and Labor or with Wellesley Aron. She would refuse passports more often than she granted them, and Aron had nightmares about this problem.[25]

Army volunteers awaiting passage to Europe or Palestine were sent to a summer camp north of New York City, near Peekskill. Aron had made arrangements with the owners of the camp to use it as a training, holding, and transit centre. Some rudimentary training was given in small arms—especially the Sten gun—and in elementary Hebrew, and each morning there was a flag-raising ceremony and a three-kilometre run. Infantry volunteers were sometimes forced to spend several weeks at the camp while they waited for passports and visas because hundreds were showing up at the Hotel Breslin by early March and it was too costly to put them all up in hotels. Aron also wanted to keep them as segregated as possible so that chances of a leak would be kept to a minimum.

Flight crews, by contrast, rarely waited around. Recruiters were alerted to be on the lookout for former flight-crew or aircraft-maintenance specialists and were told to contact New York directly to seek advice if they came across a likely prospect. These volunteers were then examined and innoculated and, once in possession of travel documents, were handed plane tickets to Paris, Rome, Zurich, or Geneva.

Volunteers destined to see action with the ground forces in Palestine travelled from New York by ship via two different routes, one direct and one through France. The direct route utilized the *Marine Carp*, a former troop-carrying Liberty ship that sailed from New York every six weeks bound directly for the Mediterranean. Land and Labor favoured this ship for American volunteers. The *Marine Carp* stopped at major ports such as Marseilles, Genoa, Piraeus, Beirut, Haifa, and Alexandria before returning to New York, and it had been used to send students and kibbutz volunteers to Palestine as early as 1946. It was clearly the fastest and most direct way of sending people as long as they had the proper passports and visas to clear British Immigration at Haifa.[26] The other route used sister ships of the *Marine Carp*—the *Marine Tiger* or the *Marine Falcon*. All three ships were operated by United States Lines. These ships made frequent sailings from New York to Le Havre, France. This route was favoured for Canadian volunteers, although Americans also travelled this way. The *Marine* ships were far from luxurious but they had two unsurpassed virtues—they sailed frequently and passage on them was cheap. The fare from New York to Le Havre was $156.[27] Because it was an ideal way for students or service-men's wives to cross the Atlantic, it also offered a modicum of camouflage for the volunteers. This was, after all, only the third spring of peace since the end of the war and young men and women, most of them oblivious to the desperate struggle then being waged in Palestine, were on the move to Paris or Rome.

IV

On a cold night in early 1948, the main auditorium of the Brunswick Avenue Talmud Torah in Toronto was filled to capacity as Major Ben Adelman, one of the Haganah's recruiters in Canada, addressed the expectant crowd. They were a disparate group, some young, some old. But probably the largest number were men in their mid to late twenties who had served with the Canadian forces in World War II. They had been phoned, had seen mysterious posters challenging them to "Stand up and be counted", or had heard rumours about recruiting for Palestine. They came to listen and, perhaps, to volunteer.

As Adelman spoke, several other well-known Toronto Jews sat on stage. Among them was Benjamin Dunkelman, a former major who had served with the Queen's Own Rifles of Canada and who had won the Distinguished Service Order. Dunkelman and Adelman were both native-born Canadians who had settled in Palestine in the 1930s. Dunkelman had eventually returned to Canada, but Adelman had stayed. He had served with the British Army during World War II and, as a Canadian, was considered a good choice to act as the Haganah's representative to the Canadian recruiters.

On this occasion, Adelman gave an impassioned speech describing the struggle in Palestine, the precarious position of the Yishuv, and the need for foreign volunteers, particularly war veterans. He emphasized that he was not asking married men, or men with children, to volunteer, but he urged others to come forward, particularly if they had skills that would be valuable to the Haganah. Almost everyone in the hall stood although few ever left for Palestine.[28]

Although Adelman had given the key speech of the evening, Dunkelman was the real sparkplug of the Canadian recruiting network. His DSO was not the highest decoration received by a Canadian Jewish war veteran, but Dunkelman's exploits on European battlefields were well known. A despatch published in the *Toronto Daily Star* in December 1944 called him "Mr. Mortar of the Canadian Army". "Wherever you go," wrote *Star* correspondent John Clare, "they know him and they know him as 'Base Plate Dunkelman'."[29]

Dunkelman was the scion of a wealthy Toronto family. His mother, Rose, had been one of Toronto's leading Zionists for many years, and Dunkelman himself had spent considerable time in Palestine in the 1930s. He was an obvious candidate to head the Canadian recruiting operation. He had held high rank in the Canadian Army, had seen considerable action, and had a strong Zionist background. When Orde Wingate's widow made a speaking tour of Canada in the fall of 1947 she directed a personal appeal to Dunkelman to consider going to Palestine to fight, but he made no commitment and bided his time. According to his memoirs, Dunkelman arrived at the decision to get directly involved after an American clergyman "described in lurid detail what the Arabs would do to the Jews in the inevitable military showdown".[30] It is highly likely that Dunkelman's decision was also influenced by Ben Adelman. In the mid-1930s Dunkelman had known Adelman in Palestine and had planned to start a new Jewish settlement with him and a number of other newcomers from English-speaking countries.[31] In addition, Dunkelman had been approached by Shamir and Marcus prior to their first trip to Palestine in January 1948.

Once Dunkelman decided to get involved, he quickly put together a Haganah steering committee that included representatives from the Jewish communities in both Toronto and Montreal. The committee tackled two main tasks—establishing and operating a recruiting network and raising the cash to pay all the expenses of sending Canadian volunteers to Palestine. Dunkelman thought he and his committee were to recruit "an infantry brigade of English-speaking volunteers" to be under his command,[32] but such a brigade—apparently fashioned after the International Brigades that had fought in the Spanish Civil War—was never formed. It is unlikely that the Haganah was ever serious about such a venture, whatever Adelman or Shamir may have proposed. The last thing the Haganah needed was infantry, and it is obvious from Ben Gurion's plans that only skilled specialists were wanted, and that these were to be used where they were most needed throughout the Jewish forces.

At least one other misunderstanding marred Dunkelman's relationship with the Haganah. When he received final instructions to begin recruiting he was told to raise "a military unit of 1000 soldiers", but the Jewish Agency later slapped a limit of three hundred on the number of Canadian recruits.[33] There was apparently serious doubt in New York about the possibility of raising one thousand volunteers in Canada and it was decided to concentrate on a more realistic target. "The daydream," Teddy Kollek later recalled, "was scaled down to a practical proposition."[34]

Dunkelman and his committee had much to draw upon. More than eighteen thousand Canadian Jews had served in Canadian and Allied

Forces during World War II.[35] Most Canadian Jews lived in Montreal and Toronto. Both cities boasted Jewish branches of the Royal Canadian Legion—the Brigadier Frederick Kisch branch in Montreal and the Orde Wingate branch in Toronto. None the less a broader national representation was necessary if the recruiting campaign was to be brought to the attention of the largest possible number of Jewish war veterans.

The effort to build a national recruiting organization began in late January 1948. Dunkelman first brought in Lionel Druker, a law student living in Halifax who had been an armour instructor during the war and who was already thinking of volunteering for military service in Palestine. Druker then contacted Arthur Goldberg, a student at the University of British Columbia and former army cadet. Goldberg had travelled to Palestine after the war and had seen the misery of the Jewish refugees living in the European displaced persons camps. Goldberg, on his own initiative, had formed a loosely organized group of students, most of whom were veterans, who aimed to fight for the Jews in Palestine but who had no idea of whom to contact or how to get there.[36]

At about the same time, Vancouver lawyer Harold Freeman was contacted by D. Lou Harris, a Toronto businessman who was a tireless and ebullient worker for Zionist causes. Harris asked Freeman to help the Dunkelman group raise money and to take charge of recruiting in western Canada. Although Freeman worried about the legality of the operation, he agreed to take the job. Within weeks he had organized his own network, which spread to the major cities in the west.[37]

Montreal had the largest Jewish population in Canada, and there a committee headed by Sydney Shulemson and Moshe Myerson worked with Leon Crestohl and other Zionist leaders. Shulemson, a former Beaufighter pilot, was widely known in the Jewish community for his exploits during the war. He had been the most decorated Jewish serviceman in Canada. Myerson, a Montreal lawyer, had joined the Canadian Army in 1940 at the age of forty-seven. Both he and Shulemson had access to the names and addresses of Jewish veterans in Montreal through the Brigadier Kisch branch of the Royal Canadian Legion.

In Toronto, Dunkelman led the recruiting network, speaking to veterans' meetings and co-ordinating his activities with the Haganah in New York. D. Lou Harris, his chief helper, took over leadership of the operation after Dunkelman left for Palestine in March. Harris took a personal interest in each volunteer. He did everything in his power to ease the volunteers' lot in the field and to provide for their welfare on their return to Canada. Harris worked closely with Sam Zacks, president of the Zionist Organization of Canada, and with Sam's wife, Ayala, who, as an underground agent in France during the war, had helped spirit downed Allied fliers to freedom.[38]

All the Canadian recruiting was locally financed. Dunkelman estimated that it would cost $1000 to equip, clothe, and transport a single volunteer from Toronto to Palestine.[39] Even after the Jewish Agency cut back the Canadian contingent to a maximum of 300 men, this meant that at least $300,000 had to be raised quietly and off the books. Across the country small meetings, usually held in private homes, were addressed by those most closely associated with the enterprise—Jewish community leaders and wealthy notables were discreetly invited to hear Druker, Myerson, Dunkelman, Harris, Adelman, and others.[40]

The campaign was an overwhelming success. After each meeting, cash and cheques were handed across the table and placed in one of a number of local funds or trusts to be used when necessary. By June 1948, $300,000 had been collected in Montreal, $100,000 in Toronto, and an additional $175,000 from Moncton, Vancouver, and cities and towns on the prairies.[41] Some of the money was later channelled to Palestine, via the Jewish Agency in New York, to supplement the volunteers' low Israeli Army pay and to provide them with their own recreational, social, and educational services while overseas.[42]

At all stages of the recruiting great pains were taken to ensure secrecy. It was not illegal to recruit Canadians for service in Palestine,[43] but Zionist leaders had no desire to make their activites a *cause célèbre* and push the government into action. In both recruiting and fundraising, however, there was competition for the support of the Jewish community from the Irgun and its North American support organizations—the American and Canadian sections of the League for a Free Palestine. These organizations believed that flamboyant publicity served the cause best. League rallies, speeches, and newspaper interviews were almost as prevalent in Canada as in the United States. These soon attracted the attention of government officials, especially when League speakers proclaimed the need to recruit fighting men for Palestine. Once government surveillance was focused on the League for a Free Palestine, the question of recruiting became a public issue.

The Haganah's efforts were also hurt by the over-enthusiastic efforts of Abba Hushi, a representative of the youth department of the Histadrut, the Jewish labour federation in Palestine. Hushi addressed a rally in Winnipeg and called on his listeners to arm themselves for the coming struggle. The students formed the "Penguin Rifle Club", ostensibly for rifle and target practice. The club promptly attracted the attention of the Royal Canadian Mounted Police, which reported club members' activities to the Department of External Affairs in Ottawa.[44]

Dunkelman was not pleased by Hushi's intervention, because several people who had intended to volunteer for the Haganah were apparently scared off by the publicity,[45] but Dunkelman's own organization was also having trouble keeping its activities secret. Many parents of volunteers objected to having their sons risk their lives for the Jews of Palestine and did everything in their power to block recruiting. In most cases, in Canada and in the United States, they visited the local recruiter to try to convince him, through persuasion, bribery, or an appeal to conscience, to leave their son behind. In one case, however, a parent approached the RCMP in Montreal and reported the existence of the recruiting network. This information enabled the police to conclude that a sudden spurt of passport applications from young Montreal Jews, forwarded through a single travel agency, was "based on recruiting for Jewish forces in Palestine".[46]

By mid-March the Canadian government was fully aware that recruiting was going on, although its information was incomplete and somewhat inaccurate because the RCMP was having severe difficulties investigating the matter. They reported to the government in May that "the whole Jewish population of Canada appears to be wholeheartedly in support of the establishment of a Jewish state in Palestine" and, as a consequence, "the sources of information that would normally be available to us in such an inquiry have been closed." They had no doubt, however, that "most of the prominent members of the Jewish Community [would] not hesitate to do anything in their power" to assist in the founding of a Jewish state.[47]

V

In the early spring of 1948, the people living near Bacher's Farm on the Main Reef Road that connected Johannesburg with Krugersdorp in South Africa must have wondered about the strange goings on in their

64

normally quiet community. Every Sunday several hundred young men and women arrived at the farm, stayed a few hours, and then left. Bacher's Farm was a Haganah training facility where courses were given in basic infantry tactics, assembly and disassembly of weapons, and calisthenics. The farm, which lay in a hollow and was surrounded by trees, was a perfect location for the discreet training that the Haganah required.

The young people seemed to learn quickly. They were eager to serve in Palestine and were enthusiastic students of the military arts, even though few had ever had any formal training or army experience. Ten to fifteen per cent of them were women; some of these were nurses, but others had served in the South African forces during the war as radar operators, meteorologists, and gunners in coastal batteries.

Although Bacher's Farm was the major Haganah training facility in South Africa, it was not the only one. There were also lecture centres at Boornfontein, Rosettenville, Berea, and other towns, an air school at Germiston, and a rifle range on the East Rand.[48] The South African Jewish community was well organized, strongly behind the Zionist movement, and ready to do more than its share in supporting the Jewish war effort in Palestine.

Hundreds of South African Jews—men and women, untrained youths and seasoned veterans—had clamoured to go to Palestine from the very first days following the partition vote at the United Nations. However, active recruiting did not begin until February, when Yoel Palgi and Boris Senior arrived. Even then recruiting was restricted to air crew. It was not until a rival organization, the Hebrew Legion, made its appearance, that attempts were made to establish a more broadly based Haganah recruiting network.

The Hebrew Legion claimed organizational and spiritual ties with Major Samuel Weiser's London-based Hebrew Legion. Now it began to advertise in the South African Jewish press, calling on young Jews to enlist. This put the South African Zionist Federation in much the same situation as the Zionist Organization of Canada had been—the kind of publicity the Legion was inviting could place the South African government in an embarrassing position and force it to take action against those aiding the Jews in Palestine. This would have been particularly unfortunate in South Africa because of the government's open sympathy for Zionism and the strong support given to partition by Prime Minister Smuts. The Zionist Federation openly repudiated the Legion; the South African Board of Jewish Deputies refused to admit the Legion as a *bona fide* Jewish organization. This made the Legion step up its attacks on the traditional leadership of the South African Jewish community.[49] By early March, the Legion had also established a training centre commanded by a former Major in the South African Army.

The Zionist Federation began its own recruiting in the second week of March under cover of the South African Jewish Ex-Service League. On March 9 about three hundred Ex-Service League members jammed a Johannesburg hall for the annual meeting. A showdown was expected between Zionist Federation supporters and Hebrew Legion allies, but the Zionist Federation representatives were in firm control. The keynote speaker was Major "Simie" Weinstein, a former chaplain in the South African Army, who was both an official of the Zionist Federation and an executive member of the Ex-Service League.

Weinstein told the gathering that the offices of the Zionist Federation had been inundated by young people who wanted to serve and that the Federation had cabled the Haganah in Palestine asking for guidance. The reply had come that "pilots, air mechanics, radar experts, telegraphists, armourers, instructors in small arms, artillery men, armoured-car drivers and naval men" were needed. There was also a need for young people willing to work on collective farms to replace those who had already been called to serve. "The registration of personnel continues," Weinstein made clear. "We want as little noise as possible for reasons which are understandable." He then attacked the Hebrew Legion for its flamboyant publicity and concluded: "We have one authority and one authority only—that of Haganah. It is to the discipline and guidelines of this body that we are required to submit."

Two motions were then put to a vote and passed with only four dissenting votes. The first welcomed the formation of the South African League for Haganah. The second condemned the formation of the Hebrew Legion and urged "all those who wish to answer the call of the Yishuv to pledge their support for the South African League for Haganah." One week later Major G. S. Gonski, one of the leaders of the Ex-Service League, told a small gathering of Jewish reporters: "The aim of the League is to enrol all volunteers who are prepared to go to Palestine when required after May 15." This was an open and explicit call to service.[50]

The two men who eventually bore the greatest responsibility for running the recruiting operation in South Africa were Weinstein and Major Lew Kowarsky. Kowarsky had commanded an infantry company in the Transvaal Scottish Regiment and later became a staff officer in the Fifth South African Infantry Brigade. He had gone into manufacturing after the war and had become national vice-president of the South African Jewish Ex-Service League and chairman of the League's Johannesburg branch. From the time of the establishment of the League for Haganah in mid-March, he neglected his factory and threw himself into setting up the recruiting and training operation.

While the Zionist Federation battled the Hebrew Legion and a deputation of Jewish community leaders (among them several members of parliament) sounded out the attitudes of the Prime Minister, Kowarsky and Weinstein pressed on quietly with their work. The job of transporting recruits to Palestine was made considerably easier when the government gave the South African Jewish community permission to "charter planes to replace the postal service [to Palestine] suspended by [Britain]".[51] This allowed the establishment of a direct air pipeline to Palestine that could carry not only "clothing and food" (as well as mail), but also volunteers and such small but vital pieces of equipment as radar and radio sets and bombsights.

The South African government was far more benevolent and permissive than the governments of Canada and the United States towards the arms-acquisition and recruiting activities of the Jewish population. The national police did not interfere with League for Haganah activities as long as there was no complaint from the public at large. This did not change even after the election of the National Party under Dr. Malan in May 1948. In later years Kowarsky observed: "The National Party was anti-semitic before it came into power and in no way tried to camouflage its feelings...but its members admired the Israeli struggle." Weinstein explained the phenomenon of National government support this way: "The Afrikaners quietly approved our rebellion against the British. They saw a parallel with their own history."[52]

From the very beginning of the recruiting effort, the Haganah had made clear that it wanted World War II veterans and others who had definite military skills and knowledge to contribute. The Haganah had as much raw manpower as it needed. In addition, it could, and eventually did, draw upon the thousands of untrained males who were brought into Israel in large numbers from the displaced persons camps

67

in Europe after the British departed and the state of Israel was declared. This group was referred to as *gahal*, a Hebrew acronym that stood for "recruits from outside the country". It was distinguished from *mahal*, which stood for "volunteers from outside the country"—those from North and South America, western Europe, and South Africa.[53]

Untrained though enthusiastic youths were discouraged and were not actively sought in any of the countries from which volunteers were recruited. Some untrained volunteers from North America went to Palestine to help with agricultural work, but there was no flood of them rushing forward and demanding a chance to shoulder a weapon in defence of the Yishuv. In North America, therefore, Haganah's insistence on recruiting trained veterans caused no real problems. In South Africa, however, the situation was very different. Thousands of young men and women demanded an opportunity to join the Jewish forces. Although their names were collected by the South African Zionist Federation, little else was done about them until early April. At that point it became obvious that South Africa's youth were being bypassed.

They were hurt and they were angry. They had been too young to serve in World War II but they objected to the idea that this should in some way be held against them. They felt that their honour was being besmirched and told the leaders of the Zionist Federation that it would be a "blot on their records" if they were not sent to Palestine.

Urgent meetings were held between the Zionist Federation and the young volunteers, and a compromise was arrived at. The Federation agreed to send "a percentage" of Zionist youth for military service while others would go to agricultural settlements of their choice.[54] The decision meant that a number of untried and untrained men and women would soon be thrown into combat, so some kind of training for them became necessary. This was the reason behind the establishment of the training facilities at Bacher's Farm and other locations around the country.

While the training went on at Bacher's Farm, Senior, Palgi, and Weinstein continued to concentrate on the recruitment of veterans. Some of these veterans who went first to Bacher's Farm were quickly disillusioned by what they considered "pretending to play at soldiers".[55] In fact, however, none of the leaders of the recruiting operation had intended to put the veterans through the rudimentary training course. For them the procedure was much simpler. After an interview at the Zionist Federation offices and a medical examination, they were assigned, as passengers or pilots, to the first available charter flight north. The first group of eight South Africans to leave, seven men and one woman, flew out of Palmietfontein airport on April 20. More than seven hundred volunteers eventually followed them.[56]

VI

By the early spring of 1948 Haganah recruiters were active in most western European countries, North and South America, Great Britain, South Africa, and even Australia. Jewish communities large and small helped with the recruiting, raised funds to cover the costs, and offered their services to screen and transport the volunteers. The Jews of Denmark, only 6000 strong, mustered thirty-five volunteers, while approximately 300 came from Argentina. Many non-Jews volunteered also. One of the most remarkable was a young Frenchman, Teddy Eytan, who had fought in the French underground and had risen to the rank of captain. The Haganah appealed to Eytan's idealism. He believed the Zionist struggle could offer an outlet for his natural youthful exuberance and help him combat the cynicism and horror which he had developed as a consequence of his wartime experiences. The Haganah offered the opportunity, he later recalled, to build, to create, and to be a part of the attainment of a worthy goal.

Eytan was inducted into the Haganah in a suburb of Lyons by Eli Overlander, a member of the Palmach who operated a small training camp at Sathonay, France. Overlander, who was later killed in action, ran a course for volunteers that included hand-to-hand combat, judo, weapons exercises, and hill climbing. Lectures were also given on Hebrew and Jewish history.[57] Eytan reached Palestine on April 29, one of a growing number of French volunteers—of whom about fifty were non-Jews—who eventually joined the Jewish forces. A large contingent came from L'armée Juif, a Jewish resistance group, founded and commanded by Avraham Plonsky, that had battled the Nazis during the war. Others came to Palestine from North Africa, mainly Morocco, via transit camps in southern France.[58]

Eytan, a non-Jew, was a starry-eyed idealist, a strong believer in the Zionist cause. He was, however, a member of a distinct minority. Unlike Eytan, very few of the more than 5000 foreign volunteers who eventually served with the Jewish forces volunteered out of a personal commitment to Zionism or to Judaism.[59]

The tragedy of the Jewish people was front-page news from the moment the first Allied troops entered the Nazi death camps in 1945. The stories and rumours that had leaked out of occupied Europe during the war seemed too monstrous to be believed, even when hard and irrefutable evidence existed to back them up. People often cope with notions and events that are, under normal circumstances, beyond their capacity to accept by ignoring the evidence. Thus, the abnormal, the unexpected, the unacceptable can be safely dismissed. Although the Nazis were capable of great evil, people reasoned, even they would not plan, execute, and cover up in cold, methodical fashion so monstrous a crime as the deliberate and wilful annihilation of an entire people. The leaders of the United States and of the other Allied countries—even the Jews of those countries—believed the stories of beatings, shootings, mass starvation, and deportation of Jews that circulated during the war; but the idea of deliberate genocide was another matter.

Then, in the spring of 1945, the horrible truth was revealed in all its grotesque detail. The mass sufferings of the Jewish people were photographed, documented, and minutely described. The ordeal was still not over for the homeless Jews of Europe, however, because another trial began at the same time. Most of the survivors were not wanted any longer in the countries of their birth. There were, for example, anti-Jewish riots in Poland in the winter of 1945–46. In any case, most did not want to return. There was no safety in Europe, many believed. There was only the memory of storm troopers and, all too often, of neighbours and friends who had done nothing to help and sometimes had aided the Nazi slaughter.

None of the western nations threw open their gates to the survivors huddled in displaced persons camps throughout Europe, sometimes mere yards from the mass graves where the ashes of mothers, fathers, or children lay. So they began to go to Palestine. Smuggled out by Palestinian Jews, they travelled in truck convoys over unlit mountain roads, hungry and cold and fearful, to Mediterranean or Adriatic or Black Sea ports. There they were jammed into reeking, leaky immigrant ships for the run to the Promised Land.

From the summer of 1946 onwards hardly a month passed without a drama played out on the high seas, as British naval units intercepted the immigrant ships. At the same time, the violence in Palestine escalated as the Irgun and the Stern Gang attacked the British. The newspapers and radio broadcasts were filled with accounts of the tragedy of Palestine in flames and stories of the single-minded desire of displaced Jews to go there. In the background was the seemingly endless wrangling between the British and Americans over the fate of Palestine and the Jewish refugees in Europe.

No Jew who thought of himself or herself as a part of the Jewish people could remain unmoved. For many if not most Jews, Palestine became the focus for the hope of redemption from the horror and the shame of the Holocaust. The partition vote at the United Nations; the forecasts of imminent war; the fear that Jews were again in danger of annihilation while the furnaces of Auschwitz were still warm; these—not some theoretical commitment to Zionism or spiritual attachment to a religious wellspring—were the main reasons why most volunteers came forward or served when they were approached.

For many non-European Jews there were, of course, other factors at work in their decision to volunteer. Some volunteers came from Zionist or religious families where awareness of Palestine was always present in the home. Many of the four thousand or so American and Canadian youths who were already in Palestine in late 1947 working on kibbutz settlements or studying at the Hebrew University were from this category; a number of the volunteers came from their ranks. Reports reaching the State Department in Washington in mid-January 1948 told of American students, studying in Jerusalem under the GI Bill of Rights, who were doing Haganah duty. An American correspondent reported to the U.S. consulate in Jerusalem that some of those students had been involved in blowing up the Semiramis Hotel.[60]

Other volunteers no doubt joined for the excitement and sense of purpose, sometimes missing in peacetime, that war offered. After several years in the army, old neighbourhoods had changed. The crowd at the local candy store was different, younger. Friends were gone—some to other cities, some married, some lying in military cemeteries from Europe to half way across the Pacific. The adjustment to civilian life was not always easy. To some the realities of peacetime must have seemed depressingly mundane—a string of meaningless jobs, a college course to prepare one for numbing work in business or the professions. Some volunteers undoubtedly wanted to experience once again the deep thrill spiced with fear of doing exciting, dangerous things, of living at the very edge of oblivion.

And some went for money. All foreign volunteers were paid something for their services. Salaries ranged from the standard pay of three Palestine pounds a month in the infantry to as much as $600 a month in the air force. Volunteers receiving bonus pay fell into two categories—those on special contracts and those serving in branches of the Israeli forces where a high standard of pay and accommodation for volunteers was accepted as the norm. A certain number of pilots, many of them non-Jewish, volunteered under the first category; most other airmen joined up under the second. Despite spectacular stories to the contrary, no bonuses were ever paid for numbers of enemy aircraft shot down and no salaries larger that $600 a month were paid. Special contracts were concluded between the local recruiter and the volunteer and usually provided for the funds to be paid directly to a wife or mother, or deposited every month into a bank account.[61] The money was raised locally as part of the funds collected for the purchase of military equipment or to finance local recruiting. This created a chaotic patchwork of pay and contractual obligations that the Israelis were later forced to straighten out.

By the end of March 1948, not more than two and a half months after the first calls went out from the Jewish Agency Committee for Overseas Mobilization, a recruiting network that spanned half the globe had been put into operation. In April the responsibility for directing recruiting was taken from the Jewish Agency by the Manpower Department of the Haganah under the command of Moshe Zadok.[62] Major Eliahu Tamkin was placed in charge of overseas recruitment and mobilization.[63]

Volunteers were already coming forward in their hundreds, each for his or her own reasons, each with a unique story. Norman Levi, of Leeds, England, had served four years as a tank driver with the British Army. His army service had included a brief stint with occupation forces near Bergen Belsen, the Nazi concentration camp. But Levi's decision to fight for the Jewish cause in Palestine was not motivated by the sights and smells of Bergen Belsen; it came from boredom. Levi was living in Leeds at the time and was looking for something to do; he had no trade and wanted to travel. At one point he and several others made plans for a driving expedition to Australia, but complications with visas forced the abandonment of the project. "I was not a Zionist," he recalled later. "I didn't know what it was to be a Zionist. It looked like there was going to be a war there, so when I saw an ad, what the hell, sounds interesting, so I went."[64]

In South Africa, Harry (Smoky) Simon and his wife, Myra, had both been very conscious of their links with the Jews of Palestine and horrified by the Holocaust. During the war, while serving with the South African Air Force, Smoky had fought two wars: one as a South African and a soldier for the Allies against the Nazis; the other as a Jew against the brutal anti-semitism of the Nazi regime. When the fighting broke out in Palestine in late 1947, Smoky and Myra advanced the date of their marriage, volunteered, and accompanied the first group of South Africans to leave for Palestine. Smoky eventually served with the air force in a variety of capacities; Myra, who had received meteorology training with the South African Air Force during the war, took up meteorology once again.[65]

Harlow Geberer of New York had served with the United States Army as a military policeman and was discharged in October 1945. His brother was a dedicated Zionist, who had been active in the left-wing of Zionism, and had sneaked into Palestine with his wife and son to join Kibbutz Kfar Blum. He wrote letters to his brother, and Harlow eventually decided to leave university to join him. He had heard of the Hotel Breslin and went there to sign up with Land and Labor.[66]

Harry Eisner, also of New York, had been a sergeant in the United States Army. His background contained little in the way of Zionist or religious affiliation. Nevertheless, he was Executive Director of the American Veterans Committee in New York City. He had agreed to help Land and Labor by passing along names of AVC members who might be persuaded to volunteer and, eventually, he decided to go himself. He showed up one day at the Hotel Breslin with his discharge papers. After being interviewed by a committee to determine his qualifications, he was sent to Mount Sinai Hospital for a "fairly decent" medical examination and a psychiatric interview he considered "a joke".[67]

During World War II, Len Hyman of Vancouver, Canada, had served aboard a Royal Canadian Navy destroyer that did convoy escort duty on the deadly run from the British Isles to Murmansk in the Soviet Union. On a bleak day in the Murmansk harbour he had met a Jewish sailor from the Soviet Navy who was one of a chorus entertaining Allied personnel aboard an aircraft carrier. The year was 1944. The Soviet sailor told Hyman that the Germans were "butchering our people" in Poland. The memory of that brief encounter haunted Hyman for the next four years. He volunteered for action in Palestine as soon as he heard that men were needed.[68]

Joe Weiner's family background was strongly Zionist. His grandfather, who had lived in Poland, had dreamed of Palestine. He had made two trips there alone while Palestine was still part of the Turkish Empire before finally deciding to settle there with his wife and children. Life in Palestine was hard, however, and they were forced to leave. Eventually, they settled in Canada. Weiner's grandfather had carried a bag of Jerusalem earth with him all his life to be placed under his head when he was buried. In 1939, when he was twenty-nine, Weiner had joined the Canadian Army. By the time he was discharged in 1945 he had worked his way up to the rank of captain. Weiner decided to go to Palestine after his father urged him to use his military skills to help his fellow Jews.[69]

One of the most promising volunteers to offer his services was George F. "Buzz" Beurling, one of the highest scoring Allied fighter pilots of World War II. With thirty-one and a third kills to his credit, he was Canada's top ace. Beurling had earned the adulation of his countrymen for his daring combat exploits, but his civilian life had not gone well. He had held a succession of jobs, mostly in flying. He hauled freight or passengers, did stunt flying, took fishing parties into the wilderness—and sold life insurance in between. His marriage fell apart. He slipped from the public view and was embittered by the memories of wartime disputes with the RCAF. In an interview published in a Canadian magazine just five days before his death, Beurling reflected, "I would be glad to get back into combat. It's the only thing I can do well; it's the only thing I ever did I really liked."[70]

Beurling had been trying to volunteer for Palestine for months before he was successful in arranging a meeting with Syd Shulemson. For a variety of reasons, Shulemson was reluctant to talk to Beurling, despite his brilliant combat record. He was not anxious to be seen in Beurling's company because Beurling had been making flamboyant public statements about his readiness to fly for pay and had attracted a good deal of attention. Besides, Shulemson did not want to recruit "mercenaries". When the two finally did meet in the home of a mutual friend, Shulemson closely questioned Beurling about his motives and stressed that he was not going to be paid. Beurling insisted on going anyway. Although his exact motives can never be determined, they

74

probably grew out of a variety of impulses including the boredom of post-war life and the strong religious background of his youth (his father had been a Plymouth Brethren lay preacher who believed that the ingathering of the Jewish people was a prelude to the second coming of Christ).[71]

Shulemson eventually agreed to take Beurling. He insists that Beurling was not paid anything more than a token amount for cigarettes and other personal needs, although one newspaper story quoted a "Haganah representative" as saying that the ace was to receive $200 per month.[72] Shulemson had cautioned Beurling about the need for the strictest secrecy,[73] but Beurling ignored the warning. He contacted at least one Canadian newspaperman before his departure for the Middle East and, in a magazine interview published in May 1948, strongly implied that he was about to go to Palestine.[74] It was not much of a secret, therefore, that Canada's top fighter ace was on his way to join the Jewish forces.

VII

By the beginning of April 1948, the winter rains in Palestine became more intermittent, then finally stopped. The warm Mediterranean sun and the clear blue skies heralded the approach of the Holy Land's long, searing summer. The leaves thickened on the deciduous trees, the roads dried, the mud turned hard, and the war intensified. The Haganah high command had drawn up a plan—called Plan D. This plan provided for a counteroffensive to be launched as soon as it was clear that the British withdrawal had advanced to the point where British forces were not likely to intervene in the fighting.

Plan D called for Jewish defences against the expected Arab League invasion to be strengthened. Complete military, civil, and economic control within those areas of Palestine designated to be part of the Jewish state by the U.N.'s partition resolution was to be regained. Arab bases that threatened Jewish areas were to be captured. Arab population centres inside the borders of the Jewish state were to be captured and controlled so that the Arabs would be deprived of bases from which they could conduct guerrilla warfare.

Operation Nachshon, which was designed to open the road from Tel Aviv to Jerusalem, was a part of Plan D.[75] The weapons that Ehud Avriel had purchased in Czechoslovakia were essential for these attacks. When those shipped on the S.S. *Nora* failed to arrive on time, a four-engine C-54 transport was chartered to fly arms directly from Czechoslovakia to an abandoned British air base in Palestine. The weapons arrived at the end of March, just in time for the offensive to begin, as scheduled, at the start of April.[76]

The fighting for control of the Jerusalem road began April 6 and raged for more than a week. Key Arab villages and fortified positions were captured after fierce fighting. One of these, the village of Kastel, which dominated the Jerusalem-Tel Aviv road, changed hands several times before the Arabs finally withdrew on April 10. Abd-el Kader Husseini, a cousin of the Mufti and one of the Palestine Arabs' most able commanders, was killed in the Kastel fighting.

Further to the north Haganah troops captured the Arab section of Tiberias and launched a major assault on the Arab areas of Haifa on April 21. Withing twenty-four hours the Haganah controlled the city, while the Arabs began a mass evacuation to Lebanon. A. J. Bidmead, Superintendent of the Palestine Police in Haifa, reported that the Jews were making "every effort...to persuade the Arab populace to stay and carry on with their normal lives",[77] but the Arab evacuation continued none the less. By this time mutual fears, fuelled by years of hatred and vivid memories of atrocities, were too deep to permit reconciliation. Less than two weeks before the Haifa fighting, Irgun forces had killed large numbers of women and children in an attack on Deir Yassin, a village near the Tel Aviv-Jerusalem road. The Jewish Agency and the Haganah had condemned the attack, but the story of Deir Yassin quickly spread through Arab Palestine, throwing much of the population into panic.

Arabs, too, tried their hand at wanton killing of innocents. On April 13 a convoy of doctors and nurses proceeding from Jewish Jerusalem to the Hebrew University and the Hadassah Hospital on Mount Scopus was attacked and seventy-seven unarmed civilians were killed. The pattern for the Palestine war had been set long ago in the streets of Jerusalem in the spring of 1920; too often no quarter, no mercy, was given. This was the war that the foreign volunteers were coming to fight.

VIII

Port officials and Jewish Agency representatives pushed through the crowd and entered the small dining room on board the immigrant ship

S.S. *Teti*. They sat down at a long table and prepared stamps, documents, and papers before beginning the laborious task of processing another shipload of legal immigrants. The *Teti*, a small, broken-down steamer, had departed from Marseilles in southern France on March 29, 1948, carrying several hundred Jewish displaced persons bound for Palestine. Unlike the "illegal" immigrant ships—the blockade runners operated by the Haganah—the *Teti* carried legal immigrants who had been granted permission to settle in Palestine under the official White Paper quota allowing 1500 Jews to enter the country each month. On this voyage, however, the *Teti* did carry contraband passengers—five Canadians who were the first foreign volunteers to arrive in Palestine.

One by one the passengers were led through a door on one side of the ship into the dining room. They sat for several moments across from the officials while their passports and visas were examined, a few questions were asked, and permission was given to enter Palestine. Sydney Cadloff of Montreal was perhaps more nervous than most. He waited, holding his passport, which was issued in the name of "Yaacov Abraham Van Zuiden" from Holland. Soon he was ushered into the little room to sit in front of the bored bureaucrat. "What's your name?" Cadloff was asked. He pretended not to understand English and stammered a few words in his less-than-perfect Yiddish. The official turned to the interpreter, who repeated the question. "I am going to 10 Frukestrassa, to visit my uncle," Cadloff replied. The interpreter repeated the answer in English. The Immigration agent then stamped Cadloff's visa and passport, said "Okay, next," and Cadloff was admitted to Palestine.[78]

Cadloff's journey had started in Montreal in late January when he attended a recruiting meeting held under auspices of the Brigadier Frederick Kisch branch of the Royal Canadian Legion. He had volunteered and, after processing, had travelled to New York by train to join a group of Canadians under the leadership of Lionel Druker and Dov Yaski of the Palmach. Yaski had been instructed by Teddy Kollek to guide the Canadians through the Haganah network to southern France and, from there, to Palestine. The volunteers were to be handled by the Mossad, the branch of the Haganah responsible for bringing displaced persons from Europe to Palestine in defiance of the British blockade. The Mossad's European headquarters was situated in Paris.[79] (This organization is not to be confused with the more famous Mossad, founded in 1951, Israel's equivalent to the Central Intelligence Agency.)

The Canadians departed aboard the *Marine Falcon* on the after-noon of March 5, 1948, bound for the port of Le Havre.[80] The late winter passage was rough—the welded Liberty ships were infamous for their rolling and tumbling in heavy seas—but, after several days, the ship reached the northern French port. There Haganah agents waited to guide the volunteers to Paris.

The delights of Paris beckoned, but the Canadian volunteers spent little time there and instead went directly from Paris to Marseilles, the Haganah's most important port in western Europe. The bustling harbour and the many small inlets nearby were the points of departure for most of the ships that carried displaced persons to Palestine. North of the city was a large transit camp, Grand Arenas. The camp housed refugees from Germany and points east who had been brought to France by the Mossad in preparation for the Palestine voyage. The camp offered perfect cover for the volunteers, and the Haganah planned to house them there and bring them to Palestine mingled with the refugees. Their passports would be taken away and held by the Haganah and they would be provided with false identity papers, usually in the name of Jews who had been murdered in Nazi death camps. They would then be spirited onto the refugee ships and brought to Palestine under the British quota system. Grand Arenas was well equipped with facilities to forge the necessary documents. Whatever training and conditioning was required could be given at Tretz, a small country manor near the main camp.

When the Canadians arrived at Grand Arenas, Dunkelman, who had flown out of Toronto days before, met briefly with them and then, carrying a false passport that identified him as an Englishman, embarked on a passenger liner for Haifa. With him was Max Brown, of Toronto, on his way to Palestine to help set up facilities for manufac-turing a submachine gun in the Haganah's underground armouries. The Canadian volunteers stayed only two days at Grand Arenas. On March 15 they moved to nearby Tretz to be trained in grenade throwing, pistol and rifle shooting, and field exercises. Some rudimen-tary Hebrew lessons were also given, as well as a short course in the history of the Zionist movement.[81]

Conditions at Tretz caused much complaint, and the Haganah was soon faced with a minor revolt—a portent of things to come. The Canadians were bored at Tretz and anxious to get into battle in Palestine. Almost all were veterans and few saw the need for the training courses they were undergoing. They felt neglected, the food was bad, and the living conditions were uncomfortable. The Haganah officers at the camp reported to their superiors in Palestine that the group "were like British soldiers, grumbling all the time".

The men complained that Ben Adelman had promised them a daily salary of 1100 *francs* while in France, and accommodation in hotels, and had assured them that they would be flown to Palestine immediately after their training was completed. Judah Ben David, a Haganah officer, and Gideon Rose, a Palmach member who was fluent in English, were dispatched to Tretz to deal with the complaints.

Tretz Commander Moshe Lipson decided that the best course was to send the Canadians to Palestine as quickly as possible. Otherwise their dissatisfaction might cause trouble among the volunteers from Hungary and the United States who were just beginning to arrive. Ben David told the Canadians that they were being accommodated in the best way possible and that they had been assigned top instructors to help acclimatize them to conditions in Palestine. He stressed, however, that the Haganah could not discriminate between them and the thousands of others who were serving the same cause.

Dov Yaski believed the opposite. He reported to Tel Aviv: "These people...enjoyed good living conditions at home and we must try to provide comparable conditions, if not on the battlefield, then in transit, i.e., in the French camps."[82] This was difficult for the Haganah to accept, and preparations went rapidly forward to send the first small group to Palestine with Yaski. Five men were chosen for the voyage and brought back to Grand Arenas, where they were photographed and provided with false travel documents. On March 29, Yaski and the five Canadians boarded the small, crowded immigrant steamer, S.S. *Teti*, for the long and uncomfortable voyage to Palestine.

5

"A Wartime Necessity"

The silver C-46 droned through the dark Mediterranean night of May 3, 1948, as the two crewmen, shielding their eyes from the glow of the instrument panel, strained to pick up the twinkling lights of Tel Aviv. Eight hours earlier they had left the small airfield at Perugia, in central Italy. They were headed for the RAF base at Ekron (formerly Aqir), southwest of Tel Aviv, which was supposed to be in Haganah hands. The plane was flown by Arnold Ilowite from New York City, a veteran of the United States Army Air Force; Jack Goldstein from Montreal, a former wireless air gunner with the Royal Canadian Air Force, occupied the co-pilot's seat and handled the flaps and the radio. As the plane passed over the coast, Ilowite banked to the south and Goldstein sent out a clipped radio transmission informing Ekron that the C-46 was approaching the airfield. They received clearance to land, and suddenly, from out of the dark, runway lights flashed on. There was no time to circle the field so Ilowite nosed down and headed straight in. Neither man was certain who would be waiting on the ground, but with less than thirty minutes of fuel left in the tanks there was no choice but to gamble.

The C-46 touched down. Instead of stopping, however, Ilowite continued to roll to the end of the strip. He pulled out a .45, handed it to Goldstein, and told him to stand by the rear door: "I'll be damned if I'm going to get caught by these Arabs on the ground. I don't know if there's Arabs or Jews here, so I'm going to taxi to the end, turn around, and let them come to us."

As the C-46 rolled, a jeep raced after it, one of the occupants waving wildly at the plane. At the end of the runway, Ilowite turned and trimmed the aircraft for takeoff, the engines running. Goldstein cautiously opened the rear door and peered into the dark, pistol in one hand, flashlight in the other. A small, dark man was standing in the jeep screaming "shalom" above the engine noise. For a split second, Goldstein thought he was an Arab and almost pulled the trigger. But on second thought he held back and yelled to Ilowite, "It's okay." The man turned out to be a Yemenite Jew. Ilowite shut the engines down, clambered back from the cockpit, and both men, bone weary, were driven into Tel Aviv to spend the night at the Park Hotel.[1]

Goldstein and Ilowite were pressed into service the very next day. They were sent north to an abandoned airfield next to Kibbutz Ein Shemer where they met several trucks loaded with food. The food was crammed into the C-46 and Ilowite and Goldstein took off to begin air-dropping supplies to isolated Jewish settlements. It was not easy. Their first objective was Kibbutz Yehiam, thirty kilometres from the Lebanese border. The kibbutz was surrounded and had not been visited by a food convoy for several weeks. Arab attacks had failed to dislodge the defenders of the settlement, but Arab gunners on the high ground held a commanding view of the settlement and shot at anything that moved. On the first few runs over Yehiam, Goldstein and Ilowite used parachutes to drop the food, but the wind was unpredictable and the containers often drifted out of the reach of the settlers.

A new and more daring method was worked out. With the rear door off its hinges, Ilowite dropped low for the approach and came in fast. Several youths stood ready to pitch out the thirty-five- to forty-five-kilogram tins of food. As the big transport approached the kibbutz, Ilowite held the controls tight, and Goldstein dropped the landing gear and lowered the flaps. As they roared low over the settlement, the food was shoved out of the doors. Then Goldstein retracted the landing gear and raised the flaps, while Ilowite shoved the throttles forward and clawed for altitude.

They flew runs over Yehiam for five days without mishap, but on May 13 their luck almost ran out. Ilowite had just banked right after the run over the kibbutz when a burst of machine-gun fire from a nearby hill shattered the windshield and blew Goldstein out of his seat. He landed atop Ilowite, struggled up and saw blood all over. "Arnie, you're bleeding!" he yelled above the wind roar.

"I'm not bleeding, you bastard, you are," Ilowite shouted back. Goldstein's face was pockmarked and he was bleeding profusely from a large number of superficial head wounds. Ilowite headed for the small airstrip at Tel Aviv, instead of Ekron, so that Goldstein could be taken quickly to a hospital.[2]

I

By the beginning of May, Jewish forces in Palestine had started to turn the tide of battle and the Palestine Arabs faced the prospect of defeat on most fronts. None of the Jewish settlements that Fauzi al-Kaukji's Arab Liberation Army had attacked in northern Palestine had fallen and Operation Nachshon had opened most of the road from Tel Aviv to Jerusalem to Jewish traffic. Convoys were still fired upon and sometimes were turned back, but the commanding hold that the Arabs had once enjoyed in the Kastel sector had been broken. The Haganah, sometimes aided by Irgun and Lehi troops, had secured Haifa, Jaffa, Tiberias, and Safed. More than one hundred Arab villages had been captured, and Jewish positions in the new city of Jerusalem had been strengthened by the taking of the Katamon and Sheikh Jarrah areas to the north and south of the old city. Jewish forces, now numbering over 30,000, had succeeded in gaining control over much of the area allotted to the Jewish state by the United Nations, particularly in the heavily populated coastal plain. In outlying areas of northern Palestine, however, and in the northern Negev and the Hebron hills, Jewish settlements were still under siege. David Ben Gurion had vowed that no Jewish areas were to be abandoned. The inhabitants of the Etzion Bloc, Kibbutz Yehiam, and other villages and settlements chose to abide by this decision, which had been made for political rather than military reasons.

If communications with the besieged settlements could not be restored by land, they would have to be maintained by air. The meagre resources of the Sherut Avir—the Austers and other light planes owned by Palestine Jews—were pressed into service to carry messages, do aerial reconnaissance, drop small quantities of food and medicine and, on occasion, evacuate the sick and wounded. But they were clearly unable to fly enough supplies to maintain settlements under siege. To do that the Haganah needed the large transports possessed by Service Airways or the Dakotas purchased by Boris Senior and others in South Africa. These large planes were also desperately needed to maintain the trickle of Czechoslovak arms. In late April and May, as political and military events in Palestine moved towards a climax,

82

foreign volunteers, aided by Haganah representatives, began to mobilize the secret airlift of planes to Palestine.

II

The C-46 flown to Palestine by Ilowite and Goldstein on May 3 had been purchased by Al Schwimmer in California in February. After reconditioning at Schwimmer's Lockheed Air Terminal facility, it had been flown to Millville, New Jersey. There it sat while the Haganah completed arrangements to secure the use of a European airfield that could be used as a Service Airways base. Although Service Airways had acquired a cloak of international respectability by leasing its planes to LAPSA, Panama was clearly too far away from Palestine to serve any useful purpose beyond providing a mailing address or a temporary refuge from American authorities.

A European base was needed, preferably out of the way, located in a sympathetic country, and as close to Palestine as possible. Italy seemed to fill the bill. In January Yehuda Arazi, who had been transferred there from the United States, began to work on the problem. Using the services of Massimo Teglio, a member of the Genoa Aero Club, Arazi approached Angelo Ambrosini, owner of the Societa Aeronautica Italiana (SAI), in Milan. Arazi proposed an arrangement between SAI and Service Airways in which the Italian company would overhaul Service Airways' C-46s.[3] Ambrosini was interested and an agreement was soon worked out that called for Service Airways to deliver as many as nineteen aircraft to SAI's shops at Castiglione del Lago for repair work. Near the end of February, Swifty Schindler wrote Ambrosini that he was "despatching several C-46s" which would begin to arrive "during the first week in March".[4]

Schindler had initially planned to send three aircraft, one of which would carry Sam Pomerantz,[5] an aeronautical engineer who had approached Service Airways as a volunteer and who was delegated to oversee ground arrangements at the Castiglione del Lago base. Permission to land in Italy was sought from the Italian government and granted, although Schindler was warned that he would have to be responsible for problems resulting from the lack of proper facilities at Castiglione del Lago because the airport was not "opened to civilian traffic".[6] This should have alerted those concerned to the fact that Arazi's European haven was profoundly inadequate, but the warning was not heeded.

83

March 6, 1948, was only seventeen minutes old when, piloted by Leo Gardner, the first Service Airways C-46 to leave for Italy threaded the parallel runway lights at Teterboro airport in New Jersey and climbed away to the northeast. Steve Schwartz, who was on the flight as navigator, co-pilot, and radio operator, sat beside Gardner. Ernie Stehlik, a mechanic who had been working with Schwimmer at Burbank, came along for the ride.[7] As Gardner set course for Goose Bay, Labrador, the men's thoughts turned to the long night ahead. The C-46 was a prodigious cargo carrier, one of the best ever built, but it was lumbering and slow. With its normal 280-kilometre-per-hour cruising speed, at least ten hours would pass before Gardner could set the plane down at Goose Bay, the first refuelling stop on the long flight to Italy.

On the surface there was nothing unusual about the flight of the Service Airways C-46. The plane had been cleared by the United States Customs Service at Newark, New Jersey, on March 5. No special permission was needed from the State Department to fly aircraft of this type out of the country.[8] Gardner had filed a flight plan that would take him from Teterboro to Goose Bay for refuelling, then to Bluie West One, in southern Greenland, to Keflavik, on the southern tip of Iceland, to Shannon, Ireland, to Geneva, Switzerland, and finally to Rome. The journey was more than 6500 kilometres, and took longer than thirty hours. The route, which was the normal one across the Atlantic for aircraft like the C-46, had been pioneered during World War II by Ferry Command, which flew aircraft from the factories of North America to England. However, despite the information filed in his flight plan, Gardner's destination was not Rome. He was headed for the airport of Castiglione del Lago.

The first twenty hours or so of Gardner's flight were uneventful. The C-46 performed well and flew above the ice-infested Labrador Sea and Greenland Strait as Gardner headed for the low hills of Ireland. At each stop, local customs officials gave the aircraft a cursory examination and then cleared it for its next leg. All was routine until the C-46 rolled to a stop at Geneva. There the Customs inspection turned up several pistols, whereupon Swiss Customs officials sent a hurried report of their find to Washington through the U.S. Embassy in Berne.[9] The State Department was now alerted that there was something strange about this particular aircraft.

To complicate matters still further, the C-46 was later reported missing over the Swiss and Italian Alps hours after Gardner had flown out of Geneva. He had forgotten to change his flight plan and, when he did not show up in Rome airport, authorities launched a search for what they thought was a downed plane. When Gardner flew into Castiglione del Lago he found no control tower and could not immediately inform Rome of his safe arrival. By the time he did report, his "missing" aircraft had caused a small uproar. In New York, Schindler was hounded by the press for information on the missing plane. More seriously, he was questioned closely by U.S. Customs agents, who asked about the purpose of the flight and wanted to know about the guns reported to be aboard. Schindler pulled out the correspondence with Ambrosini to explain the former and denied any knowledge of the latter.[10]

In Italy Gardner found, to his chagrin, that the airport was little more than a primitive dirt strip and was certainly not suitable for Service Airways' operations with heavily loaded transports. He, Schwartz, and Stehlik flew the C-46 to the nearby city of Perugia where they checked in at the Bufani Hotel to await further instructions.[11] Within a few days they were back in the C-46, circling over the Adriatic, searching for the small steamer Lino, which was reported to be carrying a cargo of Czech rifles and ammunition from a Yugoslav port to Beirut. The Haganah had learned of the Lino's departure and was determined to sink it; Gardner was ordered to locate the ship and send it to the bottom. Gardner took part in the adventure reluctantly because the C-46 could only attack a ship by having crew members throw bombs out the door—a dangerous business. Gardner was willing to conduct an air search for the freighter,[12] but he and his crew found nothing and the C-46 was soon back at Perugia. It was locked up and abandoned there until May. Schwartz and Gardner returned to the United States, and Stehlik remained in Italy.

The failure to secure a viable European operating base was serious because time was short. The FBI's investigations following the January 3 debacle at the Jersey City dock were leading it steadily towards Service Airways, and the airline's U.S. cover was starting to fall apart. The FBI was quite certain by early February that there was a direct link between Service Airways and the Jewish Agency and was convinced that Service Airways would "establish a Trans-Atlantic Air Service for either freight or passengers between the United States and Palestine".[13] The situation in Palestine was also getting more desperate by the hour. Moreover, there were arms in Czechoslovakia that were needed by

Jewish troops on the road to Jerusalem. It was no longer possible to wait in the United States while another, more suitable, European base was found; the planes would have to be moved quickly to Panama. At 4.00 a.m. on March 14, Lineas Aereas de Panama's flagship, Constellation RX 121, lifted off from Newark, New Jersey, with Sam Lewis at the controls, and turned south for Kingston, Jamaica. Lewis left two C-46s and the Constellation RX 123 behind at Millville. Constellation RX 121 carried a load of tools and spare parts for LAPSA's new base at Tocuman, Panama. Newark was the only airport in the vicinity that possessed both the long, hard runways for the takeoff of a fuel-laden Constellation and the customs facilities required by U.S. law. Lewis had had no trouble clearing Newark because the local customs office believed that since the plane was "in foreign trade" and was foreign owned, "export licenses were not required".[14]

By mid-day Lewis had flown over Cuba and was on his approach to the airport at Kingston. His touchdown caused great excitement. No Constellation had ever landed there before. Lewis played the genial host and invited several British officials and other local residents aboard the plane to look it over while aviation gas was being pumped into the large wing tanks.[15] Then RX 121 took off for the 960-kilometre hop to Tocuman. It arrived at 4.30 p.m. to great fanfare and celebration. This was, after all, the beginning of a mighty Panamanian air fleet that would sail the skies and bring commerce and tourists to the tiny Central American republic.[16]

Lewis's departure landed Service Airways into more trouble with the U.S. government. Schindler had not thought an export licence was required for RX 121 because "there was no transfer of ownership of the planes and the registration was temporary", or so he told Customs investigators.[17] His belief had been confirmed by the Customs office at Newark airport. But they were wrong because the U.S. embargo of December 5, 1947, stipulated that heavy aircraft such as the Constellation required a State Department licence for export purposes, and no such licence had been obtained. On March 22 the Bureau of Customs office in Philadelphia was ordered to investigate Schindler's operation at Millville, and Customs agents John W. Yale and H. E. Moore took charge.

They drove to Millville Airport for a look around and found that Service Airways had three planes parked on the apron—Constellation RX 123 and two C-46s. All were under Panamanian registry, and all were "in fly-away condition". Service Airways had no office at the airport and there were no Service Airways people around but Schindler had recently rented a storage room from the airport manager. When this was unlocked, it was found to contain spare wings, tires, and different aircraft parts. The two agents learned little about Service Airways' operations or its employees. They knew that "one Sam Lewis" may have flown RX 121 to Panama, and that RX 123 had flown in from California twelve days before "fully loaded with spare plane gear and parts obtained in California" but that was all.[18] Although the on-the-spot investigation turned up little, it did provide tangible evidence to Schindler that the government was closing in on Service Airways and was keeping a close watch on Millville.

On March 26, 1948, President Truman issued a proclamation that, from April 15 on, all exports of aircraft and aircraft parts, components, and accessories had first to be cleared by the State Department. This meant that Service Airways' C-46s would have to leave the United States before April 15 or they would probably not leave at all. There were now four C-46s and one Constellation at Millville, and five C-46s at Burbank. The ten aircraft were still not in the best possible flying condition and only twenty or so air crew had been cleared to fly the planes, but there was little choice. On the night of April 10, four C-46s cleared the runway at Millville and headed south. The departure had been delayed for twenty-four hours by difficulties with Customs which had tried to stop the planes from leaving. Nahum Bernstein interceded and forced the release of the aircraft, since they were carrying no contraband and were breaking no laws by leaving prior to April 15.[19] By the afternoon of April 11, the four transports had landed safely at Tocuman, joining RX 121.

The leader of the flight down and the man responsible for organizing the daily routine at Tocuman field was Hal Auerbach, a thirty-one-year-old former lieutenant commander in the U.S. Navy. He and another pilot, William Gerson, were called back to the United States along with Sam Lewis three days after their arrival in Panama to help fly the last five Service Airways C-46s out of the Lockheed Air Terminal at Burbank. The planes were flown to Los Angeles Municipal Airport and given a cursory Customs inspection before taking off for Panama. Three planes left Los Angeles on the night of April 13 and the last two flew out twenty-four hours later, just before the April 15 deadline.[20]

The departure was hurried; the loading of the aircraft at Burbank

87

was haphazard and carried out without regard for normal margins of flying safety. In effect Schwimmer's entire Burbank operation was loaded aboard the transports, along with spare parts, tools, and communications equipment. The C-46s took off carrying loads much heavier than the Federal Aviation Administration regulated maximum gross weight of approximately 20,000 kilograms. This, Sam Lewis later observed, was "a wartime necessity". The heavy loads exceeded the single-engine takeoff-performance limit of the C-46, which meant that failure of one engine on takeoff would spell disaster.[21]

The C-46s flew from Los Angeles to Tijuana, Mexico, for refuelling and then flew on to Mexico City via Mazatlan. On the takeoff from Mexico City, disaster struck. The Mexican capital is more than 2100 metres above sea level and aircraft takeoff performance suffers at these heights. Longer runways and lighter loads are necessary, especially if daytime air temperatures begin to climb. Lewis was first to roll and used most of the 2200 metre runway before lifting off. Then came a second C-46 piloted by Gerson. There was a flat, dry riverbed not far from the end of the runway, and Lewis had told the other pilots to abort the takeoff and head for it if they had trouble on takeoff. Gerson's transport began to move, gathered speed, and bore down on the end of the runway. The plane rose briefly, nosed down towards the riverbed and crashed, killing Gerson and his mechanic, Glen King.[22] The following day the remaining four transports continued on to Tocuman, their loads lightened. The off-loaded equipment was left behind in storage at the Mexico City airfield.

III

Deputy Chief Prosser of the British Police Mission in Athens was a former officer in the Palestine Police; he knew Palestine. More important, he knew the secret ways of the Haganah underground. The U.S. Embassy in the Greek capital had received a curious report. It concerned impounded British civilian aircraft flown by American crews that had been seized on the island of Rhodes apparently en route to Palestine. The Americans asked Prosser to help with their investigations. On April 17, 1948 Prosser flew to Rhodes accompanied by three U.S. Embassy officials to interrogate the crew members. The crew, one of whom was Sam Pomerantz, claimed that they were employees of Service Airways and that they had been dispatched by one Danny

Agronsky in Rome to ferry the planes to Singapore.[23] When Prosser and the Americans began their investigation, the Service Airways employees stuck to their story. The planes, they added, had been purchased by Willem Van Leer, a wealthy Dutch Jewish businessman, who was acting for Australian interests. Prosser was not fooled: he knew Danny Agronsky was an old hand at Haganah underground operations. Moreover, documents found aboard the impounded air-craft looked forged. Prosser concluded that the planes were bound for Palestine and, within days, the British government had revoked the aircraft registration and officially requested the Greek government to "prolong [the] internment of [the] planes…".[24] The Greeks did so, but no formal charges were laid against the crews, who were allowed to leave. Shortly after this, British security in London reported to the British Embassy at Athens (which passed the information along to the Americans) that "Van Leer and associates" were connected with a "large organization established for [the] purpose [of] furnishing planes to Palestine".[25] The head of that organization was the man who had sent the British registered planes to Rhodes—Danny Agronsky.

The Haganah's air operations in Europe centred on Rome. There Agronsky, the American-born son of the publisher of the *Palestine Post* and a former collaborator of Yehuda Arazi,[26] ran an ever-growing network that procured aircraft, trained pilots, dispatched contraband planes to Palestine, and tried to outsmart the investigators of half-a-dozen countries. Agronsky, who was already known to the British for his involvement in"Jewish illegal activities", posed as the Rome man-ager of Service Airways and local representative of LAPSA. His head-quarters were located at the Hotel Massimo d'Azeglio.[27] The pilots, air crew, and others associated with Agronsky were accommodated at a number of other small hotels around Rome.

Agronsky maintained a link with his counterpart in Paris, Freddy Fredkens. Fredkens lived with his wife at the Hotel California[28] and travelled frequently to England in search of aircraft and air crew volunteers.

Later, when regular airlifts were being flown out of Czechoslovakia, Benjamin Kagan was assigned to oversee Haganah air operations in Prague.[29] Kagan was a former officer in the Polish Army who had lived in Palestine from 1933 to 1936. He had escaped from Poland to England in June 1940. During the war he fought in the commandos and took an active part in the Italian campaign. At the end of the war he asked to be repatriated to Palestine where he rejoined the Haganah.

The British soon learned about Agronsky's Rome operation and concluded that he was working with the tacit approval of the Italians. They feared that the Italian government was about to allow Agronsky to export thousands of kilograms of arms and ammunition by air and sea, and they were convinced that fifty Palestinian pilots were undergoing flight training on light aircraft at Urbe[30] airfield near Rome. Not surprisingly, the Italians denied this[31] but it was, in fact, true. Palestinian pilots were training at Urbe under the auspices of the ALICA flying school, and the airfield was used as the Haganah's main staging base in Italy.

The four planes seized on Rhodes had landed at Urbe on April 10 after a flight from England. They were ostensibly being exported to Singapore under a U.K. licence issued to an Australian company. In fact, however, they had been purchased by Fredkens in Britain earlier in the year and were being smuggled to Palestine along with a number of other planes.[32] Fredkens had planned to have the planes fly to Palestine by a somewhat circuitous route, avoiding normal flight paths and major airports. The small Greek island of Kos, which lay just off the Turkish coast about 125 kilometres northeast of Rhodes, was chosen as a refuelling stop en route. Greek authorities had reported curious goings on there in late March. A mysterious plane had landed at Rhodes on March 26 without clearance. It had taken off the following day for Nicosia, Cyprus, but had landed at Kos instead. When the plane was approached by airport authorities, it had hurriedly taken off. The landing was not recorded in its flight plan and investigators later concluded that the crew had been searching for a secret fuel cache which they had apparently failed to find.[33] The authorities, then, were on the alert when the four planes landed at Rhodes.

Although Fredkens's planes never got to Palestine, another of his projects, also financed by Van Leer, was far more successful. In mid-January 1948, David N. Miller, a former U.S. Army officer working as an aircraft broker in Paris, purchased a contract from Victor M. Oswald, a Swiss national, to take delivery of fifty surplus U.S. Army UC-64A Noorduyn Norseman single-engine transports. The Norseman was a rugged Canadian-designed bush plane used extensively for ferrying supplies during the war and was ideal for Haganah use in the Palestine fighting.

In the spring of 1947, the U.S. government had sold these planes, which were based in Germany, to Oswald (who was represented by Miller). As far as is known, neither man had any connection with Agronsky or the Haganah. In August 1947, the first two planes had been delivered to Oswald in Frankfurt. In December one of these was then flown to Schipol Airport near Amsterdam. KLM Royal Dutch Airlines had agreed to renovate the planes and, in particular, to extend their range by installing long-range fuel tanks. Subsequently, each Norseman delivered in Frankfurt by the U.S. Army was sent on to Schipol for overhaul and renovations. Meanwhile the first two were flown to France and stored at Toussus le Noble, a small airport near Paris. Miller bought out Oswald's contract in January 1948. Shortly after this, Miller was approached by a Belgian company, known as Somaco, which told him it was interested in buying planes for use in the Belgian Congo. Miller agreed to sell Somaco twenty Norseman aircraft and to deliver them by June 1, 1948.[34]

Somaco was not what it appeared to be. The company was financed by Van Leer;[35] and the approach to Miller had been worked out by Fredkens. Fredkens was apparently steered to Miller after Miller's sister, Mrs. Sol Silverman of Roanoke, Virginia, had told a speaker at a fund-raising meeting for Palestine that her brother was an aircraft broker in Paris. The information was passed on to the Hotel Fourteen which, in turn, sent it to Fredkens.[36] Whether or not Miller was aware of the Palestine connection, he dutifully turned over the two aircraft at Toussus le Noble to Somaco, as well as three more that were still being worked on by KLM at Schipol. Somaco later advised Miller that "the first batch of five Norseman... aircraft [from] the original purchase of twenty, for account of Messrs. H. G. Turse, Fredkens and Company of Belgian Congo, have been duly received by this firm in Rome."[37]

Three of the single-engine transports left Rome on May 2 for the long flight to Palestine. The morning after they arrived they were pressed into service to drop supplies to the encircled Etzion Bloc of settlements. Thereafter Norseman aircraft were flown out of Rome at regular intervals after their arrival from Holland. In June Miller's connection to Palestine was discovered by the American Embassy in Paris. The Embassy asked the French to ground all aircraft owned by Miller and took action to revoke his U.S. passport for any travel apart from a direct return to the United States. Further delivery of the planes from Germany was also stopped.[38]

Miller's planes were a welcome addition to the small but vitally important Jewish air fleet in Palestine. They arrived shortly after the Haganah had pressed a South African Dakota into service between points in Palestine and Europe. The plane, which was flown by two non-Jews, Claude Duval and Del Webb, had been owned by Pan African Air Charter. It was in the air between Athens and Cairo, on a flight from London to Johannesburg, when Duval received a radio message to head for Lydda airport in central Palestine. On landing, the crew were met by a company agent who told them they were to fly Arab refugees out of Palestine from Haifa to Beirut. Haifa had just been won by the Haganah after a short but bitter fight.

On April 24 Duval had just left Haifa for Lydda when the tower radioed that Arab forces had gained control of the airport at Lydda and instructed him to return. Duval flew back to Haifa, parked the Dakota, and registered at a local hotel. Shortly after this he and Webb were approached by the Haganah and told of the sorry state of the Jewish air force in Palestine. The Dakota would be a great help, they were told. Duval suggested that the Haganah approach Pan African Air Charter and offer to buy the plane outright. He and Webb agreed to stay in Palestine to fly it. A deal was soon struck and the Dakota, with the two South Africans at the controls, began to fly between Palestine and Europe. Duval kept the South African registration on the plane to allow him to land at European airports without having to explain the origins or mission of the aircraft.[39]

IV

The settlers at Kibbutz Niram, in the northern Negev, shielded their eyes from the hot desert sun as they searched the sky for the source of the barely audible droning engine noise. Soon a speck appeared in the southwest, coming from the direction of Egypt—a lone Beechcraft Bonanza was approaching the kibbutz. As the plane began to spiral down, the settlers clutched their Sten guns warily and prepared to open fire. The Bonanza turned again, straightened out, and came in low, flaps and wheels down, landing with a puff of dust at a small dirt strip near the kibbutz. Armed men and women ran across the field towards the plane. Among them was Elly Eyal, the young German-born Palmach flier who commanded Sherut Avir's "Negev squadron" as the two Jewish light planes parked at the kibbutz were designated.

The door of the Bonanza pushed open and the smiling face of Boris Senior looked out. "Hi Elly," he called.

Eyal stared for a moment. "Where did you come from?" he asked.

"I came from South Africa," Senior told him.

Later Senior learned that the kibbutz defenders were convinced he was an Arab pilot because he had flown from the direction of Egypt and his plane was brand new, not like the flying wrecks the Jews possessed. It was, he later recalled, "the only dangerous moment of my whole trip".

His odyssey had started in South Africa on a bright and sunny morning one month before. On April 3, Senior and Cyril Katz, "a little, nervy kind of fellow", as Senior described him, had climbed into two brand-new Bonanzas for the trip to Palestine. Katz, like Senior, was an experienced pilot who had flown Dakotas in the South African Air Force during World War II. They cleared customs at Pietersburg, declaring they were businessmen off to the British Industries Fair in London, and flew north into Rhodesia, trying to keep each other in sight. The weather soon began to deteriorate, and Senior lost Katz, whose plane was slightly faster. After a long flight, Senior touched down at Lusaka but saw no sign of Katz. A half hour or so later, the airport radio operator came up to the South African and told him that Katz had landed at a small emergency strip next to the Zambesi River. Senior sought help from a local mechanic, and together they flew south. Senior landed at the little strip and taxied up to Katz who told him that he had started to get sick when the weather began to close in and had decided to land. Now his flaps were not working. Senior decided to fly off for help. He taxied back to the landing strip with the mechanic but, as he eased into his takeoff run, there was a loud crash and the nose wheel seemed to bury itself in the runway. The propeller banged to a stop and the engine was practically torn from its mountings: the baked mud surface of the strip had given way.

The three men spent a hot and uncomfortable night on the floor of a small nearby police post. In the morning they went back to inspect the planes. The strip was in the middle of the jungle and there were clear signs that elephants, lions, and monkeys had carried out their own inspection during the night. There was nothing to do but leave the two planes there, hitch a ride to Salisbury, Rhodesia, and arrange to have the damaged plane trucked out and the other repaired at the strip and flown to Salisbury. Senior then flew the Bonanza back to

Johannesburg while Katz returned by train.[40]

On April 11, an unlikely convoy of three Fairchilds and a Rapide took off from South Africa and headed north. The Fairchilds were flown by Les Chimes, Arthur Cooper, and Tuxie Blau, while Alf Lindsay flew the Rapide. The planes ostensibly belonged to Pan African Air Charter, a company owned by South African Jews, but in fact they had been purchased by Senior and Cecil Wulfsohn, a former South African Air Force pilot, in March. The cover story, in case they were challenged en route, was that the planes had been sold to a party in London and were being delivered there as fast as possible. With the limited range of the Fairchilds—no more than eight hundred kilometres—and flying by day in short hops, the little air flotilla covered the distance to Khartoum, Sudan, in nine days. The South Africans did not arouse any suspicion during their trek across British East Africa, but at Khartoum a British official questioned them closely on the real intent of their mission. The South Africans stuck to their story and showed him the documents they carried to back it up. They were warned that if they ever landed in Palestine the landing rights of Pan African Airways in Sudan would be taken away, and their departure was delayed while their story was checked.[41]

While Blau and the others sweated away nine days in Khartoum's heat—they spent long hours lying in tepid baths sipping cold drinks—Senior was completing arrangements for a second try. In addition to the aircraft Katz had flown on the first attempt, there was now a brand-new Bonanza, just flown in from the United States. Senior lined up Cecil Wulfsohn and Cyril Steinberg, an ex-South African Air Force navigator with a Distinguished Flying Cross, to help out. Senior feared that, because of his many escapades, he was being watched by the South African Police, and was convinced he would never get out of South Africa in the cockpit of a plane. The safest course was to fly out by commercial airliner and meet one of the planes en route. Wulfsohn agreed to pilot a Bonanza to Khartoum and turn it over to Senior who would fly it to Palestine. Katz and Steinberg would fly the other Bonanza all the way.

Senior and Wulfsohn left first. Wulfsohn flew to Khartoum without incident and handed the plane over to Senior. Senior flew on to Wadi Halfa, just a few kilometres south of the Egyptian border, and then on to Luxor. The ancient Egyptian city had several good hotels and was crowded with British troops on leave from the Suez Canal

94

zone. Senior yearned to stay a few days, but Palestine awaited. On the morning of May 4 he filed a flight plan for Beirut and took off. Before he left the Egyptians warned him that war was looming in Palestine and that he would be well advised to stay clear. He repeated his assurance that he was heading for Beirut. Senior flew towards Beirut then veered towards the Negev and, by 10.00 a.m., was over Kibbutz Niram. After refuelling, he flew on to Tel Aviv and went into action later that day, flying the Bonanza on reconnaissance runs over the Jerusalem front.[42] Katz and Steinberg arrived two days later.

On April 29, just a day or so before Senior and Wulfsohn had arrived in Khartoum, Blau, Lindsay, Chimes, and Cooper left Khartoum for Cairo. It was the last time anyone ever saw Lindsay, who became separated from the other three and never arrived in Cairo. The Egyptians were deeply suspicious of the South Africans but had no concrete reason to detain them. On May 7, Blau, Chimes, and Cooper flew off once again. They had debated the wisdom of feigning flight to the west then turning east for a dash to Tel Aviv, but Egyptian Spitfires rose to escort them in the direction of Libya. By the time the last Spitfire turned home, they were out of range of Tel Aviv and were forced to continue across North Africa and the Mediterranean to Rome.

V

Half way across the world the pilots, crews, and maintenance workers of Service Airways, alias LAPSA, were preparing to depart for Palestine. At 4:00 a.m. on the morning of May 8, Jules Cuburnek and the others were awakened and driven out to the airfield at Tocuman, Panama. When they reached the airfield the sun was up and the tropical heat was already creating shimmering mirages on the long concrete runways. The crews gathered near the five loaded and fuelled C-46s that were to take them to Paramaribo, Dutch Guiana. It was the first leg of a route pioneered by the Allies during the war to ferry planes from the United States to the Middle East or the China-Burma-India theatre of operations. None of the men had ever flown the route before and all knew the absolute necessity of keeping their destination and purpose completely secret. The atmosphere was charged with the crews' barely suppressed excitement. The disaster in Mexico City and the long weeks of waiting in the rain in Panama had depressed spirits, lowered morale, and brought a quick end to the earlier devil-may-care adventurousness. Now, however, the men were about to come alive again. During the three weeks between the arrival of the last of the C-46s in mid-April and the May 8 departure, pilots, crew, and mechanics had been practising night flying and working to ready the planes for the long trip to the Middle East. Cabin fuel tanks had to be installed, compasses had to be calibrated, engines needed overhauling. After the deaths in Mexico City, caution was the operational byword. Bad feelings and accusations about the cause of the fatal crash further depressed morale: Schindler blamed Schwimmer; Schwimmer and Lewis blamed the necessities of war. The personality problems were eventually ironed out when Schwimmer flew down from New York with Heyman Shamir and took personal control of the operation. Schindler resigned as president of Service Airways but insisted on piloting one of the C-46s to Palestine.[43]

The crews were split up and lodged at three hotels near Tocuman field. There were still not enough pilots and navigators to fly the nine planes to Palestine and more volunteers were hurriedly flown in from New York. Aboard one flight were Jules Cuburnek, Eddy Chinsky, and Trygve Maseng. Chinsky, who was from Windsor, Ontario, had been a wireless air gunner in the Royal Canadian Air Force. Maseng was a Protestant who had flown in the United States Army Air Force.

Hal Auerbach had drawn up the daily routine, which usually began before dawn when the mechanics were trucked out to the airfield to begin work on the planes. The crews were awakened at 6:45 and by 8:15 were on their way to the field to begin their test flights, engine run ups, radio instruction, or compass calibration.[44] While the planes were being worked on they were loaded and carefully checked to ensure that they stayed in balance. Engines and parts went aboard some of the C-46s, fuselages and wings of two BT-13 trainers went aboard the others. In the evening, navigational classes were held and the pilots practised night flying. On Tuesday night, May 4, Auerbach circulated the operations schedule for the next day, "D Day Minus Two". At the bottom of the long list of duties to be performed he typed instructions to all crew members to give navigator Moe Rosenbaum an envelope containing "whatever confidential data may be needed in event of serious illness or accident. Include your blood type." He added, almost as an afterthought, "Last day for one-day laundry service."[45]

At 7:00 a.m. on the morning of May 8, five Service Airways C-46s took off from Tocuman and headed for Paramaribo, Dutch Guiana.

They kept together as they flew over the rugged northern tip of Colombia and the steamy jungles of the Orinoco River headwaters. They climbed gently to clear the hilly country of eastern Venezuela and then nosed down to fly low over the jungles of northern British Guiana. Finally, after slightly more than ten hours in the air, they landed at Paramaribo. Three of the planes had been stricken with mechanical problems on the flight and stayed over until Tuesday, May 11,[46] but the remaining two took off the next morning for the nine-hour-and-forty-minute haul to Natal, Brazil. Their passing was noted by the American consul at Paramaribo who observed their origin and destination and took down their Panamanian registration numbers.[47] The five C-46s were reunited at Natal on May 11 and the crews began to prepare for the 2700-kilometre flight to Dakar, French West Africa. The planes were in poor condition and some of the men insisted on staying in Natal until they were completely overhauled. However, a local newspaper story had named them as the vanguard of the Jewish air force in Palestine. Their journey was now an open secret,[48] and they would have to leave soon, while they were still free to do so.

Three planes flew out of Natal before midnight on May 12: RX 130, piloted by Hal Auerbach; RX 135, flown by Martin Ribakoff, with Ray Kurtz, a former B-17 pilot who had left his job as a New York fireman to join Service Airways, sitting in the co-pilot's seat; RX 138, piloted by Larry Raab, with Jules Cuburnek navigating. The crews took off in a driving rain unsure what weather awaited them on their flight route.[49] They had been using weather information provided by British Overseas Airways Corporation until the Palestine story broke in the Natal newspaper; they were now on their own. Auerbach was soon forced to return to Natal because of engine trouble and Ribakoff and Raab flew on without him.[50] The two planes climbed above the weather and, after about two hours, Cuburnek took a star shot to check their course. He was an expert navigator thoroughly familiar with the exacting business of determining his position by stellar navigation. For most of the night, however, his skills were not needed because Dakar in French West Africa, a main station on the south-Atlantic air route, had a strong radio navigational beacon. All Raab had to do was keep the correct signal coming into his earphones by slight course corrections.[51]

The C-46s flew on, Ribakoff and Kurtz in the lead, Raab somewhere behind in the dark. Radio operators sat through the night at their sets, earphones on, fuses open, listening for the signal that would tell them that their mission was unmasked and their odyssey would end at Dakar.[52] The signal never came. Cuburnek made periodic star shots from the Plexiglas dome atop the C-46 to check the accuracy of the Dakar beacon. The pilots concentrated on steering down the beacon and staying awake. At about 5:00 a.m., dawn broke over the ocean with a ribbon of pink glowing on the eastern horizon. Soon the hot tropical sun rose high and began to bake the silver transports. At about 9:00 a.m. on May 13, the long coastline of Africa slid above the horizon. Within minutes the two aircraft touched down at Dakar, one not far ahead of the other. It was ten hours and thirty minutes since they had lifted off from the rainswept runway of Natal.[53]

VI

Ben Dunkelman was the first Canadian volunteer to arrive in Palestine. When he sailed into the port of Haifa in early April 1948, the sights and sounds of war mingled strangely with the normal peacetime bustle of a busy harbour. Each arriving boat was greeted by Palestine Immigration officials, some of whom were Arab employees of the Mandatory government, some of whom were officials of the Jewish Agency. The dock area was guarded by troops of the Transjordan Arab Legion, who were stationed in Palestine to augment British forces. They were withdrawn just before the Mandate ended on May 15. Dunkelman and Max Brown made their way through Immigration with false identity papers and boarded a bus to Hadar Hacarmel, the Jewish section of the city, half way up Mount Carmel. At the Carmelia Court Hotel, Brown was soon led away by Haganah officials who were eager to put his expertise in arms manufacture to work.[54] Dunkelman was not so fortunate. He spent several days pondering the sights and sounds of Haifa before travelling by armoured bus to Tel Aviv where he was installed at the Brandstater Pension. He was given forty Palestine pounds for subsistence and provided with an identity card.[55]

Although Dunkelman was impatient to get into action, the Haganah was not quite ready to receive volunteers in April. There were no facilities for integrating arriving volunteers quickly into the Jewish forces and there was no set procedure for equipping and training the volunteers or assigning them to established units. The Haganah could easily make immediate use of air crews arriving from South Africa,

Europe, or Panama. Planes were needed for supply and reconnaissance, and the crews were quickly put to work flying missions in Palestine or shuttling back and forth to Europe. But for volunteers destined for the infantry, or for specialists in armour, artillery, mortars, radar, and maintenance, there was as yet little more than chaos.

Dunkelman soon found that the Haganah had no intention of establishing a separate brigade of English-speaking soldiers and, despite his protests to Haganah leaders, including Ben Gurion, no such unit was set up.[56] He soon tired of the waiting and asked to be assigned to the Jerusalem front, where the Palmach's Harel Brigade was fighting to re-open the road between Tel Aviv and Jerusalem. He arrived on April 20 after a hazardous journey under fire in a Palmach supply convoy.

The men he had hoped to command began to arrive in early April. The first group of five Canadians had sailed from Marseilles the night of March 29 aboard the S.S. *Teti*. The 4000-ton freighter, which had been designed to carry eighty passengers and cargo, now had 700 immigrants jammed into its holds.[57] When the *Teti* docked in Haifa, the five Canadians were taken to a hotel on Mount Carmel, where they stayed for several days. An armoured bus then took them to Tel Litvinsky army camp a few miles southeast of Tel Aviv. Within ten days they were joined by the rest of the Canadian contingent, led by Druker.

The trip to Palestine aboard the immigrant ships was an education in itself. In Marseilles the volunteers had been kept pretty well separate from the displaced persons and had gone for training and indoctrination to some of the smaller farms near the main refugee camps. On board the ships, however, they were jammed together with the rest of the passengers for the whole voyage to Palestine. For the first time the volunteers saw the remnant of European Jewry at close quarters. After the ship left port a thriving black market sprang up in food, chocolate bars, and cigarettes. In the packed holds the heat and stench were intense. The latrines were usually nothing more than wooden platforms built over the ship's railings. Even though the volunteers were given the best places on or near the decks and fed the best food, direct exposure to the overwhelming sickness and misery of many passengers was unavoidable—and often shocking.[58]

Americans and Canadians usually came by sea, but most South Africans flew in. In late April several volunteers arrived from South Africa via Europe. The very first group landed at Lydda airport on

April 21. No Jewish officials were there to greet them—all the Customs and Immigration officers in the arrival hall were Arabs, although they were guarded by a few British soliders. The South Africans were fortunate that a Jewish taxi owner had driven to the airport in an armoured car to bring the last Jewish employees out before Lydda field fell into Arab hands. They hitched a ride with him to Petach Tikvah on the outskirts of Tel Aviv.[59]

Also on April 21 a second South African contingent landed at Lydda, but the situation there was so unsettled that the volunteers were instructed to stay aboard the aircraft and proceed to Rome. From there they were taken to Milan and lodged at Costelumbra, a large villa on the Swiss border that served as a displaced persons camp for Jewish refugees heading for the port of La Spezia. These volunteers were soon joined by another South African group that had come by way of Cairo. At Costelumbra the South African volunteers met the remnant of European Jewry for the first time. One of the South Africans later spoke of the impact this meeting had on him:

> I had gone through the Zionist movement and had studied Jewish history. Logically, I should not have been as one hit by revelation. But I was. . . . These people had spent days and nights crossing mountains in the snow. They had concentration camp marks on their arms. Some told of watching parents marched off, others of parents killed in front of them. . . .

The South Africans and the refugees celebrated the Jewish Passover festival at the camp and the experience left a lasting impression on the volunteers. The refugees prayed and sang freedom songs until the early hours of the morning, because as far as they were concerned going to Palestine meant going home.[60]

The South Africans at Costelumbra were also anxious to get to Palestine, but there were no ships available for several weeks. The transport shortage left a growing number of volunteers waiting in Italy and France in late April and early May. The delay was a blessing in disguise, however, because it gave the Haganah time to begin organizing facilities and procedures for the reception and integration of foreign volunteers into the army. Tel Litvinsky, a former U.S. Army camp that had been sold to the Jewish Agency in December 1947, became the main reception centre for volunteers.[61] It was a typical Middle East installation, with rough, sun-bleached concrete buildings scattered over a terrain of sand, rock, and shrub. The camp had no anti-aircraft defences, not even slit trenches, and had fallen into disrepair after it had been abandoned by the U.S. Army. Little or nothing was done to upgrade Tel Litvinsky after it was purchased by the Jewish Agency and the volunteers were forced to put up with the bad food and primitive living conditions that were an ever-present part of the war in Palestine.

In the early months of the war Tel Litvinsky was little more than a crowded way station where men whiled away the hours and days until they were assigned to specific duties or unofficially recruited by officers who competed with each other to attract volunteers to their units. The twenty-seven Canadians who made their way to Tel Litvinsky were almost all specialists. In the rush to press men into action, however, they quickly became foot sloggers—infantry armed with rifles and grenades and equipped with a few Czech-built machine guns. Neither uniforms nor ranks were assigned to the individual soldiers at Tel Litvinsky, but further training was given in grenade throwing, rifle firing, and the bayonet. Here, also, the official induction into the Haganah took place.

The Canadians languished in Tel Litvinsky for about two weeks, impatient to get into action and increasingly upset by the Haganah's failure to put them to good use. All the old problems that had plagued them in the French training camps re-emerged and the old grievances were again trotted out. They sent a petition to the Haganah bureau in charge of foreign volunteers complaining that they had received false information about army pay and claiming that they had been forced to spend as much as $100 each for clothing and equipment. They charged that, because they had been allowed to bring only one small suitcase, they were forced to do without personal effects like towels, shaving kits, and kitbags. They were also upset at having to pay to send telegrams to their families in Canada. Most of all, they were dismayed by the apparently complete lack of preparation for their arrival.[62]

The Canadians were moved out of Tel Litvinsky before an investigation could be conducted into their petition. On May 3 they were sent to the Givati Brigade based at Camp Bilu near the town of Rehovot. There, they were assigned to the 2nd Battalion, which was known as Givati 52. Givati was one of six Haganah field brigades formed in the general reorganization of February 1948. (The others were Alexandroni, Carmeli, Etzioni, Golani, and Kiryati.) The largest of the six—

Golani—contained about 4100 men; the smallest—Kiryati—mustered about 2500. Together the six fielded 18,810 men by mid-May. This, plus the 6000 men of the three smaller Palmach brigades—Harel, Negev, and Yiftah—comprised the effective mobile strength of the Jewish forces in Palestine.[63]

Each brigade was responsible for conducting operations in an assigned geographic area. Givati was responsible for the southern approaches to Tel Aviv, the district around Rehovot—about nineteen kilometres south of Tel Aviv—and the western portion of the Tel Aviv-Jerusalem road. By early May the Haganah high command expected the Arab League armies to attack immediately after the Mandate ended on May 15, and military operations were primarily designed to strengthen Jewish positions in the expected path of the attack. Links with isolated Jewish settlements had to be established, roads had to be cleared, and Arab fighters had to be expelled from positions to the rear of, or in between, important concentrations of Jewish population.

The town of Bash-shit, home to about 1600 Palestine Arabs, was situated at the junction of five dirt tracks, about three kilometres east of the Tel Aviv-Gaza highway. It was a small, out-of-the-way place that in peacetime would hardly have been noticed by anyone but those who called it home. In war it was a military objective, a small part of a larger Haganah picture known as Operation Barak.

Barak, which was planned for early May, was designed to clear Arab resistance from the area between Tel Aviv and Gaza. The operation was to be mounted by the Haganah's Givati Brigade and the Negev Brigade of the Palmach, and was specifically designed to secure roads and communications routes in the region, demoralize the enemy, and break the Arab blockade of Jewish settlements in the northern Negev.[64] There were several major Arab towns and a number of smaller villages in the way; one of these was Bash-shit. The first Canadian volunteers were never to forget Bash-shit. There they were introduced to the war in Palestine. For most of them it was the first time they had been under fire.

On the night of May 10 a Haganah reconnaissance patrol was sent to Bash-shit to probe village defences. The patrol estimated that about one hundred of the villagers were fighters, most armed with rifles, one or two with machine guns. There were no signs of the Arab Liberation Army or the Moslem Brotherhood guerrillas from Egypt that were known to have infiltrated across the border. The patrol suggested that

102

Bash-shit's defences were strongest on the north side and recommended that a surprise attack be mounted from the south and west. The patrol's report left the impression that Bash-shit would be an easy conquest and took no heed of the fact that the Bash-shit fighters had already proved their abilities in attacks on Jewish settlements and convoys in the area.[65]

In the early morning hours of May 11, under cover of darkness, the soldiers of Givati's 2nd Battalion moved in. Two companies, each consisting of two platoons, were bused from the nearby Kibbutz Yavneh to a spot southeast of Bash-shit. The twenty-seven Canadians made up about half of the second company, which was under the command of Dov Elduby. They were already known in Givati as "the Canadian platoon". The commander of the 2nd Battalion had been reluctant to order the Canadians into action because, although they were all World War II veterans, few had any combat experience.[66] They had been eager, however, and, under Lionel Druker's leadership, had proved themselves to be a disciplined and cohesive body while training at Camp Bilu.[67] When Elduby was given over-all command responsibility for the platoon, he agreed to insert them into the order of battle.

The two 2nd Battalion companies were split up. The first crept into position on the north side of the village. There, the men worked their way to the top of the two low hills overlooking Bash-shit and set up a machine gun to ambush any Arab attackers who might rush to the defence of Bash-shit from the Arab town of Yibna, which lay to the north. Other soldiers laid mines on the dirt track that ran west of Bash-shit. Their primary job was to block the reinforcement of the village while the second company was penetrating the town from the southwest. A "Davidka"—a homemade mortar—and a standard 80-millimetre mortar were positioned in the fields to the east of Bash-shit, while homemade armoured cars patrolled the main highway farther east. The attack was planned as a quick blow so that British troops would not have time to intervene.

Ironically, in light of their plan, the Israeli attackers sent an ultimatum to Bash-shit demanding its surrender. Surprise was immediately lost. When Elduby's company advanced towards Bash-shit on the main dirt track leading from the west, the Arabs opened fire from a well-house on the north side of the road. Elduby had thought the well-house empty and, as his men dived into the dirt and took cover behind rocks and sabra cactus, he called in mortar fire. The Davidka proved useless. Its large, bucket-shaped charge sailed lazily through the early dawn and landed with a massive explosion in the field outside the town. The weapon was extremely inaccurate at the best of times and was more valuable for the sound of the explosion than for the actual damage it caused to enemy installations. The mortar was more accurate, and managed to lob at least seventy-five rounds into Bash-shit before Elduby called it off to allow his men to move in.

When the commander of the northern company heard shooting, he ordered one of his two platoons to stay in its defensive position atop the hills to the north of Bash-shit and sent the other to attack from the north. It was a rash decision. The men ran into heavy fire from the town and were forced back to the hill where they had been most of the night. As the sky lightened, the Arab defenders in the village easily spotted them atop the hills and began to shoot. The Givati men had not dug trenches or foxholes and were easy targets: two were killed and eight wounded in the short fire fight, and three armoured cars were needed to evacuate the wounded.[68]

To the southwest of Bash-shit, Elduby was still under the impression that his men were part of a co-ordinated assault. He ordered the Canadian platoon to advance down the road into the centre of the village, and sent the other platoon to skirt the village and link up with the northern company in its hilltop positions.[69] The Canadians advanced cautiously, shooting from behind the corners of buildings, lobbing grenades into houses and courtyards, racing across open spaces between cover. The Arab machine gunners in the well-house were dislodged in a grenade attack and pulled back into the village. Murray Cappell, Irving Kaplansky, and Moe Dankovy, three Toronto volunteers, carried a Spandau heavy machine gun mounted on a tripod. They would grab the gun, race a few metres over the stones and debris left by the mortar bombing, then fling themselves down behind a pile of rubble or other cover and open fire. They had to make the Arabs think there were many such guns, so, after a minute or two of squeezing off bursts, they grabbed the gun, dashed off, and set up in a new position.[70]

The Canadians pressed ahead despite heavy shooting at close quarters and were well inside the town before they suffered their first casualties. Syd Cadloff was firing while lying prone in the midst of a small group of men. The platoon radio operator was crouched beside him. During a short lull in the shooting, some of the others raced forward to throw grenades into a nearby courtyard. Cadloff heard a shot ring out, and the radioman screamed and fell forward with a bullet in his thigh. Then a burst of machine-gun fire stitched the ground beside the two men, kicking dust into their faces. An Arab gunner had climbed a tree in a courtyard and poked his gun over the top of the wall to fire a few bursts. Cadloff had no time to roll away before a second burst cut across his left leg from his knee to his ankle: he screamed from the painful burning sensation.[71] Moments later another Canadian was wounded in the head as he peered from behind the corner of a building.

Up ahead, Cappell, Dankovy, and Kaplansky had penetrated to a small courtyard in the centre of the village. They hacked away at the wall until they broke through and set up the machine gun to fire through the hole towards the central square. Suddenly a grenade sailed over the courtyard and exploded on the other side of the wall. One of their own men had been ordered to throw it by an officer who had heard the digging and firing and assumed that the Arabs had installed themselves there.[72]

Now Elduby learned that the northern attack on Bash-shit had been driven back and that the Canadians were in the centre of the village facing the combined strength of the Arab defenders shooting at them from three sides. They were dangerously exposed and Elduby ordered them to withdraw. All except the three-man machine-gun crew began to pull back, taking the wounded with them. However Cappell, Kaplansky, and Dankovy failed to receive the order to retreat and kept firing through the hole in the courtyard wall. When Druker realized they had not pulled out he ran back to get them, and the four then made their way slowly out of Bash-shit, firing as they retreated.[73]

When they had pulled clear of the village, Elduby ordered the Canadians to join the other 2nd Battalion troops on the hilltops to the northeast thus blocking any attempts by Arabs in surrounding villages to reinforce Bash-shit. Elduby himself fought a rear-guard action. With six or seven of his men, he sighted a small group of Arabs waiting in ambush and killed all of them with grenades and machine guns. When Arab reinforcements were spotted moving along the dirt tracks towards Bash-shit, the Givati troops opened fire and drove them off.

At this point the brigade commander decided to throw another battalion into the fight. The second attack on Bash-shit was begun at about 9:20 a.m. Within an hour the village defenders were killed, driven off, or taken prisoner, and the town was demolished. Inside Bash-shit the Arabs had suffered twenty-five dead and fifty wounded, the Jews four killed and seventeen wounded including the two Canadians.[74]

Cadloff's leg could not be saved. After several days he began to run a high fever, and when the doctors opened his leg cast they discovered gangrene had set in. The surgeon told Cadloff that it was dangerous to wait any longer for the fever to subside before surgery and the decision was made to amputate. The leg was so badly smashed that the doctor was forced to cut it off above the knee. Cadloff wrote to his brother: "I am learning to hop around on crutches, and later on I'll get an artificial limb and everything will be hunky dory. . . . I'll bet you wouldn't tell the difference whether I had an artificial limb or not."[75] Though many of these twenty-seven men saw heavy action in the months that followed—in other infantry units, in the Seventh and Eighth brigades, even in the navy and air force—they never forgot the little village of Bash-shit. It had been their first time under direct fire and it was, in their opinion, a botched operation.[76]

VII

As May 15 and the end of the Mandate approached, the Zionist movement faced its moment of truth. Jewish forces in Palestine were gaining the upper hand over the Palestine Arabs. The Etzion Bloc south of Jerusalem remained under siege, however, and finally, on May 14, surrendered after a combined onslaught of local Arab fighters and units of the Transjordan Arab Legion.

At the United Nations and in Washington, Chaim Weizmann and other Zionist leaders were receiving mixed signals. The U.S. delegation to the U.N. was pressing as hard as ever for the adoption of its trusteeship proposals and had succeeded in lining up what appeared to be a majority of the General Assembly. At the same time, however, President Truman sent word to Weizmann that if partition survived the current U.N. debate and a Jewish state was declared after the British Mandate ended, he would give it very quick recognition. There was no longer any doubt in anyone's mind that the British Mandate would end May 15, but the establishment of a Jewish state was still a matter for conjecture. Some Zionist leaders, including Moshe Shertok, believed that in view of the international political situation and the virtual certainty of an Arab League invasion, the best course was to delay the proclamation of Jewish independence. Shertok was in a minority position, but the mere fact that some leading Zionists were advising caution made the final decision less than certain.

In the "Alice-in-Wonderland" world that the United Nations had become, events seemed to move with exaggerated slowness as the clock ticked away the final days and hours of the Mandate.[77] In the General Assembly, a U.S. resolution to establish U.N. control over Jerusalem—the first step in the move towards trusteeship—was given solemn attention. Delegates chose to ignore the obvious fact that Arabs and Jews were fighting and dying by the hour in a block-by-block struggle to dominate the Holy City in preparation for the final British departure. No U.N. soldiers kept the peace of Jerusalem. No Arab or Jewish soldiers were likely to honour any U.N. resolutions that ignored the reality of spilled blood. Rabbi Abba Hillel Silver of the Zionist Organization of America told the U.N. delegates early on the afternoon of May 14 that a Jewish state, the State of Israel, had been declared to exist as of the end of the Mandate, at 6:00 p.m. New York time. The delegates listened, but many doubted that such a move would actually take place. At 4:45 p.m. the President of the General Assembly opened the last meeting of the special session that had been called a month earlier to deal with the U.S. proposals on Palestine. In an effort to beat the deadlines, a time limit of five minutes was imposed on each speaker, but it was a futile gesture. As the debate ended and the voting began, the clock showed 6:00 p.m. Anything the United Nations now decided would be illegal. The Mandate was over; British authority in Palestine had ended and with it the United Nations' right to impose a political solution. Half way around the world, and a world removed from the empty diplomatic manoeuvrings at the United Nations, the State of Israel was being born in an agony of bloodshed.

6

"Like a Flying, Burning Stake"

On the afternoon of May 14, 1948, the crews of the Service Airways C-46s flown by Ribakoff and Raab sat huddled together in the airport coffee shop at Casablanca, Morocco, and tried to relax after a nine-and-a-half-hour flight that had started before dawn at Dakar, French West Africa. After crossing the south Atlantic, they had rested for only a day at Dakar before pushing on to Casablanca, and the exhausting pace was beginning to wear them down. Soon they would be on their way to Catania, in Sicily. As they ate, the news that Israel had just declared its independence began to spread through the restaurant. The Service Airways flyers "had to suppress a shout", Cuburnek later remembered, for fear that they and their mission would be exposed while they were still in the heart of the Arab world. Despite their desire to get away from Morocco as quickly as possible, they were forced to spend two nerve-wracked days in Casablanca while awaiting word on the fate of the other planes. It seemed wise to post a constant guard near their aircraft. Athough no one in Casablanca seemed to catch on to the real mission of these Service Airways planes and crews, the French airport officials had no doubt about their eventual destination. When Raab and Ribakoff filed their flight plans for Catania, they were told: "We hope you win in Palestine."[1]

I

Most of the important political leaders of the Yishuv began to gather nervously in the Tel Aviv Museum after lunch on May 14. Some, like Ben Gurion, wore a white shirt and tie for the first and last time in their public lives. They were there to hear Ben Gurion read the Declaration of Independence of the State of Israel. The National

Council of the Yishuv had decided only in the last few days prior to the end of the Mandate to go ahead with the declaration. Some important members opposed this daring step and wanted, instead, to make one last effort at a compromise solution. The name of the new Jewish state had been chosen only hours before. The Declaration of Independence was typed out on a plain sheet of paper. The scroll signed by the delegates that afternoon was blank; the design and words were added later.

Ben Gurion stood up to read as the photographers popped their flashbulbs: "Eretz Israel was the birthplace of the Jewish People. Here their spiritual, religious and political identity was shaped. Here they first attained statehood, created cultural values of national and universal significance and gave to the world the eternal Book of Books." The statement epitomized fifty years of Zionist hopes and centuries of Jewish dreams. It declared the establishment of the State of Israel with a Provisional Government upon the expiration of the Mandate at midnight. Ben Gurion ended with a plea for peace: "We extend our hand to all neighboring states and their peoples in an offer of peace and good neighborliness and appeal to them to establish bonds of co-operation and mutual help with the sovereign Jewish people settled in its own land." It was a hopeless gesture; the invasion had already started.[2]

At dawn on May 15 Egyptian fighter bombers swooped low over Tel Aviv as air-raid sirens moaned. The strafing attack did little damage and one fighter was shot down. However, it was an ominous sign of the days to come, when Egyptian fighters and bombers—usually converted Dakotas—attacked southern Israel at will. During one bombing of Tel Aviv the central bus station was destroyed. There were more than 40 killed and 100 wounded. The May 15 air raids came as Egyptian troops, supported by tanks, artillery, and armoured cars, were pouring over the border and starting to push north along the coast towards Tel Aviv. They advanced quickly up the coastal highway attacking Jewish settlements on their eastern flank and putting several under siege. The Egyptians managed to raise 7000 combat troops, which were then divided into two groups. A 5000-man group advanced on Tel Aviv, and a 2000-man contingent was ordered to cut across the northern Negev by way of Beersheba and follow the Beersheba-Hebron highway to link up with the Transjordan Arab Legion near Jerusalem.

The Arab Legion had been stationed in Palestine during the Mandate, but as May 15 approached it started to withdraw east of the Jordan River. On May 15 the Legion recrossed the Jordan River at the Allenby Bridge near Jericho and began to deploy around Jerusalem. Transjordan's objective was clear—to occupy Arab Palestine and annex it to Transjordan. To secure these objectives the Arab Legion began to move towards the proposed boundaries of the Arab state and, on May 17, it took control of the police fort at Latrun overlooking the Tel Aviv-Jerusalem highway. Prior to May 15 the Haganah had succeeded in breaking the Palestine Arab blockade of Jerusalem, but after May 17 the blockade was re-established by a much stronger, better-organized, and better-armed Arab force. The Legion began shelling western Jerusalem and placed the Jewish quarter of the ancient walled city under siege.

In the hills of Samaria north of Jerusalem, the Iraqi Army deployed in Nablus. It had tried to cross the Jordan River near Gesher, about eight kilometres south of Lake Tiberias, but had been blocked by Jewish forces. It then swung south, crossed the river near Jericho, and established its headquarters in Nablus where Kaukji's Arab Liberation Army was also based. On May 25 the Iraqi troops attacked west, aiming to reach the sea near Netanya, about twenty-five kilometres north of Tel Aviv. Had they succeeded they would have cut the coastal strip in two, but they were stopped ten kilometres east of their objective by the Alexandroni Brigade.

The Syrians had been expected to launch their main assault north of Lake Tiberias, and thus their attack on Samakh, on the southern tip of the lake, came as a complete surprise to the Israelis. The Syrian troops were tired and untrained, however, and their attack was listless and ineffective. The Syrians eventually succeeded in capturing Samakh, but were unable to advance further west past Kibbutz Degania. Lebanese troops also invaded on May 15 but, instead of pushing south along the coast, concentrated their efforts on an eastward attack towards the Jewish settlements in the upper Galilee. They captured Malkiya from the Palmach who were forced to retreat east to Kadesh. If the Lebanese thrust had been properly co-ordinated with the Syrian forces driving west, it might have reached the Jordan River and cut the main road from Lake Tiberias to the most northerly Jewish settlements near Metulla. However, after their initial success, the Lebanese chose to stop and consolidate inside the borders of Israel.[3]

These initial Arab assaults were carried out without any substantive interference either from the United Nations, which had sanctioned partition and the birth of a Jewish state, or from Great Britain, which continued to supply arms to Iraq, Transjordan, and Egypt as if the invasion had not taken place. Even U.S. action was more apparent than real. In a surprise move that caught his own State Department off guard, President Truman issued a de facto recognition of the State of Israel only minutes after it was born, and on May 17 the U.S. delegation at the United Nations began to push for an immediate ceasefire, with sanctions imposed for non-compliance. The British, however, opposed this, claiming doubt that the Arab League countries were aggressors or had broken the peace.[4] As long as Arab armies appeared to be advancing on all fronts, Britain stood behind Arab claims that they had been invited into Palestine by the Palestine Arabs to restore order in the wake of the British withdrawal. The United States was obviously willing to push diplomatically for a quick end to the fighting. However no moves were made to send troops to protect Israel and to enforce partition, and no threats of unilateral sanctions against the Arabs were issued from Washington. If Israel was to survive its first days, it would have to do so on its own, supported by those Jews and non-Jews in the rest of the world who knew that action, not talk, was required.

II

Israel's defence plan in the first weeks of the Arab invasion can be summed up in one word: survival. Somehow, Arab armies would have to be held off, roads would have to be kept open, and outlying settlements would have to be supplied. At the same time Israel's main population centres would have to be protected against air attack. None of this would be possible without a quick infusion of heavy weapons and other vital military equipment that would enable the Haganah to face the firepower of the Arab invaders.

The planes from South Africa and the United States, still en route to Israel, were now needed more than ever, both to help maintain communications inside the country and to airlift any weapons that the Czechs were willing to sell. On May 15, Israel's first full day of independence, the first of the planes that had left South Africa on April 11 arrived. Tuxie Blau, Les Chimes, and Arthur Cooper (and Alf Lindsay, who vanished en route) had left Cairo on May 7, but had been unable to fly directly to Palestine and had been forced to detour via Rome. When the first plane, a Fairchild flown by Tuxie Blau, touched down at the Tel Aviv airstrip just before dusk, an Egyptian bombing raid was in progress. Blau quickly turned off the runway, leaped from his cockpit, raced across the field with a group of men, and dived into a hole just as a stick of bombs exploded. One day later Chimes and Cooper landed at Haifa. They had been en route for thirty-five days, had covered almost 10,000 kilometres, and had spent more than one hundred hours in the air. They were met by an Immigration official of the newborn state who used an old Mandate stamp to admit them. It read: "Government of Palestine, Immigration Department, admitted for temporary residence...." Underneath, the official wrote, in Hebrew, *harishon* (the first).[5] It was not accurate, but it somehow seemed appropriate.

On the day Chimes and Cooper landed in Israel, the two Service Airways C-46s flown by Larry Raab and Martin Ribakoff left Casablanca and flew to Catania on the east coast of Sicily. There they were greeted by Danny Agronsky and Heyman Shamir, who had flown ahead on commercial airlines from Panama. In March, Agronsky had chosen Catania airport as a substitute for Castiglione del Lago after Leo Gardner had reported the latter unusable. Agronsky had approached the airport manager and presented himself as the representative of Service Airways of New York City and Lineas Aereas de Panama of Panama and obtained landing authorization for a number of C-46s "under Panamanian registry manned by American crews", as he described it. Shortly after Agronsky had left Catania, a general "from the Air Ministry in Rome" had appeared and told airport officials "not to examine too closely the papers of crewmen on the C-46s landing at Catania".[6]

It was early afternoon on May 18 before Ribakoff and Raab, with Shamir along in Raab's plane to guide them, left Catania for Israel; and it was pitch dark by the time they approached the coast. Tel Aviv was blacked out, but the crew could make out the shoreline by the light of the full moon. In RX 138 Shamir said to Raab and Cuburnek, "Look, there's a power station in Tel Aviv and I know it. It'll give us a perfect check."

Raab descended to look for the power station and flew over one of the few anti-aircraft gun positions in all of Israel, which promptly opened fire. Tracers reached out for the low-flying transport, but Raab quickly pulled up and took evasive action. By the time he was flying straight and level again, however, they were lost. Out of the cockpit window, they spotted green airport lights in the darkened countryside, and Shamir called, "That's it." Raab flew over and began to circle, waiting for a red light to signal that it was time to begin final approach. But no light came on.

Just then the Ekron radio operator crackled through the head-phones: "Get the hell away from there. Come back 180 degrees and we'll put the lights on for you." They had been flying over the Jordanian-controlled field at Lydda. Within minutes, Raab and his crew joined Ribakoff and the others who had flown in RX 135 without trouble and had landed first.

The crews, exhausted, spent a hot night trying to sleep in several cabins by the airstrip while, Cuburnek remembered, members of the ground crew stole anything they "had not nailed down".[7] Early the next morning, after a fitful sleep, the crews flew the two planes to Brno, Czechoslovakia, to pick up a cargo of arms. When they landed at Catania for refuelling, their planes were impounded by the suspicious airport manager, who was convinced they were smugglers. Agronsky was forced to fly down from Rome to "pay off" the airport officials and secure the release of the two aircraft.[8]

When Agronsky flew on to Sicily, he left behind a mess of major proportions. On the morning of May 20, one of the Somaco Norse-man aircraft, bound for Palestine with George "Buzz" Beurling and Leonard Cohen aboard, had lifted off from the main runway at Urbe. The plane, bearing the United States registration number NC 79822, had barely lifted fifty metres off the runway when a lick of flame appeared out of the engine and quickly grew into a trailing inferno of smoke and fire. Whoever was at the controls tried to land, but the damage to the plane was so serious and the heat and smoke in the cockpit so unbearable that he could do little. The Norseman dived, whirled, and skidded, hitting the ground with one wingtip before finally falling "like a flying, burning stake on the runway". Horrified ground personnel sprang into action. Men with extinguishers rushed frantically towards the burning wreck, while two airport fire fighters' trucks raced across the field; but it was too late. The plane was a twisted wreck; Cohen and Beurling were burned to death.[9] Both men were war heroes whose exploits had become the stuff of legend. Cohen, an Englishman, known as "The King of Lampedusa", had been forced down on the small Mediterranean island of Lampedusa, near Tunis, during World War II only to have the entire detachment of the island's Italian defenders surrender to him.

No direct proof has yet been unearthed that Beurling and Cohen were killed by sabotage. In Canada, Syd Shulemson was satisfied, after an informal investigation, that the crash was caused by an engine fire, and other accounts bear this out. The Norseman was prone to such fires under certain circumstances. However, a Haganah agent in Rome filed a secret report which—if it is true—rules out accidental death. The Haganah man claimed that a British agent—an ex-sergeant in the British Army who had served with the Palestine Police between 1946 and 1948—had sabotaged Beurling's Norseman. The British agent was supposed to keep tabs on the Agronsky operation, including the comings and goings at the hotels and the Urbe airfield, and he was to do whatever he could to prevent the planes and volunteers from proceeding to Palestine. The undercover Haganah man claimed that the saboteur was intercepted as he left his hotel after the crash and "in a distant lane near the Tiber [he] was hit, [and] his corpse was thrown into the river."[10] There is no independent evidence to corroborate this story.

III

In the first weeks of the war foreign volunteers played little part in the heavy ground fighting on the five fronts. Volunteers had begun to arrive in the final days of April and the two weeks preceding the Israeli Declaration of Independence, but they were still few in number. As long as the British maintained the last vestiges of control under the Mandate, each volunteer had to be smuggled into the country using false identity papers. As May 15 and the end of British control approached, however, the Israelis began moving larger numbers of refugees from the European displaced persons camps to Palestine. Along with those refugees came thousands of *gahal* recruits from the camps. They were picked for their age and physical condition and given rudimentary training with wooden rifles before being thrown into battle. Hundreds were pressed into action with the Seventh Brigade formed under the command of Shlomo Shamir on May 14 and many of them died within days, even hours, of reaching their promised land. Mixed in with these recruits and the other refugees were the volunteers who had waited for transport to Palestine. The *Marine*

114

Carp was one of the ships involved in carrying those volunteers to war.

The *Marine Carp* cleared port at Athens a few days before May 15 bound for Beirut. It was carrying its normal complement of passengers—businessmen, vacationers, tourists—on a leisurely cruise around the eastern Mediterranean. It also carried a contingent of Land and Labor volunteers, including forty Americans, twenty-four Jewish Palestinians returning from the United States, three Canadians, one Mexican, and one Pole.[11] The *Marine Carp* took the quickest and most direct route from New York to Palestine. However, it normally stopped in Beirut before proceeding to Haifa, and this had caused problems in the past. In November 1946, a group of American Jewish veterans sailing to Palestine aboard the *Marine Carp* had been confronted by Lebanese port authorities in Beirut and denied permission to leave the ship. Several of the passengers who refused to obey the injunction and tried to go ashore had been prevented from doing so. They had complained to the American Legation. Lebanese authorities had told the United States chargé d'affaires that the ban had been issued "for security purposes only" to protect the passengers. At the same time an official from the American Legation had tried to convince the veterans that there was "considerable tension" in Beirut over the Palestine issue and "strong anti-Jewish sentiment". He had warned them that they must expect "occasional incidents and embarrassments" in the area. The State Department later told the American Zionist Emergency Council that it regretted the incident but that they must bear in mind "that Beirut is an Arab port situated within less than a hundred miles of Palestine and that tension in this area is a matter of concern".[12] Despite this incident, however, and despite the looming invasion of Palestine, Land and Labor had continued to send volunteers aboard the *Marine Carp*.

As the ship sailed towards Beirut the news of the Israeli Declaration of Independence was received over the radio, and the word spread quickly. A spontaneous celebration that lasted throughout May 15 and into the early morning hours of May 16 broke out among the Jewish passengers. Even Arab passengers joined in, but on May 16, dawn brought the cold realization that the ship was headed for Beirut, capital of a country that had just invaded Palestine. The arrival of the *Marine Carp* in Beirut would be a provocation the Lebanese could not ignore. A delegation of Jewish passengers approached the captain and asked him to change course so that the ship would stop at Haifa before sailing to Beirut. The captain refused and, apparently, also failed to contact the U.S. government, which was, in effect, the owner of the vessel.[13] On the morning of May 19, the S.S. *Marine Carp* glided to a stop beside a pier in the bustling harbour of Beirut. The dockworkers made the ship fast and the gangplank was raised to its side. Lebanese Customs officials then scrambled aboard while soldiers, rifles at the ready, stood on the dock. As soon as an officer from the American Legation showed up, the Lebanese began a slow and methodical search of every nook and cranny of the ship, paying close attention to the baggage of the Jewish passengers. The proceedings dragged on until evening, when the Jews were gathered in the ship's dining hall and told that all males of military age would have to disembark. The American Legation had tried to persuade the Lebanese Foreign Office to allow the American citizens to proceed, but had been told that public opinion in Lebanon and the other Arab countries made this impossible. When the American official aboard the ship protested the order, he was told that the passengers in question would be taken off by force if necessary. He then informed the passengers that physical resistance would lead to bloodshed and advised them to leave quietly.[14]

The men took what little personal baggage they had with them—the rest was left in the hold—and walked down the gangplank to waiting trucks parked on the other side of the freight shed. Kit bags and suitcases were thrown in, the men hopped aboard, and the trucks drove off with a clashing of gears. They soon left the streets of Beirut and headed into the mountains. The drivers drove quickly through the dark on the twisting roads, seemingly oblivious to the sharp hairpin curves and the steep slopes just beyond the headlights. Sometime around 4:00 a.m., the convoy rolled into the former French Army barracks at Beka, next to the magnificent Roman ruins of Baalbek.[15]

On May 22 the American Legation in Beirut sent an officer to Beka who reported that the "detainees" were in good health and spirits and "loud in their praise of the treatment accorded to them".[16] The British Vice-Consul visited the three Canadians among the men on June 1 on behalf of the Canadian government. He found the men "in good health but subdued". The imprisonment was not harsh, but it was long and filled with uncertainty. At the mercy of an enemy country, isolated from homes and families, they had no idea of how long their imprisonment would last.

Diplomatic efforts to secure the release of the sixty-nine began almost as soon as they were seized, and the United States took the initiative on the day after the volunteers were trucked to Baalbek. The U.S. chargé d'affaires in Beirut told the Lebanese that in Washington's view all bearers of U.S. passports, "regardless of race, color or creed" were entitled to "an equal measure of protection". The U.S. government took a serious view of "discrimination of this character. . . against United States citizens" and insisted that the internees be released.[17] The message was clear, but the Lebanese rejected it. The "Lebanese Army of occupation" was attempting to maintain "order and security" in Palestine, they said. In blocking young Jews from joining the Zionist forces in Palestine, the Lebanese claimed to be acting in self-defence. It was obvious, the Lebanese government declared, that these men would "join elements of trouble and anarchy in Palestine" and would "attack the Lebanese forces which have intervened with other Arab forces to reestablish order and put an end to the violence and acts of terrorism committed by the Zionists."[18]

Despite the tough talk the Lebanese were not willing to defy the United States indefinitely and, on May 24, they sounded out the American Legation on a possible solution. They were prepared to release the U.S. citizens provided arrangements were made for their "direct repatriation to [the] U.S." The same terms were extended to the Canadian government via the British mission in Beirut, which reported to London that the U.S. authorities in Beirut were "trying to arrange transport for the whole party. . . ".[19] It was far from certain that the internees would accept these conditions, since some of them had told a visiting American newspaperman that they wanted to go to Palestine "to fight alongside their people".[20]

As long as the matter remained unsettled and the internees were in Lebanese custody, the United States pressed its case. A State Department legal advisor told the Secretary of State that, since the Lebanese had interned the men without charging them with the violation of any Lebanese law, the arrest was purely arbitrary. Following this advice the State Department sent a protest note to Beirut claiming that the seizure of the sixty-nine *Marine Carp* passengers was "in disregard of the established principles of international law" and requesting their immediate release.[21] On May 27, the U.S. chargé d'affaires in Beirut reported that the American citizens interned at Baalbek had agreed to return directly to the United States and would not try to get to Palestine "during [the] existence of [the] present fight". The American internees were also anxious to secure the release of the other passengers, particularly the Jewish Palestinians, whose lives, they feared, would be in jeopardy if they remained.[22] Two days later the U.S. government accepted Lebanon's terms and State Department officials began making arrangements for the return of the volunteers to the United States. The Canadian Department of External Affairs worked closely with the U.S. State Department and the British Foreign Office to secure equal treatment for the Canadians.[23]

The internees were going back to the United States. Ironically, however, they had to await the return of the *Marine Carp* to Beirut before they could leave. The ship was not due to clear New York until June 11 and would take three more weeks to reach the Lebanese capital. The men at Baalbek were not told that they were leaving until two days before the ship docked in Lebanon, when a representative from the U.S. Legation told the internees they would embark shortly and informed them that they would be taken directly back to the United States. There was no argument with this—there was little choice in any case—but some of the volunteers were determined to get to Palestine despite the assurances given Lebanon by Washington.[24]

IV

The Egyptian armoured column that had spearheaded the invasion of Israel on May 15 had fought its way up the coast for two weeks. Stiff opposition had delayed its advance at Kibbutz Yad Mordechai. Now, at dusk on May 29, it sat stalled at the Ashdod bridge, forty kilometres southwest of Tel Aviv. Haganah sappers had blown the bridge ahead of the Egyptians and Egyptian officers had ordered a halt until they could find a way around the obstacle. As the officers at the head of the column surveyed the wreckage, Egyptian soldiers sprawled along the dusty road contemplating the coolness of the approaching evening. Suddenly the sound of aircraft was heard. Egyptian anti-aircraft gunners leaped into their seats and began to crank their guns around, bringing them to bear on the four greyish-green fighters approaching low from the sea. The planes, Czech-built Avia S-199s, had taken off from Aqir only minutes earlier. They were flown by two Israelis—Modi Alon and Ezer Weizman—and two volunteers—Eddie Cohen from South Africa and Lou Lenart from the United States. With Lenart in the lead, the fighters had flown out to sea immediately after takeoff, and then had swung back towards the Egyptian column, which was parked almost bumper to bumper on the highway. The fighters passed low over the column, dropping their bombs and strafing the scattering troops as they zoomed over the line of trucks and armoured cars. Eddie Cohen was killed when his fighter was hit by anti-aircraft fire and crashed, and another fighter was badly damaged, but the Egyptians were unnerved by the attack and halted their advance on Tel Aviv.[25] It was the closest they ever got to the Jewish city.

Israel's mysterious fighters had been purchased on April 23. On that date, the Czech government had agreed to sell ten Avia planes—along with spare parts, cannon, machine guns, and bombs—and to provide training for pilots, for $190,000 cash per plane. The Czechs also agreed to place part of a military airfield approximately 120 kilometres west of Prague at the disposal of the Jewish forces. This was to serve both as a training base and a base from which the Israelis could fly military supplies to Palestine. The field—Zatec—was located in the Sudetenland and had been used as a Luftwaffe fighter field during World War II.[26]

The Avia S-199 was based on the highly effective German Messerschmitt Bf-109 fighter of World War II. The Germans had built large numbers of Bf-109s at the Avia company in Czechoslovakia during the war and Avia had continued to turn the fighters out for use by the Czech Air Force after the war ended. In September 1945, fire destroyed a warehouse in which the entire stock of Daimler Benz DB 605 engines used on the Bf-109 was stored, and almost all were lost. The Czechs, who now had a large number of airframes but very few engines, decided to adopt another German-built engine, the Junkers Jumo 211F, for use in the Bf-109 airframes. Since this engine, which had been used to power Heinkel He-111 bombers during the war, was totally unsuitable, the S-199 was a far cry from its German predecessor in handling, performance, and pilot comfort. Czech pilots dubbed it *Mezec*, meaning mule, an appropriate nickname.

The S-199 was uncomfortable, unwieldy, and dangerous. The cockpit was cramped, the seats were not adjustable, and the canopy was hard to open. The landing gear was too close together for operations from rough airstrips, and the plane had a tendency to flip over on takeoffs and landings. The fighter was armed with two 20 mm cannon slung under the wings and two 13.5 mm machine guns mounted on either side of the nose. The cannon tended to jam; the machine guns were supposed to be synchronized to fire through the big three-bladed propellor, but sometimes shot it right off.[27]

Because of its extremely short range, the S-199 could not possibly fly to Israel, so the planes had to be disassembled and flown in by the LAPSA C-46s and the previously chartered C-54. The first fighter left Zatec in the early morning of May 20, its wings and fuselage packed tightly inside the C-54. Also on the plane were two Israeli pilots who had learned to fly the S-199 and a number of Czech mechanics who would teach the Israelis how to put it together.[28] The fighter was flown to Ekron and was soon joined by others. It was not possible to fit an entire fighter into a C-46 so the fuselage was loaded into one plane while the wings and propellor were loaded into another.

By May 22 a constant relay had been established between Zatec and Ekron. After the C-46 seizure on May 19, Catania was no longer suitable for a mid-journey refuelling stop, so operations were switched to Ajaccio on the western coast of Corsica. When the remaining C-46s of the original LAPSA fleet showed up at Catania a few days after Raab and Ribakoff, they were directed on to Zatec, as were the two other LAPSA C-46s that had departed from Tocuman on May 17. Sam Lewis left Panama in the Constellation at about this time and flew to Zatec carrying an entire workshop for delivery to the Czech end of the air bridge.[29] The last C-46 to arrive, RX 134, left Tocuman June 4, just as the U.S. government was beginning to take a direct interest in the activities of the peculiar airline known as Lineas Aereas de Panama. On June 10 the U.S. Embassy in Panama was instructed to ask the Panamanian government for a "thorough investigation...of the past and projected activities of LAPSA, and if facts warrant [it], [to] prevent use of Panamanian facilities for smuggling arms and ammunition to Palestine".[30]

As the airlift from Czechoslovakia started into operation, Aharon Remez called a meeting with Heyman Shamir and Munya Mardor, a Haganah arms-collection specialist who had been based in Europe. It was decided to forge the Constellation and the C-46s into a somewhat autonomous group to be known as Air Transport Command, under Mardor's direction. Offices from which Mardor and Shamir could direct the airlift were set up in Jaffa. Sam Lewis was to be chief pilot in charge of operations at Zatec, and was to work with Ben Kagan who was based in Prague.

The first airlift on March 31 had been dubbed "Operation Balak" after Balak, son of Zippor, in Numbers, 22.2, in the Bible.[31] (Zippor means "bird" in Hebrew.) The name stuck and each outbound flight thereafter was named Balak 2, Balak 3, and so on. A pall of gloom was soon cast over the Balak flights when on May 24, a C-46 approaching Ekron at night, piloted by Norman Moonitz, flew into a heavy fog and crashed. Moe Rosenbaum, the navigator, was crushed when the load shifted on impact. Back in Panama, Hal Auerbach had assigned him to carry the personal envelopes and blood type information of the LAPSA crew members. Rosenbaum was the only one killed.

Air Transport Command's priority mission was to bring the Avia S-199s to Israel. There were usually only three serviceable C-46s for the job, since mechanical failure kept most out of commission.[32] The lack of air cover in Israel also meant that the operational C-46s had to be gone by daylight so they would not present fat targets for roaming Egyptian fighters. These considerations, combined with the urgent need for the Avias, meant a punishing schedule for planes and crews. Each empty transport, usually flown by a crew of four—pilot, co-pilot, radio operator, and navigator—flew out of Ekron at about 4:00 a.m., while it was still dark. It was normally a ten-hour flight to Ajaccio, Corsica, and the planes flew at 8-10,000 feet. When they were an hour or so from the coast of Palestine, the sun rose to reveal the wide expanse of the deep blue Mediterranean. The planes flew over Crete and the Greek islands and made course for Brindisi, a small city on the eastern coast of the Italian heel. From there the C-46s flew directly to Ajaccio, Corsica, for an hour or two of rest and refuelling before starting on the four-hour flight to Zatec.[33]

Although the run from Corsica to Zatec was the shortest part of the trip, it was also the most hazardous. The planes headed north and began to climb soon after crossing the Italian coast. The white sawtooth peaks of the Alps loomed on the horizon as the lumbering transports began the long climb to 15,000 feet. The Linz radio beacon in Austria was the chief navigational aid for this leg. At last the planes cleared the Alps and began the descent into western Czechoslovakia, passing almost directly over Pilsen before landing. The main runway at Zatec was long and wide and the C-46s touched down and rolled past Czech Air Force jets and Avia fighters in various stages of disassembly before coming to a stop. The crews were then driven into Zatec to spend a night or two at the Zloty Lev or the Hotel Stalingrad before starting the long flight back to Palestine.

The return trip was, if anything, more hazardous. The transports, fully loaded, left at 7:00 a.m. and strained to reach maximum altitude in order to clear the mountains. The unstable air over the peaks—updrafts and downdrafts—bounced the planes around like bobbing corks. Pilots and co-pilots strained and sweated at the controls to keep the planes flying level and stop the load from shifting. It was not unlike the backbreaking work many had known during the war keeping fully loaded bombers tightly in formation as they moved into the dangerous air over Germany. There were more obstacles as they landed in Ajaccio with their contraband cargo. Their manifests always read "Glassware for Morocco" or "Machinery for Tunisia", and the local airport authorities had been well taken care of; nevertheless, the risk of discovery was high and added to the tension.

The crews left Ajaccio about mid-day, planning to touch down at Ekron after dark. There were no navigational aids to guide them to the Israeli coast, and planes could make landfall at any point from Beirut to the northern Sinai. After landing at Ekron, the crews were driven to the Park Hotel in Tel Aviv for rest and recreation. The bars in the Park and at the small, sun-bleached hotels that stood on the sea side of Hayarkon Street in Tel Aviv were soon famous as the watering spots for the air crews that maintained Israel's precarious lifeline to the outside world.

It was bone-wearying work, but there was a sense of high achievement and intrigue to it that, for most, cancelled out the fatigue and the frustration. The mystique of secret flights to foreign places had its allure, as did the beauty of the Mediterranean—the ancient sea of the Greeks, Phoenicians, and Romans which lapped historic shores from Gibraltar to Istanbul. At Ajaccio, a minor crossroads of the Mediterranean airways, crews from many nations mixed in airport coffee shops and bars, and whorehouses beckoned with the warmth of flesh. At the freezing summits of the Alps some felt an intimacy with the nearby peaks slowly drifting past under a throbbing metal floor. Death and triumph were so close together. There was also a sense of shared destiny with other men who knew well the close comradeship forged in airplane cockpits and yet who revelled in their own uniqueness and had their own informal insignia—a nickname proudly worn, perhaps, or a crushed flying cap or wrinkled leather bomber jacket, or a way of dragging on a cigarette or draining a beer glass. The bars of the Zloty Lev or the Stalingrad or the Park were the team locker rooms after the fourth quarter, except that winning was bringing another load of guns and ammunition, another pair of Avia wings, or another fuselage safely to Ekron. Losing was dying.

In Israel the first Avias to arrive were assembled by Czech mechanics and were flown by pilots who had graduated from the training facilities established by the Czech Air Force at Ceské Budejovice. Three of the first five fighter pilots were volunteers—Eddie Cohen from South Africa and Cy Rubenfeld and Lou Lenart from the United States—and two, Modi Alon and Ezer Weizman, were Israelis. On May 29, 1948, the Avias and their pilots and groundcrew formally became the 101 Fighter Squadron of the new Israeli Air Force under the command of Modi Alon. For their first operational mission, using the only four fighters assembled, they planned a surprise attack on the Egyptian air base at El Arish, home to the fighters and bombers that had been attacking Tel Aviv since May 15. However, as the Egyptian Army made slow but steady progress up the coast, the situation on the approaches to Tel Aviv became serious. The commander of the Givati Brigade, Shimon Avidan, requested an air attack on the Egyptian column now near Ashdod on the main Gaza-Tel Aviv highway. It was only a few minutes' flying time southeast from Ekron, where 101 Squadron was then based, and the request, placed through Chief of Staff Yigael Yadin, could not be refused.[34]

In the days following the May 29 attack on the Egyptian column, constant mechanical problems and delays in delivery kept the number of serviceable aircraft to a bare minimum. The day after the attack against the Egyptians a third Avia was lost in an attack on a railway station. On June 3, however, a victory greatly boosted civilian morale in Tel Aviv. On that day Egyptian bombers escorted by a small number of Spitfires were sighted approaching Tel Aviv from the sea. Alone, in the sole serviceable Avia, Modi Alon took off from Ekron, climbed above the droning Dakotas, and dived on them out of the sun. He fired at the tail of the first aircraft, which burst into flames and began to spiral down to the sea. Next he turned head-on into the second bomber and shot out the cockpit. The escorting fighters scattered at the first sign of the attack and Alon was credited with having shot down the first two enemy aircraft in the history of the new Israeli Air Force.[35]

The newly founded fighter squadron was hampered by a lack of pilots and aircraft, but at least the Avias were real fighters. This was not true of the developing bomber force, which used any and all available planes—from fabric-covered single-engine light planes to Dakotas and C-46s—to carry out its missions. The Israelis had no aircraft that were designed and built as bombers, so they were forced to combine nerve and ingenuity to fill the gap—this included throwing the bombs out by hand. This was called "bombchucking" and was done from light planes and larger aircraft. In the smaller craft someone sat behind the pilot with a load of small bombs (two to three times the size of hand grenades) beneath his feet. On most of these planes the door had been removed prior to takeoff and, when the plane approached the target, the pilot banked to allow the "bombardier" to lean out and drop his missiles. Sometimes empty pop bottles were thrown out with the small bombs because of the whistling noise they made as they plummeted to earth.

In the Dakotas the process was more complex. The cargo doors were removed prior to takeoff. The bombs (generally fifty pounders) were loaded into large wooden bins on the floor of the cargo hold, with two bombs side by side in each bin. Five or six men flew in the rear, with one or two assigned as "bombchuckers" and wearing parachute harnesses that were attached to a static line that ran down the length of the cabin. As the plane approached the target a small "bucket brigade" was formed from the bomb bins to the door. The bombs were passed from hand to hand down the line to the bombchuckers, who threw them out when the pilot flicked the green light that was designed to tell paratroopers when to leap into space. There was nothing scientific about it, but on the night of June 1, 1948, three "bombers" were able to dump 1500 pounds of bombs on the Transjordan capital of Amman in about eight minutes, bringing an indignant British protest.[36]

V

When the hot sun rose over the hills of Latrun on the morning of May 25, the battle for control of the squat, fortress-like police station that dominated the Tel Aviv-Jerusalem road was already raging. The Haganah attack on the Arab positions in and around the police fort was supposed to have started at about 1:00 a.m., but a mix-up in communications, difficulties in getting into position, and a recent, unexpected change in command for one of the attack groups had delayed the assault by three hours. To make matters worse, Arab observers had

Israel's first Spitfire is pieced together in the open. (L. Shapiro)

Irvin Schindler's B-17 at the Royal Canadian Air Force Station, Dartmouth, Nova Scotia. (I. Schindler/M. Minnich)

Lionel Druker, leader of the
first Canadian contingent. (M.
Cappell)

South African Syd Cohen,
Second Commanding Officer,
101 Squadron. (S. Simon)

Len Fitchett from Canada in
his World War Two RCAF
uniform. (Israel Defence Forces
Archives)

False identity card carried by Canadian volunteer Murray Cappell.
(M. Cappell)

Cappell in a Seventh Brigade armoured car. (M. Cappell)

Pilots of 101 Fighter Squadron. Top row (l. to r.): John McElroy, Chester Baker, Rudy Augarten. Second row: Arnie Bare, Sandy Jacobs, Cesar Dangut, Denny Wilson, Jack Doyle, Ezer Weizman, Syd Cohen. Third row: Syd Antim, unknown. Bottom row: Wayne Peake, Lee Sinclair, Cy Feldman, Arnie Cohen, Sam Pomerantz. (D. Wilson)

The *Altalena* lies beached and gutted off the Tel Aviv sea front. (D. Drutz)

The first homemade Spitfire. (Israel Defence Forces Archives)

Czech supplied Avia S-199. (Israel Defence Forces Archives)

Harvards smuggled from Canada and used as dive bombers by 35 Squadron. (Israel Defence Forces Archives)

Norseman aircraft. (Israel Defence Forces Archives)

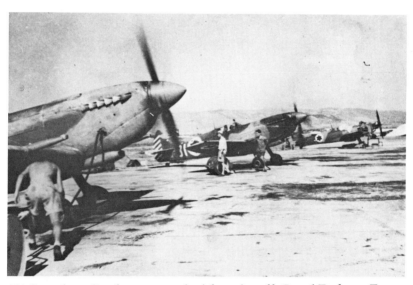

101 Squadron Spitfires are readied for take off. (Israel Defence Forces Archives)

Bill Katz of the United States, Commander of 69 Squadron, along with squadron personnel, in front of a B-17. (Israel Defence Forces Archives)

Palmach troops ready to climb aboard a C-46 on the flight to Ruhama during Operation Dust. (Israel Defence Forces Archives)

spotted the Jews moving into position in the dark, and Arab gunners had suddenly poured a withering fire into the midst of Haganah troops in the wheatfields around the fort. The Haganah soldiers were part of the Seventh Brigade, a newly formed unit that had been assigned the task of attacking Latrun from the west while the Palmach's Harel Brigade attacked from the east. Many of the Seventh Brigade soldiers were gahal—untrained refugees who had come to the front almost directly from immigrant ships. They knew little or no Hebrew, had never been in battle, and were in poor physical condition. When they were caught in the Arab barrage, any semblance of military discipline broke down and they became a mob of frightened, panicky men. As Arab shells, mortar bombs, and tracer bullets set the wheatfields aflame, the sun rose higher in the sky and the dreaded desert khamsin wind began to turn Latrun into a virtual blast furnace. These refugees of Hitler's hell had come to Israel to die in the inferno of Latrun.[37]

Shortly after the Arab League invasion had begun on May 15, Jewish Jerusalem was once again put under siege. It had happened because of a Haganah blunder. For approximately forty-eight hours the Latrun fort stood empty, but Haganah intelligence failed to discern this crucial fact. On May 17 the post was occupied by troops of the Transjordan Arab Legion who also placed observation, mortar, and artillery positions on the high ground above the monastery that lay up a gentle slope several hundred metres south of the fort. The post itself was a Tegart fort, built at the direction of British security advisor Charles Tegart during the Arab revolt of the late 1930s. Tegart had suggested that a number of police posts—squat buildings with thick walls—be built to dominate key road junctions throughout Palestine. The Latrun post had been placed on a low rise several hundred metres from the two-lane asphalt road that connected Tel Aviv with Jerusalem. From the firing slits of the fort, the Arab Legion had a commanding view.

The Legion had originally planned to mount the siege only as a supporting operation for a major armoured assault on Jewish Jerusalem. When the assault plan was abandoned in the face of stiff Jewish resistance,[38] the Legion changed its tactics. It now concentrated on drawing a noose ever tighter around the Jewish quarter inside the walls of the old city while starving out the inhabitants of the new city and pounding them constantly with shellfire. The situation in new Jerusalem deteriorated daily as food and water rations were cut and cut again.

The need to raise the siege became imperative and the fate of Jewish Jerusalem clearly hung on Israeli success in breaking the blockade.

The Haganah attack on May 25 was a total disaster; hundreds of Israeli troops were killed or wounded and Latrun remained firmly in Arab hands. Ben Gurion had chosen Colonel David "Mickey" Marcus, who had returned to Palestine only shortly before, for the special task of co-ordinating operations of the Seventh and Etzioni brigades in the drive to break the Jerusalem siege.[39] Although Marcus was unsuccessful in driving the Arab Legion out of Latrun, he was instrumental in developing an alternate route to Jerusalem. The Israelis promptly dubbed this the "Burma Road", because it was a pale imitation of the route once used by the Allies in China to truck supplies to the beleaguered armies of Chiang Kai-shek during World War II.

The "Burma Road" was a narrow dirt track that ran through several wadis and rose and fell over steep rocky hills. It ran several hundred metres south of the Jerusalem-Tel Aviv highway and was protected from Arab Legion observation posts at Latrun by a low range of hills. It was only a little more than sixteen kilometres in total length. It was not marked on the maps, but it had been used by local Arabs trying to avoid the mined roads in the area, and had first been driven by a lone Jewish armoured truck on May 15.

At dusk on May 18, Ben Dunkelman and three other men under the command of Amos Horev also tried it out. They set out from Jerusalem in a small armoured car and picked their way westwards through Arab-controlled territory until they reached a Jewish sentry who did not, at first, believe they had broken through from Jerusalem.[40] The route was kept in mind as an alternative, but little was done to improve it until after the assaults on Latrun had failed. By then the situation in Jerusalem was desperate and there was little choice but to use the dirt track.

At first food and arms were carried by truck from Tel Aviv, loaded on the backs of soldiers and mules, and hauled over the hazardous track to meet trucks that had driven from Jerusalem. Later the track was improved by hundreds of workers, labouring after dark, until it was just suitable for motor vehicles over its entire length. Although the Arab Legion continued to hold Latrun, the siege was broken and, on June 10, the first motorized convoy to travel from Tel Aviv to Jerusalem since May 17 traversed the completed road and brought food and ammunition to the beleaguered people of Jewish Jerusalem.

VI

At the start of the Arab invasion, Britain had done nothing to restrain its Middle East allies. It had opposed U.S. efforts to impose a ceasefire in Palestine and brand the Arab League countries as aggressors, and it continued to send weapons and supplies to the invaders. On May 19, when Egyptian forces were bombarding Kibbutz Yad Mordechai on the road to Tel Aviv, the Arab Legion was completing the encirclement of Jerusalem, and the Iraqi Army was moving in force into the mountains of Samaria, the British Foreign Office told the British High Commissioner in Canada that arms supplies to Egypt, Iraq, and Transjordan would continue. Stopping the flow of arms would "ruin [British] relations with those States for a long time to come", he maintained.[41] The next day Harold Beeley of the Foreign Office told a State Department representative much the same thing. Assistance to Transjordan's King Abdullah and the other Arab leaders would continue unless the United Nations acted to make British aid "contrary to U.K. obligations under the [United Nations] charter".[42] On May 21, Sir John Balfour, the British chargé d'affaires in Washington, told State Department officials that London was worried that the United States and Britain were drifting apart on the Palestine issue. The British government had no intention of recognizing the Jewish state and hoped that Washington would maintain its arms embargo. He reminded them that Britain was obligated, under its treaty with Transjordan, to assist that country if it were attacked from the outside, and pointed out that this could happen if the Jews gained military successes and pursued retreating Arab forces into Transjordan.[43]

There was uproar and confusion in the State Department. George Kennan thought the United States should do nothing to bring itself into conflict with Britain on the Palestine issue, but Lovett did not agree. He believed the United States should not join the British in "actions [felt] to be improper merely to avoid the conflict" and did not think the United States had any special responsibility for ending the war in Palestine, although he did believe it shared some responsibility as a member of the United Nations. It was clearly the job of the United Nations to preserve peace and security because failing to do so "seals its own doom".[44]

Lovett's views carried the day and, with Truman's approval, he laid down a new and tougher line for Senator Austin to follow at the United Nations:

If the Security Council is unable to take effective action to bring about a cease-fire or to impose a general arms embargo, the United States will inform the Security Council that we shall resume our freedom of action with respect to the licensing of arms shipments.[45]

Lovett had not become an instant convert to the Zionist cause, but he and others in the State Department were undoubtedly worried about a further escalation of the Palestine conflict. A civil war had now become a full-scale war, pitting the new State of Israel against the entire Arab world. What was next? Britain had given repeated assurances over the previous six months that the arms situation in the Middle East was under control, but events showed that this was untrue. British shells, tanks, and planes were already being used by Arab armies in Palestine and more shipments were in the pipeline. There was a chance that Britain would remain deaf to U.S. and U.N. pleas and that Washington would have to respond by allowing Israel, which the United States had recognized, to buy arms. But Lovett and the others probably figured that there was a better chance of British compliance, however reluctant, because, since the early days of U.S. participation in World War II, the British had increasingly learned that their place in the western world was to follow the United States.

The next several days were filled with diplomatic sparring while the fighting in Palestine continued to rage. A Security Council resolution was passed on May 22 urging the parties to the conflict to arrange their own truce. This was not effective, and a further resolution, calling for a ceasefire in Jerusalem, also went unheeded. The fighting did not go well for Britain's allies, however, and by late May it was apparent that the Arab invasion was failing to achieve its major objectives: the Egyptian and Iraqi advance had been halted; the Syrians had accomplished little or nothing; and the Lebanese had not penetrated more than a few kilometres inside Palestine. Only the Transjordan Arab Legion, which had captured the Jewish quarter of the old city of Jerusalem on May 28 and had a continuing stranglehold on the remainder of Jewish Jerusalem, could claim to have had any success.

The Arab forces, whatever their strategic or tactical positions, had used up tremendous quantities of ammunition and fuel and needed a break for resupply and reorganization. The Arab Legion was particularly low on stocks. Britain feared that, if fighting did not end soon,

U.S. policy might shift, giving Israel an opportunity to replenish its stocks and add new American equipment to its arsenal. The Israelis also welcomed the prospect of a break in the fighting because, although they had stopped the main Arab assaults, they were hard pressed on many fronts and were running low on supplies. When Ernest Bevin, Clement Attlee, and the leaders of the British armed forces met the U.S. Ambassador in London on the morning of May 25, a ceasefire had become a high priority for Britain.[46] Within forty-eight hours the British were ready to present their own proposals to the Security Council. They made it clear to the United States that, if their resolution was adopted, they would suspend arms shipments and order all British fighting personnel presently seconded to the Arab Legion to be withdrawn from Palestine.[47] On May 29 the British resolution was adopted by the Security Council. It called for a four-week truce and imposed a strict embargo on the import of war material to "Palestine" (it did not mention Israel) and the Arab countries. The governments concerned were not to bring in new fighting personnel, and the British gave assurances to the Arabs that they would not allow Jews of military age interned on Cyprus to go to Palestine. Two days later all British arms shipments to the Middle East finally stopped.[48]

The ceasefire was arranged by a U.N.-appointed mediator, Count Folke Bernadotte of Sweden, who was first approached by Secretary General Trygve Lie on May 18. Bernadotte accepted the assignment the following day and was given a fairly free hand to arrange for a cessation of the fighting and to try to find the basis for a political settlement. However, because he lacked strong U.N. backing, his task was doomed to failure. The May 29 Security Council resolution gave him the necessary support and he was soon able to arrange a four-week ceasefire to take effect on June 11—the Arabs refusing to agree to a longer term. The ceasefire contained provisions for a continuation of the embargo on arms shipments to the Middle East, called upon both sides not to improve their situations through augmentation of weapons or manpower, and established International Red Cross supervision for convoys to Jerusalem.[49]

As the hour of the ceasefire approached, both sides fought fiercely to add new territory or to solidify positions already held. On the night of June 8-9, Marcus launched a new assault on Latrun in which Israeli troops gained at least a part of their objectives and briefly broke into the police fort. By dawn, however, they were again thrown back with heavy casualties. In the north, on June 10, the Syrians succeeded in capturing the settlement of Mishmar Hayarden, their only success of the war. In the south, the Egyptians had been pushed farther from Tel Aviv. However, they were able to consolidate their positions in the northern Negev, to cut off the Jewish settlements to the south, and to secure the road from Majdal on the coast to Faluja several kilometres east of the key Iraq Suweidan road junction.

At 2:10 a.m. on the last night before the ceasefire, an Israeli Dakota lifted off from Ekron. The air force had decided that an attack on an Arab capital on the very eve of the truce would deal a psychological blow to the enemy. Cyril Katz (who had flown a Bonanza from South Africa less than a month before) was at the controls. Leslie Chimes, who had brought in one of the three South African Fairchilds, was in the right seat. Smoky Simon was navigator and one of six bombchuckers. The Dakota climbed to 3050 metres and headed northeast towards Damascus. Lydda airport, sliding by on the left side of the aircraft, was brilliantly lit, and Haifa, away in the distance to the north, looked "like a Christmas tree", as Simon noted in his flight log. Damascus was also brightly lit and could been seen from seventy kilometres away. At 3:12, the bombchuckers got busy and began passing their deadly load to the back and shoving it out the door. There was no opposition from below and Katz kept the twin-engine transport droning over the Syrian capital for fifteen minutes. The plane made six passes, while Simon and the others dropped 2400 kilos of bombs and three boxes of incendiaries. At 3:27 Katz turned for Ekron. The Dakota landed, completely unscathed, at 4:35 a.m.[50]

That same night, in his tent in Abu Gosh to the west of Jerusalem, Mickey Marcus was having difficulty sleeping. The third attack against Latrun had failed within the last twenty-four hours and his troops were fighting off Arab Legion counterattacks in and around the village of Gezer, which had changed hands twice in several hours. Marcus was uneasy: during the day he had remarked to an aide that he felt a sense of foreboding, a conviction that he would not survive. At about ten minutes to four, wrapped in a bedsheet against the chill of the night air, Marcus left his tent for a walk. Out of the dark came a challenge from one of his own sentries and Marcus, who knew no Hebrew, failed to respond. He was shot dead.[51] Only hours later, the guns fell silent in Palestine for the first time since November 1947.

7

"Dew from Heaven"

Miami airport was the civil aviation gateway for U.S. air traffic to the Caribbean and Central and South America; hundreds of planes from scheduled and non-scheduled airlines and cargo carriers took off and landed every day. On the airport's back lot, far removed from the terminal building, an odd collection of planes was usually parked. Customs officers and aviation officials were generally too busy to pay close attention to every plane and crew that used the airport; it was a good exit point for those like Schwimmer and his associates who needed to slip planes or cargoes out of the country without too much difficulty.

On June 12, 1948, less than twenty-four hours after the ceasefire had gone into effect in the Middle East, three weatherbeaten B-17s, former heavy bombers with the United States Army Air Force, taxied out from a remote corner of the airfield, stood at the edge of the main runway while crews ran up engines, and commenced their takeoff roll. As they climbed away from the airport they turned southeast, bound for San Juan, Puerto Rico. The planes were part of a contingent of four owned by the Irwin L. Johnson Company, a dummy corporation established by Al Schwimmer and Teddy Kollek.[1] The planes had been purchased around the country—one in California, one in Oklahoma, and two from Charles Winters, a Miami businessman. The two Miami planes were already in use hauling produce between Miami and San Juan while the other two badly needed repairs and overhauls. It had been decided, for the sake of maintaining secrecy, that the planes would not be brought together until shortly before their departure. While the planes were being readied to leave the United States, crews were collected to fly them.

131

Schwimmer, working with Winters, chose Miami as the U.S. point of departure for the B-17s because there was constant movement of planes in and out of the airport.[2] He and Winters planned to fly the planes to San Juan with skeleton crews and there to take aboard "cargo handlers"—air crew recruits funnelled through New York—for the flight to Zatec, Czechoslovakia. These recruits were kept moving until the B-17s were ready to leave Puerto Rico; one small group was flown to Mexico City, Havana, and Miami before arriving at San Juan.[3] One volunteer wrote home that Mexico City boasted "some of the most cultured prostitutes" he had ever met.

On June 12, 1948, three of the B-17s left for San Juan. Winters, who was aboard one of the bombers, had deposited money with a fuel company to pay in advance for aviation gas along the route. Puerto Rico was within the territorial jurisdiction of the United States and the B-17s did not require any special government clearance or an export licence to fly there from Miami. At San Juan the "cargo handlers"—about ten to each plane—climbed aboard. A flight plan showing that the three aircraft were about to make an aerial survey of the Azores was filed. Since this appeared to mean that the planes were only leaving U.S. jurisdiction for a short stay abroad, they were granted takeoff clearance. As one State Department official laconically commented: "Due diligence on the part of customs officials at San Juan was lacking...."[4]

For two of the planes the flight to the Azores was both long and uneventful, but in the bomber flown by former Lieutenant Colonel James B. Beane everything seemed to go wrong from the start. Shortly after takeoff Beane's plane developed engine trouble and he was forced to return to Puerto Rico for repairs. Beane apparently forgot to notify the Azores of the delay, because he was later—after the first two bombers had landed—reported missing. He himself was not in very good condition to fly because of a prolonged drinking bout in San Juan the night before departure, so his co-pilot, David Goldberg, flew for several hours while Beane slept off the night's revelries in the rear of the plane.

The navigation equipment aboard all three bombers was inadequate—the radio compasses had a receiving range of only 320 kilometres or so—and the navigators were forced to shoot the sun by standing out in the slipstream while fellow crew members hung on to them. Most of the Plexiglas domes and turrets had long since been removed from the planes, and the holes in the fuselage had been covered with plywood. This caused one of the most hair-raising episodes of Beane's flight. The navigator, Eli Cohen, crashed through a piece of plywood on the floor of his bomber and fell halfway into space. He found himself with his legs dangling 3000 metres over the ocean being slowly sucked out by the slipstream. By this time Beane was back at the controls. Goldberg, who was resting in the rear, heard the shouts and ran up to the cockpit to tell Beane to slow down, while several crew members tried to pull Cohen inside. Cohen was soon pulled back in but he was in no condition to do any navigating for the remainder of the flight.[5]

The three bombers arrived at Santa Maria, Azores, late at night on June 13, refuelled, and then took off and headed for Zatec, flying non-stop across Spain, France, and Germany. After landing in Czechoslovakia, a telephone call was put through to a Haganah representative in Geneva who relayed news to Ajaccio, Corsica, of the planes' and crews' arrival. There, by arrangement with Agronsky, an announcement was made that three bombers had arrived in Ajaccio from the Azores. For several days the ruse worked and the State Department was convinced that the bombers were in Corsica.[6]

The three planes were kept at Zatec for several weeks. There they were overhauled and refitted with bomb racks and rudimentary bombsights. Meanwhile crews already in Israel, most of whom were flying with Air Transport Command, were picked to bring the planes in from Zatec. Three days after the arrival of the B-17s in Zatec, the American press carried stories of the mysterious bombers smuggled out of the country for the Jewish forces in Palestine. When a C-46 made a forced landing at an Italian air force base at Treviso on June 23, it became clear that the smuggling was going on on a regular basis. The plane, carrying a crew of six, five cases of machine guns, and thirty-five cases of ammunition, had developed engine trouble over the Alps. The pilot's documents alleged that the weapons were bound for Nicaragua via Corsica and Casablanca. The papers, which were signed by Anastasio Somoza, Nicaraguan Minister of War, authorized Dr. José Y. Irazi (Yehuda Arazi) to act as Nicaraguan agent in the purchase of machinery, planes, trucks, ships, arms, and ammunition to the value of 5 million dollars.[7] The document with Somoza's signature had been obtained with a huge bribe brought to the Central American republic over several months in early 1948 by a distant relative of Al Schwimmer acting for the Haganah in New York.[8]

The cover story did not work; the Italians arrested plane, crew, and cargo. They reported the incident to the U.S. government, which made arrangements to have the passports of the crew members picked up and validated only for return to the United States.[9] For several weeks the crew were kept in custody on the base while their fate hung in the balance. The pilot decided he had had enough and returned to the United States, but the others stayed put and, before they could be reached by the long arm of the State Department, Agronsky swung into action. He sent Danny Rosin, who had arrived in Rome from South Africa several weeks before, to Treviso with "a wad of money" and insructions "to see what could be done with regard to springing the boys from jail". It took all of Rosin's persuasive powers, plus the small fortune he had brought with him, to get the crew members released and to persuade the base commander to turn the C-46 over to them. The Italians kept the cargo, but Rosin and the others were allowed to leave. Rosin had never flown a C-46 before, so he manned the co-pilot's seat while the original co-pilot, Julian Sween, piloted the plane.[10] Despite their lack of experience with the C-46, the two managed to reach Zatec, where the aircraft was put back into operation on the Balak flights.

I

When the U.N.-imposed truce began on June 11, Arabs and Israelis were supposed to honour an embargo on the import of weapons and other military supplies and were not supposed to augment their fighting forces. However, the unstable situation on the ceasefire lines and Israel's precarious position made it virtually certain that a new round of battle would begin sooner or later. In the north, the Lebanese Army still held an area around Malkiya in the upper Galilee, which placed them a mere five kilometres from the shore of the shallow Lake Hula and less than ten kilometres from Syrian positions around the fallen Jewish settlement of Mishmar Hayarden. A push to the shore of the lake or a link-up with the Syrians would totally isolate Jewish settlements to the north. The Syrians at Mishmar Hayarden were perhaps two kilometres from the main Metulla-Tiberias road and less than ten kilometres from Safed. The Iraqi Army, which had invaded across Samaria, had been halted about ten kilometres from the sea to the north of Tel Aviv.

The most serious situation facing the new State of Israel was in the Jerusalem sector: the Jewish quarter of the ancient city had surrendered; the Etzion Bloc of settlements to the south of Jerusalem had fallen; the Transjordan Arab Legion still held Jewish Jerusalem in a partial siege. Under the terms of the truce, the Red Cross and the United Nations supervised food and medical-supply convoys on the main Jerusalem-Tel Aviv highway, but the Israelis refused to allow them to inspect traffic over the Burma Road. In the south, the Egyptian advance on Tel Aviv had been stopped, more by the lack of Egyptian will than by any feat of Jewish arms. The Egyptians, however, held the northern Negev tightly, cutting off Jewish settlements to the south and linking up with Jordanian forces south of Jerusalem. The Egyptian troop concentration along the coast still pointed, like a finger of destruction, straight at Tel Aviv.

In battle after battle—at Latrun, in the Etzion Bloc, at Mishmar Hayarden—a combination of green troops, untried leadership, and poor equipment had meant defeat for the Israeli forces. Some mistakes of command had been horrific in their consequences. In the first attack on Latrun, for example, untried immigrants, some of them straight from the refugee ships, had been thrust forward in a searing heat wave to assault the thick walls of the police post defended by the Arab Legion. The attack should have started at midnight but was delayed while all attack elements moved into position. The assault should have been called off, but instead Israeli troops were sent forward in broad daylight to be slaughtered under the hot sun.

The sloppiness and leadership failures of the Israeli forces were, however, surpassed by those of the Arabs, who, for the most part, demonstrated a lack of will and conviction. With the exception of the Arab Legion, which fought well and achieved most of its objectives, the Arab forces proved themselves almost completely incompetent on every front. This gave Israel its one real victory, a triumph that counted above all the failures—it had survived.

The truce that began on June 11 gave Arabs and Jews an opportunity to reorganize and reassess the performance of their forces in the first round of fighting. The Israelis were well aware that they were still at a material disadvantage: their lack of armour had proved costly at Latrun; the scarcity of artillery had put them at a serious disadvantage in the fighting southwest of Tel Aviv; their initial lack of anti-aircraft defences had exposed their cities and towns to Arab bombers. Wherever Arab forces had used their armour, artillery, and air power effectively they had been irresistible.

The material disadvantage at the end of the truce was serious, but not as significant as it had been on May 15. The Balak flights had brought fighters, mortars, and machine guns as well as ammunition; several anti-aircraft guns and small artillery pieces had been procured, while arms factories, emerging from the underground, continued to turn out homemade mortars, bombs, and even armoured cars of a sort. The Arabs had also shown themselves incapable, in most cases, of using their greater material wealth effectively. The Israeli lack of air power did not significantly hamper Israel's military operations, for example, because the Arab air forces, while better equipped, were used piecemeal and without regard to the close support tactics developed during World War II. One U.S. Military Intelligence estimate of the Egyptian Air Force, completed just before the ceasefire, concluded that the "combat effectiveness of the R[oyal] E[gyptian] A[ir] F[orce]" was "so low it [could not] be considered an adequate defensive force".[11] The eight to ten Avia S-199s acquired by Israel via the Balak flights from Czechoslovakia had proved to be the most effective air contingent on either side, and had probably achieved more far-reaching results than the Egyptian, Syrian, and Iraqi air forces together.

None the less, large areas of Israel were still held by strong Arab forces that remained in excellent strategic positions. Israeli military leaders were determined to use the truce to prepare for the next round of fighting. At that point they hoped to push back the major Arab troop concentrations at least to the borders sanctioned by the United Nations for a Jewish state.

II

Count Folke Bernadotte had earned his reputation for fairness and effectiveness in international dealings through hard work, concise thinking, and even-handed coolness in dealing with especially difficult problems. During the war he had worked tirelessly for the Swedish Red Cross, saving thousands of Jewish refugees from extermination. When he accepted Secretary General Trygve Lie's invitation to assume the position of U.N. mediator for Palestine, he was determined to put together an effective truce-supervision team that would nip ceasefire and embargo violations in the bud. Even before the ceasefire went into

136

effect, he approached the United States, Britain, Belgium, France, and Sweden with requests to provide personnel and equipment for his truce-supervision force. By the time the fighting stopped on June 11, more than 150 observers, technicians, and guards made up the truce-supervisory machinery. Britain and the United States supplied jeeps, trucks, and a small number of aircraft; France and the United States placed ships at Bernadotte's disposal.[12]

Bernadotte's men tried to police the truce in and around Israel, but they did not reach into Europe, South Africa, or North America. There, underground Jewish efforts to procure and ship war material and to gather and send *gahal* recruits and *mahal* volunteers continued without interruption. Israel refused to gamble on Bernadotte: the obvious shortcomings that had plagued Israeli forces in the first three and a half weeks of the Arab invasion would have to be overcome quickly in case the truce broke down and fighting resumed. Defeat in the field meant annihilation, and the violation of a U.N. truce was a small matter measured against this stark reality.

The U.N. embargo that Bernadotte's team was supposed to police had called upon "all governments and authorities concerned" not to "introduce fighting personnel . . ." into the warring countries.[13] Bernadotte fleshed out the original Security Council resolution of May 29 with his own interpretation, which was sanctioned by another Security Council resolution, giving him the right to limit the number of men of military age arriving as immigrants in any of the belligerent countries if he believed their arrival would "give one side a military advantage" over the other. These men were to be kept in detention camps under U.N. observation to ensure that they were not mobilized into the armed forces or given military training during the truce. In order to enforce this interpretation of the ceasefire, U.N. personnel would police the ports and be placed aboard immigrant ships. To carry out these responsibilities, the Security Council called upon the belligerent countries to notify the mediator "well in advance as to the port of embarkation of any ship bearing immigrants".[14]

Britain and the United States began to try to prevent the entry of men of military age into Israel as soon as the truce was put into effect. The United Kingdom's most potent weapon was a blanket refusal to allow such men to leave the Cyprus detention camps for Israel along with other refugees.[15] Bernadotte did not request this and, in fact, made "no specific statement positively affirming his support and approval of it". He told the Security Council that the action was taken on Britain's responsibility alone. He did "explicitly state", however, that the Cyprus situation should be governed by the "general truce rules in force".[16] The United States was as zealous as Britain in its interpretation of the Bernadotte guidelines. Washington gave "secret instructions" to the military governor of the United States Zone of Occupation in Germany, General Lucius D. Clay, to keep "Jews of military age" in internment camps. Also, on the first night of the truce, ten passengers were taken off the *Marine Carp* just before the ship cleared New York harbour on its regular voyage to the Mediterranean.[17] U.S. officials explained that the action was taken in accordance with the May 29 Security Council resolution. (All ten persons had been bound for Haifa.) To further ensure that U.S. ports were not used as points of embarkation to Palestine, the State Department asked Vice-Admiral W. W. Smith, Chairman of the United States Maritime Commission, to inform shipping companies operating to Palestine of the May 29 Security Council resolution and "urge" them to "refrain" from carrying "fighting personnel" to the countries named in it.[18]

III

The escape of the B-17s and the Treviso incident confirmed British and American suspicions that a vast clandestine airlift was bringing planes and arms to Israel despite the truce. Britain was anxious to co-ordinate its embargo efforts with the United States and wanted a joint effort to create an agreed list of prohibited goods.

The British also wanted to co-ordinate the two countries' policies on the export of civil aircraft to the Middle East and the licensing of special charter flights.[19] They were under considerable pressure from Arab governments, particularly those of Transjordan and Iraq, to drop their embargo and resume arms shipments. The British Ambassador in Amman could only reply that stocks of weapons would be kept on hand in the Middle East to be released to the Arab forces "as circumstances permit".[20] His colleague in Baghdad told the Iraqi government that Britain's ban on weapons shipments to the Middle East was the only way of ensuring the United States embargo on the export of arms, without which Jewish dollar resources would have ensured a large flow of war material to the Jewish forces...." The Jews' lack of such supplies, the ambassador suggested, "had no doubt contributed substantially to the successes which the Arabs had gained".[21]

While Britain was keeping its Arab clients at bay, the United States launched a diplomatic offensive to line up international support for the embargo. The government of Panama was again approached with a request that something be done to shut down Lineas Aereas de Panama.[22] The Panamanian Foreign Minister assured the American Ambassador that his government "had already initiated measures to prevent misuse of Panamanian facilities". Several weeks later, Panamanian President Enrique A. Jiminez issued a proclamation that prohibited Panamanian-registered air and sea carriers from violating the U.N. embargo. The penalty was to be confiscation of the contraband material and cancellation of Panamanian registration.[23] It was only enforceable in the event that a LAPSA plane somehow fell into the hands of a government willing to co-operate with Panama. This obviously excluded Israel and Czechoslovakia.

Panama, however, was not the only culprit involved in the clandestine air operations. The British and Americans had known since April that the Italian government was not interested in closing down Jewish operations on its soil. On the eve of the Palestine truce, therefore, both governments began to put diplomatic pressure on Italy to "take appropriate measures to ensure adequate checks and controls of movements of men and materials during the four-week truce".[24] No such pressure was necessary to convince Greece to back the embargo.[25] The Greek government had abstained on the November 1947 partition vote in the General Assembly and had remained distinctly cool to the Palestine Jews ever since. Since the spring, Greece had been co-operating with Britain and the United States to end the Haganah's clandestine use of Greek landing strips for transit stops on the way to Palestine.

Czechoslovakia was a much tougher nut to crack. At the start of the truce, the U.S. military attaché in Prague informed the State Department that machine guns, ammunition, and disassembled fighter planes were being flown to Israel. Within a week the U.S. Embassy in Prague was instructed to "recall" to the Czech government "its responsibility under [the] S[ecurity] C[ouncil] resolution of May 29 to prevent the introduction into Palestine or the Arab States of war material".[26] It was apparent very quickly that the plea had fallen on deaf ears. On June 21 the British air attaché in Prague reported that a "ground reconnaissance" of the Zatec airfield in the previous forty-eight hours had revealed the presence of three C-46s and three B-17s sporting the Panamanian flag and registration.[27]

The U.S. government also acted to stop the flow of Norseman aircraft to Israel from KLM's repair shops at Schipol Airport. At first Washington tried to order its American officials in Paris to cancel further deliveries of the planes to Miller. However, since none of the provisions of his contract had been violated, at least not on the surface, the agreement could not be broken arbitrarily.[28] On June 26 the U.S. Embassy in Paris asked the governments of France and the Netherlands to ground the Norseman aircraft, pending completion of an Embassy investigation into the real destination of the planes. The two governments initially co-operated with the U.S. request, and four aircraft were grounded in each country. However, both governments were also reluctant to withold takeoff permission indefinitely, and on June 30 the Dutch allowed two planes to leave for Paris via Brussels.[29] These planes were later flown directly to Czechoslovakia before proceeding to Israel.

The embargo, as it applied to Israel, was not popular in France or Holland. This, when combined with the active sale of arms to Israel by Czechoslovakia, left gaping holes in the embargo. Material continued to flow to Israel despite the best efforts of Britain and the United States. On July 7 a twin-engine Mosquito fighter, purchased by a mysterious "Mr. Farnfield", took off from Cambridge in England on a flight to Exeter. The plane landed at Nice, in southern France, was refuelled, and took off with the full knowledge and permission of the French authorities.[30] It proved a valuable addition to Israeli air power.

The Israelis also continued to receive Avia S-199s. On May 20, Ehud Avriel had signed a second contract with the Czech government for the purchase of a further fifteen fighters, most of which were delivered during the truce. The C-46s continued to ply the air lanes from Zatec to Ekron, bringing the Avias and other military equipment. Great pains were taken to maintain secrecy, and the precaution paid off because, as late as June 23, the U.S. Embassy in Prague reported to Washington that it had "not yet been able to learn whether flights [from Zatec to Israel] had been discontinued",[31] while Bernadotte's post-truce report to the Security Council concluded that "no evidence was found that any [aircraft destined for the Jewish forces] arrived in Palestine during the truce".[32]

140

IV

For Tel Aviv bar owners, the "angels of death" were truly and aptly named. These men of 101 Fighter Squadron of Israel's fledgling air force soon developed the type of boisterous unit spirit that characterized fighter squadrons in every air force. They wore red baseball caps, and one squadron member designed an insignia that was soon sported on the noses of their fighters—a skull wearing a flying helmet with two large black wings curling around above, almost touching, on a round red crest. They seemed to drink prodigious amounts—the three Israelis among them, by all accounts, keeping up with the more experienced volunteers[33]—and they good-naturedly cut a swath of destruction from the Atom Bar to the Gali Yam Café. One English newspaperman, writing about Israel's "secret air force", described the Gali Yam as "full of the unmistakeable World War II spirit".[34]

It was not all fun and games, however. The truce provided a good opportunity to train additional pilots and integrate more volunteers into the unit. Although most of the pilot volunteers from abroad were veterans with many hours in single-engine fighters, none had ever flown a Messerschmitt, let alone the bastardized version built in Czechoslovakia. Most of these men had left the forces in 1945 to pursue civilian careers and had not sat in a fighter cockpit for three years. Syd Cohen of South Africa, for example, had flown Spitfires with the South African Air Force in North Africa and Italy during World War II but had entered medical school at the war's end. He had volunteered for service with the Israelis in May 1948. Towards the end of that month, he was sent to Ceské Budejovice via Rome with two other South African pilots, Lesley Shagan and Issy Noach. All three spent several weeks learning how to fly the Avias before being posted to Israel to join 101 Squadron.[35]

In Czechoslovakia, Israeli and foreign volunteer trainees received flight instruction at two bases—Ceské Budejovice and the new Czech air academy at Hradec Kralove east of Prague. The Czechs were well paid for the training and gave good service in return.[36] German-designed dual-instruction trainers were used, and pilots then graduated to special two-seater versions of the S-199 before going solo in a single-seater plane. Training was somewhat complicated by the use of German-type calibration on the instruments, but the Israeli and volunteer pilots soon learned many of the idiosyncrasies of their new craft.[37] Flying time was not extensive, however, and American pilot

Gideon Lichtman later estimated that he had received less than an hour in the air before he was transferred to Israel.[38]

In early June, 101 Fighter Squadron was moved from Ekron to Herzliya. Herzliya was a small town on the Mediterranean coast just a few kilometres north of Tel Aviv, where a single landing strip of packed earth had been prepared amidst orange groves and banana orchards. There were a small mess hall, a few concrete block huts, and several tents scattered among the trees, but there were no hangers or barracks; most of the daily routine of operating an air base—maintenance and repair work, arming, fuelling, and engine testing—was done under the shade of the trees.

The informality of the setting matched the casual air of the squadron: there were no uniforms, insignia, or rank badges. Many of the mechanics and ground crew frequented an army club in Herzliya, while the clean white sand close to the runway beckoned on the hot days of mid-summer. Pilots were off in the bars and hotels of Tel Aviv or in the small beach hotel of Herzliya when they were not flying, and cars and jeeps were taken with little regard for the niceties of ownership. The odd assortment of surface transport collected at Herzliya seemed to grow larger each time another group of pilots returned from a night in town.[39]

V

In all her years of nursing, Ray Brunton thought she had seen just about everything, but as she watched the Israeli nurse passing from bed to bed with a hypodermic needle filled with penicillin, she was immediately curious. "I told you to give them injections," she called out. "But Ray," the other nurse answered, "that's what I am doing." Brunton was suspicious. "You're going from bed to bed with one syringe," she exclaimed. "Yes," came the reply. A shocked realization registered. "You don't know that each patient has to have his own syringe and needle?"[40]

Ray Brunton was one of a number of doctors and nurses from South Africa who had gone to Israel to lend their valuable medical knowledge to the Jewish war effort. In April, Arthur Helfet had been the first doctor to arrive. He had come at the invitation of Michael Comay, who had stressed that the medical organization of the Jewish underground in Palestine was very poor.[41] In his first weeks in Palestine, Helfet visited and advised upon military and civilian casualties in different hospitals. In May he was attached to Yigal Allon's Palmach headquarters at Rosh Pina in the northern Galilee. Towards the end of the month, Helfet prepared a report for Dr. Haim Sheba, head of the army medical committee, in which he outlined the changes in medical services that would be necessary in the event of a prolonged war.

The report stressed the importance of using medical services to maintain morale and mental well being. Helfet suggested that the wounded should be rehabilitated as quickly as possible, that eye and plastic surgery should be assured to soldiers and civilians, and that artificial limbs should be made available when necessary. He stressed the desirability of recruiting Hebrew-speaking psychiatrists experienced in war and pointed out that many more medical specialists were needed in the country.[42]

On May 28 Helfet left for South Africa to recruit Jewish doctors; when he returned to Israel in early July, he had succeeded in persuading several to join him. Among them were Dr. Lionel Melzer, an anesthetist and public-health specialist, and Dr. Jack Penn, "South Africa's leading plastic surgeon", in the words of Michael Comay. Both doctors had had extensive military experience during World War II.[43]

By early June, before the ceasefire, more South African medical personnel were arriving to join Helfet. Ray Brunton, a nursing sister, was among them. She was assigned to open a military hospital near Jaffa. For its location she chose a former nursing home once patronized by wealthy Arabs. It was called Djani and became known as Military Hospital 2. The place was in a mess: the Arab staff, fleeing Jaffa during the April fighting, had buried most of the instruments, including the operating table, in the ground around the building. There was no electricity. There weren't even any beds.

Brunton consulted a residential map to find the offices of Arab doctors who had fled Jaffa and, accompanied by guards and a truck, made the rounds, taking all the medication and bedding she could find. Then she and a surgical nurse cleaned up the building in preparation for the first casualties from the fighting near Jerusalem. The Latrun battles took a heavy toll, and wounded men soon filled the building to overflowing. Brunton worked twenty hours a day and was sometimes horrified by the inexperience of some Israeli doctors whose standard cure for almost every battlefield wound seemed to be amputation.[44]

Brunton later modified her judgment of the Israeli medical staff when two refugee doctors, Moses from Poland and Spira from Czechoslovakia, arrived to practise at Djani. Dr. Moses had fought with the Polish partisans and had performed surgical miracles with a penknife. Dr. Spira, an orthopedic surgeon, used sculptor's tools in place of proper surgical instruments. Eventually about twenty doctors were labouring at Djani. All worked under tremendous pressure, and none harder than Sister Brunton. She was so popular that there was a minor revolt among the hospital staff when she accepted an invitation to join Dr. Penn in Haifa. Brunton agreed to stay a while longer but eventually left Djani for the hospital at Kfar Giladi in the northern Galilee.

The South African medical teams accomplished wonders in Israel and helped reorganize the different departments of the army medical service. Dr. Lionel Melzer submitted a plan, modelled after one used by the South African medical corps, with special officers and directors in charge of separate areas like medical personnel, hospitals, supplies, hygiene, malaria control, administration, etc. During the truce Melzer visited practically every brigade in the army. As a result, senior medical officers of the different brigades began to make regular visits to the battalions, medical posts, and other medical units under their command. Medical supplies began to flow to the fronts in larger quantities. Also the medical services provided within the brigades by, for example, orderlies, stretcher bearers, and ambulance attendants was vastly improved. New hospitals and clinics were established and new initiatives taken to control malaria. Rapid amputation was stopped; triage procedures were improved; specialties such as anesthesia, plastic surgery, and general surgery became widely available.[45]

One South African doctor made her contribution in the Cyprus detention camps. Mary Gordon had been the first woman doctor at the Johannesburg General Hospital. There, during a thirty-year career, she had been physician in charge of wards and a senior physician doing part-time and honorary work. She had also lectured at the medical school in anesthesia and clinical medicine. She had planned to emigrate to Palestine; however, when war broke out in 1939, the government refused to allow her to leave and she joined the South African Army with the rank of captain. In 1946 she managed to wangle a transfer to duty in Palestine, but she was returned to South Africa after only three months.

Her third try at emigrating to Palestine was a success. In the summer and fall of 1946 Mary Gordon resigned her commission in the army, closed her practice, and left the hospital, the university, and the Transvaal Education Department. On October 19 she departed for Palestine as a "temporary labourer for WIZO", the Women's International Zionist Organization. She went to work in Cyprus in the Jewish wing of the British Military Hospital in Nicosia. There she provided a liaison between the Jewish wing and staff and the British authorities. She became a listening post and mother confessor to most of her patients. Many of her charges benefited from her immense compassion and understanding. As a colleague later recalled: "[she] had a deep feeling for her people. . . . The Jewish people were her life. Her private life was incidental. She stood completely by herself. She never asked for anything, always gave. She made decisions firmly and was beyond consideration of status and prestige." When the Arab invasion began on May 15, Gordon insisted on staying in Cyprus because of the great need that remained there, and she persuaded many of the Israelis on her staff to stay with her. She finally returned to Israel in October 1948.[46]

VI

Shortly after the truce began, Israeli brigade commanders assembled in Tel Aviv with Ben Gurion and the directors of the General Headquarters branches. They came from every fighting front and had an opportunity, for the first time in months, to discuss the general military situation and internal conditions in the army. One commander called the truce "dew from heaven"—the fighting units were tired and casualties in some had been very heavy. The commanders, who were dismayed by the fire power of the Arab armies, particularly the large number and variety of armoured vehicles, pleaded for anti-tank weapons. They discussed the lack of co-ordination between brigades that had led to costly mistakes and failed operations. They also dwelt on the problems posed by lack of discipline in the army, a failing that had had direct and disastrous consequences in the field. Attention was drawn to a deterioration in the morale of the ordinary soldiers, whose families at home were often neglected by the government. When the men knew that parents, wives, and children had little or nothing for food and subsistence, one commander recounted, they "refused to eat their meals because they knew that their families were hungry." Another cause of low morale was the lack of such minor but necessary things as shoes and clothes. "They do not demand planes nor tanks," one commander said of his men, "but small things, concrete small things."[47]

The foreign volunteers were materially better off than the newly arrived *gahal* troops, many of whom had neither hats nor shoes. Even so, the *mahal* were having problems adjusting to life in the Israeli forces. This did not directly affect their fighting spirit, but it did cloud their ongoing relations with many Israelis.

Most of these foreign volunteers were war veterans; they had spent years in the Allied forces and had contributed their share to the victory over Hitler. In early 1948 they had been approached to serve, and they had done so out of a conviction that they were sorely needed. That need was real enough. However, when the volunteers started arriving, the Israelis were unprepared for them, and trained men were sometimes not used to the best advantage. This was one source of discontent.

The biggest problem facing volunteers, however, was one of status: they were in, but not part of, Israeli society. They served with the Israeli forces, but they were not Israelis. South Africans tended to accept this because, for the most part, their service was based upon an ideological or religious support for Israel and Zionism. They were far readier than Americans to accept the poor pay, bad food, and the often meaningless and confusing bureaucratic practices that afflicted the Israeli forces. But most Americans and many Canadians had not volunteered out of a yearning for Zion, and they were ready, when pushed, to push back. They were not children, and they bitterly resented being treated as such.

The relationship between the volunteers and the Israelis often got off to a bad start right at the point of embarkation. Haganah agents usually took the volunteers' passports away before they left the Marseilles refugee camps prior to the sea voyage to Palestine.[48] This was generally done without explanation, although reassurances were given that the passports would eventually be returned. When the volunteers arrived in Israel they were initially assigned to units without much consideration of their areas of expertise or their ability to understand Hebrew. By mid-May volunteers had started to arrive from Scandinavia and France as well as from North America and South Africa. Many had been led to believe that they would serve in units with others who spoke the same language, but this did not usually happen. Canadians and others complained that promises made regarding pay, accommodation, training, and so on were not kept.

It is clear that Israelis did not believe that foreign volunteers had enough of a feel for the Arab-Jewish conflict or enough knowledge of warfare in Palestine to command at the highest levels. At the beginning they also tended to think that many volunteers were naive and lacking in self-discipline.[49] Episodes like the near revolt of the Canadians at Grand Arenas in April probably strengthened these prejudices. Israelis also discovered that some of the volunteers who claimed combat experience or specialized knowledge were actually frauds who knew little or nothing about weapons or the army. The Israelis learned to be sceptical, to test volunteers out before passing judgment, and to be careful about entrusting scarce, specialized equipment to glory-seeking liars. This attitude was deeply resented by many of the veteran volunteers, who soon complained that command in Israel was given out according to political considerations. This was a quick and harsh judgment. Although few volunteers were quickly placed in command positions (David Marcus being an obvious exception), many did reach command by the end of the war.

Much of the morale problem was caused by the unavoidable misunderstandings that arose from the meeting of people with different cultural, ethnic, and national backgrounds, not to mention different expectations and desires. In May and June 1948, Israel's first priority was to hold back the invasion of five Arab countries and to reestablish land communications among the Jewish areas of Palestine. Volunteers were thrown into action where they were needed. There was little or no time to attend to the personal and emotional needs of a handful of foreigners, mostly Jews, who sometimes took the view that they had arrived to "save" Palestine. Nevertheless, the special problems involving volunteers prompted the Israeli Chief of Staff to establish a *mahal* department of the army under Harold Jaffer, who had formerly been connected with the Sonneborn Institute in New York. Ayala Zacks of Toronto was appointed civilian advisor to this department and became responsible for the general welfare of the volunteers, while Gideon Bartz administered the office and acted as Jaffer's assistant.[50] This was, at least, an admission that a problem existed. In fact, however, very little of concrete value was done until the autumn, when more serious difficulties arose within several units.

The morale difficulties that emerged in July during the first truce fortunately affected very few of the volunteers. Most were determined to do whatever was asked of them, with few complaints other than the normal grumbling that is part of every army. In fact, many strongly resented the swaggering boastfulness of some of their colleagues who seemed to do most of their fighting in the bars and cafés of Tel Aviv. These people were derisively called *shvitzers*, and were identified by their ostentatious display of weaponry. One observer claimed that those who wished to see "this species of humanity" had only to stand on the corner of Allenby and Ben Yehuda streets in Tel Aviv to see a "parade of enough equipment to stock a fair-sized arsenal...all hanging from belts". There were "pistols and knives, pistols and bayonets, pistols and pistols, and pistols". A story was told of three "Tel Aviv cowboys" sitting around a table in a café, each with a sawed-off shotgun on his hip, who grunted, "Huh, look at the big *shvitzer*," when an unarmed but obviously battle-tested army captain walked in.[51]

It is likely that morale problems had something to do with the break-up of the "Canadian platoon" in Givati shortly after the truce. The Canadians were released from the brigade with the explanation that the army did not want serious repercussions in Canada in the event that the entire platoon was wiped out.[52] However, in the following weeks large numbers of volunteers were assigned to the 32nd Battalion of the Alexandroni Brigade and about three hundred men, mostly from Canada, South Africa, the United States, and Britain, were put into the 72nd and 79th battalions of the Seventh Brigade.

There had, in fact, been continuing difficulties between members of the Canadian platoon and the army over conditions of service, pay, and other matters. At one point in late May, Eliyahu Tal complained to Dunkelman that he did not want "to hear in the future anything from Lt. Druker in the presence of other volunteers that I did not keep my word and fulfil promises to him and his men". Tal was so upset over the trouble that he asked Dunkelman to relieve him of any duty in connection with the Canadians.[53]

VII

Late on the evening of June 11, 1948, the *Marie Annick*, a small 120-ton schooner, slipped into the little bay of La Ciotat not far from Marseilles, and 150 Jewish passengers who had been trucked from the Grand Arenas camp trooped aboard. Most were refugees, but about

148

thirty were foreign volunteers carrying false documents identifying them as concentration camp survivors. At 2:00 a.m. on June 12, after about twenty tons of medical supplies had been loaded aboard, the *Marie Annick* slipped away into the dark.[54] The ship was old and small; the berths reminded Arthur Goldberg, who was aboard with many of his original group from Vancouver, of pictures he had seen of the inside of concentration camp barracks.[55] The holds were foul; the rations were meagre; and the toilet facilities consisted of a blanket draped over a frame by an opening in the railing. Cooking was done on a single stove on the main deck, until the wooden planks underneath caught fire and the stove fell through into the hold below. Each time a plane or a ship was sighted everyone aboard scrambled down into the hold, and the main hatch opening was covered with a tarpaulin. The Italian crew were drunk much of the time and managed to run the ship aground off the coast of Corsica. The voyage to Israel took almost two weeks. When the *Marie Annick* finally approached the coast off Tel Aviv, immigrants, volunteers, and crew were shocked to see a large plume of black smoke rising from a spot just off the beach. It came from the still-burning wreck of the *Altalena*.

The *Altalena* was a war surplus LST (Landing Ship, Tank) that had been purchased in 1947 from the War Assets Administration in the United States by the American League for a Free Palestine. It was owned jointly by the League and Three Star Lines, and was registered in Panama.[56] The ship had been reconditioned at Gravesend, Brooklyn, and, in accordance with U.S. export requirements, rendered unfit for military use primarily by having her bow landing door welded shut. The ship then sailed for Europe under the command of Monroe Fein, a former LST captain in the United States Navy. By April 1948, the *Altalena* was berthed at Port-de-Bouc, France. There, further work was done to make the craft useful to the Irgun (the welded door was cut open), and arrangements were concluded to load arms and volunteers for use by the Irgun in Palestine.[57]

On May 26 the Provisional Government of Israel issued Order No. 4 uniting all land, naval, and air forces in the new state into the Zvah Haganah Le Israel (Zahal)—Israel Defence Forces or IDF in English. The order applied to the Irgun and the Lehi, except in Jerusalem, which was then cut off and technically not under the control of the Provisional Government. Despite this, however, the Irgun continued to make plans to send arms and volunteers to Israel from France aboard the

149

Altalena. Loading operations began in June. Six hundred tons of arms and 853 volunteers were placed aboard before the LST sailed from Port-de-Bouc on the night of June 11.[58] The *Altalena's* passengers were men and women from all over Europe, Canada, and the United States. Fein was in command and Jack Blank, a Canadian, was gun captain. The LST, unlike the *Marie Annick*, was large and fast. Within eight days it was approaching the coast of Palestine.

Ben Gurion knew about the *Altalena* and its cargo and agreed to allow it to land on two conditions: the arms and ammunition were to be turned over to the IDF, and the volunteers were to be absorbed into IDF units. When Menachem Begin, leader of the Irgun, insisted that his organization keep 20 per cent of the *Altalena's* arms, Ben Gurion refused, interpreting the move as a challenge to the authority of the government and the IDF. He therefore issued orders that the *Altalena* and its cargo were to be seized.[59] When the LST finally anchored off the beach of Kfar Vitkin, about thirty-five kilometres north of Tel Aviv, units of the Alexandroni Brigade surrounded the settlement while the *Wedgwood*, a former Royal Canadian Navy corvette, and a smaller craft were sent to block *Altalena's* escape route to the open sea.

The 32nd Battalion of the Alexandroni Brigade had a number of volunteers in its ranks and there were many volunteers serving aboard the *Wedgwood*. They, like the Israelis with them, had little taste for the exercise. Aboard the *Wedgwood* a meeting was called and a representative of Ben Gurion's Mapai party explained the government's viewpoint. The men were told that there could not be any division in the armed forces of the new state and that the arms aboard the *Altalena* had to be surrendered to the legitimate government of the day. Few could argue with this reasoning and none did.[60] Battle stations were manned. At about 9:00 p.m. on June 20 the *Altalena* began unloading and small boats carried the volunteers and the cargo to the beach at Kfar Vitkin. By morning about 750 volunteers and fifty tons of cargo had been taken off. In the dawn light, Fein noticed two warships standing out to sea but, since he received no signals or instructions from them, he continued the unloading operations. During the day about fifty more tons of cargo were taken off the LST. All was going smoothly until, just before sunset, firing was heard from the beach. The IDF troops had begun to move in.

Fein received an urgent instruction over his walkie-talkie to move out to sea, and the *Altalena* began to raise its forward landing doors and back away from the surf.[61] Aboard the *Wedgwood*, Canadian Jerry Rosenberg manned the Aldis lamp and blinked out a message to the LST. He told the *Altalena* that these were Israeli warships, instructed her to proceed to Tel Aviv, and gave the LST captain a course and speed to follow.[62] Ben Ocopnik, also of Canada, was manning one of the *Wedgwood*'s Bofors guns when a burst of machine-gun fire hit the bulkhead just above his head.[63] The *Wedgwood* returned the fire and, after a short burst, Rosenberg signalled again to ask if the LST had any casualties aboard. The reply was brief but cocky: "We don't, but maybe you do."

In later years Jack Blank claimed that the *Altalena* had not opened fire on the *Wedgwood* until fired upon, and it is possible, as Ocopnik believes, that the burst that almost killed him came from the beach.[64] Irgun supporters are convinced that the *Wedgwood* began the exchange by firing several shots across the *Altalena*'s bow as she appeared to head out to sea. What is certain is that after the shooting both ships headed south along the coast towards Tel Aviv, with Fein keeping as close to shore as possible and the *Wedgwood*'s captain trying to head the *Altalena* farther out to sea. Fein thought he might find a safe haven in Tel Aviv. He also knew that if he allowed the corvette to sail between his ship and the shore it would be able to open fire without fear of hitting anything on the coast.[65]

The two ships approached Tel Aviv at about midnight and exchanged fire again for about two minutes before the *Altalena* ran aground about half a mile from the surf in front of the Katae Dan Hotel. The streets near the Tel Aviv waterfront came alive with rushing, shouting men and the roar of jeep and truck engines, as the Irgun and IDF forces moved into position. After dawn, firing broke out along the shore between the Irgun and the IDF. When a small boat from the *Altalena* approached the beach, it was driven back by gunfire. At about 4:00 p.m., mortar rounds from the beach hit the *Altalena*, which caught fire. The ammunition on board began to explode, and Fein gave the order to abandon ship. One U.N. observer watching the events noted that about forty people began to swim to shore under machine-gun fire. When the shooting stopped, fourteen Irgun men and two IDF soldiers had been killed. The *Altalena* continued to burn for several days, a funeral pyre marking Israel's brief civil war.[66]

Since daylight on June 20, U.N. observers had been aware that something out of the ordinary was occurring with the mysterious LST at Kfar Vitkin. When they tried to approach by land in a jeep, they were turned back by IDF roadblocks, and when they tried to fly over the unloading ship, their light aircraft were driven back by gunfire. The events could not remain hidden for long, however, because, ironically, the Katae Dan Hotel housed a large number of U.N. observers, who watched the unfolding drama in front of them with horrified fascination.

The Israeli government's explanation to Bernadotte was designed to hide the real purpose of the fighting. It claimed it was attempting to uphold the ceasefire and stop the landing of arms and ammunition in violation of the truce. It stated that no arms had been off-loaded at Kfar Vitkin and that the weapons confiscated there by IDF forces were actually the personal weapons of the Irgun troops that had surrendered.[67] In putting forward this specious explanation, the Israeli government tried to cover its own implication in the landing of *Altalena* arms and place full responsibility for the events on the Irgun. Some of the volunteers who fought the *Altalena* were also given this explanation. They were profoundly saddened by the affair. They knew little about the bitterness and intense rivalries of Yishuv politics, and they cared less. For them no explanation could wipe away, or completely excuse, the killing of Jew by Jew. This was not, after all, what they had come to Israel for.

On June 29, 1948, the *Altalena* issue was, in one sense, closed when all members of the armed forces of Israel—Haganah, Irgun, and Lehi—swore an oath of allegiance to the State of Israel and its government. The volunteers, for the most part, stood aside or else swore a different oath, not of allegiance but of obedience,[68] since great care was taken not to jeopardize their own citizenship by an oath to a foreign state. There was good cause for this, and indeed the volunteers themselves usually demanded it, but it underlined their separate treatment arising out of different obligations.

VIII

All immigrants of military age brought to Israel during the truce aboard ships such as the *Marie Annick* were taken to U.N.-run internment camps. These were only loosely guarded and the foreign volunteers among the internees usually managed to slip away within a few days. In twos and threes they soon ended up in the sprawling, teeming Tel Litvinsky army camp, where they whiled away the hot hours by trying to make contact with some branch of the armed forces that needed them. Some ended up in the artillery. A company was being formed under the command of Michael Landshut, a tall, blond Australian, to fight the Syrians at Mishmar Hayarden. Landshut was a mysterious figure: some said he had served under Orde Wingate in Burma; others that he had fought the Japanese in the Pacific. He was specifically looking for English-speaking volunteers and he chose a mixed group composed of Americans, South Africans, and Arthur Goldberg's Canadian group from Vancouver. The men were told they were to begin training on new "secret" weapons and were soon taken to an abandoned winery near Herzliya, where they saw two old French-built 75 mm anti-aircraft guns pulled by trucks.[69] They trained on the guns for about one week and then broke camp to leave for the north.[70]

By the beginning of July it was growing increasingly apparent that the war would soon resume. Bernadotte had proposed a peace plan that would have stripped Israel of the Negev in return for the western Galilee, which—in the original partition plan—had been assigned to the Arabs. The Israelis, particularly Ben Gurion, saw the Negev as the future frontier of their new state and rejected Bernadotte's proposals. The Arabs, who objected to any plan that included a Jewish state regardless of its size and boundaries, also rejected the proposal. They were determined to keep fighting until Israel was wiped out.

Although Israel wanted more time to prepare, it was also eager to resume the war in order to broaden out the Jerusalem corridor, open the road to the Negev, and drive the Arabs out of the western Galilee.[71] The Seventh Brigade was chosen to achieve the last of these objectives. It had been severely battered in the Latrun fighting and, during the truce, had been withdrawn to Ein Shemer, in central Israel, for rest and reorganization. At the beginning of July, Ben Gurion picked Ben Dunkelman to command it. Before departing for Ein Shemer, Dunkelman sent for Joe Weiner, another Canadian, and asked him to command the brigade's 79th armoured battalion.[72] Weiner agreed. There were two other battalions in the Seventh, the 71st, commanded by Yehuda Werber, an Israeli, and the 72nd, under the command of Jackie Nursella, an American-born Israeli.

Dunkelman was well aware of the poor condition of his new command; he expected to have at least two weeks to whip it into shape but, in fact, he had little time. He assumed command at Ein Shemer on July 5. Soon after he was ordered to move the brigade north to the vicinity of Haifa, and to be there by July 7.[73] The truce was due to expire at 6:00 p.m., July 9, and Dunkelman ordered his battalion commanders to prepare for the move north while he started out to conduct an aerial reconnaissance of the western Galilee and the eastern approaches to Haifa.

Dunkelman's new opponent was to be the Arab Liberation Army of Fauzi al-Kaukji, and the main prize was the ancient city of Nazareth. As Dunkelman was flown over the rough, hilly terrain that was to be his forthcoming battleground, Bernadotte began to withdraw the U.N. truce observers from the different fronts. On the morning of July 8, thirty-six hours before the truce was due to expire, fighting broke out along the Egyptian front in the south. Within hours, the killing had resumed on all the fronts.

8

"You'll Never Get a Chance Again"

It was late in the afternoon of July 16, 1948. Joe Weiner was certain that an Arab roadblock, backed by armour, lay between the spearhead of the 79th Armoured Battalion and the town of Nazareth, but he had only three armoured cars and a half-track with which to lead the Israeli attack. He instructed the three armoured-car drivers to lead, and positioned the half-track, which carried a 20 mm anti-aircraft gun, to follow. Then he held a roadside meeting with the crews. "All right," he instructed, "go up the road, and when you get to the top there'll be a roadblock there. I don't know what it is, but as soon as you see it, front armoured car, you open fire, move to the left; second, open fire and move to the right; third, to the left, and that will leave a passage in between for the twenty millimetre to fire through." He turned to the half-track gunner: "As soon as you see they've moved aside, you open fire and pull." "How many shots?" the gunner asked. "Pull it until it jams," Weiner emphasized. "You'll never get a chance again."[1]

The men climbed aboard their vehicles, started their engines, and moved off down the road towards the waiting town. As the small Israeli column crept up a hill, the first crew spotted two British-built Staghound armoured cars with 37 mm guns drawn up across the road. The Israeli armoured cars opened up with machine guns, but the bullets bounced off the thick armour of the Arab cars. The Arabs began to traverse their turrets to open fire but, just before they brought their cannons to bear, the 20 mm opened up, hit the first Arab armoured car in the turret rim, freezing the turret, and struck the second Arab car over the drivers' positions. The ammunition inside began to explode and the crews of the two Arab armoured cars leaped out of their hatches and were cut down by Israeli machine guns. A third Arab

155

armoured car, which was waiting just beyond the road block, turned quickly to escape the onrushing assault force but was hit in the front suspension. It spun out of control and tumbled down the hill. Six other Arab Liberation Army armoured cars then beat a hasty retreat into Nazareth and the entrance to the city was open.[2]

I

The attack on Nazareth was the climax to Operation Dekel or "palm tree". The operation was designed to eliminate the Arab Liberation Army threat both to the coastal plain north and east of Haifa and to the largely Jewish settled areas of the northern and eastern Galilee. Dekel was part of Israel's over-all strategy for pushing Arab forces away from major Jewish population centres and for breaking the Arab hold on key roads and positions in or near the areas allotted to the Jewish state by the U.N. partition plan. When fighting had ended on June 11, Arab armies had dominated, controlled, or occupied much Israeli territory outside of the coastal strip from just south of Tel Aviv to Haifa. On each front, therefore, Israeli forces were given specific objectives designed to fit the larger plan of pushing the Arabs back as far as possible.

In the south, Israel's claim to the Negev, based on the November 1947 partition plan, had been questioned by Count Bernadotte. Israeli troops were therefore charged with opening the road to the Negev and clearing out Egyptian forces. In central Palestine the blockade of Jerusalem had been broken by the building of the Burma Road, but the Transjordan Arab Legion still held Latrun. Here the Israeli objective was to strengthen Jewish access to the Holy City. In the north, Israel aimed to force the Syrians back across the Jordan River at Mishmar Hayarden, block the Lebanese army from advancing any farther south or east, and secure areas controlled by the Arab Liberation Army.

During the truce, the Israeli high command had been reorganized, and a number of front commanders had been appointed to assume responsibility for operations in their areas. The northern commander was Moshe Carmel while the co-ordinator for Operation Dekel was Haim Laskov. Laskov directed a task group consisting of the Seventh Brigade, under the command of Ben Dunkelman, and an infantry battalion from the Carmeli Brigade with a small battery of medium-range artillery.[3] The task group was ordered to attack southeastward from Acre to open the road to Nazareth and eliminate Arab resistance

156

in the hills and villages along the route.

II

Tel Kissan is a small knoll about four kilometres east of the main coastal highway north of Haifa and five kilometres south of Acre. It was the only position on the coastal plain occupied by the Arab Liberation Army, but it gave the small ALA contingent based there an excellent point from which to observe and harass Jewish traffic on the coastal highway. Tel Kissan was therefore chosen as the first objective of Operation Dekel. Under cover of darkness on the night of July 11, men of the 71st Battalion crept around to the rear of the position and opened fire, catching the defenders by surprise; surrender was almost immediate. Dunkelman then ordered the 71st to attack Damun and Ruweis—two villages lying just at the eastern edge of the coastal plain— while the infantry battalion from the Carmeli Brigade captured two smaller villages to the north. By the night of July 10, the Seventh Brigade was firmly in control of the coastal plain east of the Bay of Haifa.[4]

To attack Kaukji's main body in the Nazareth area, the Dekel task group had to fight its way upwards. North-central Israel east of Haifa rises steeply from the coastal plain to heights of about 550 metres, before plunging below sea level at the Sea of Galilee. From the highest spots it is possible to see all the way to the coastal plain and sometimes to the Mediterranean itself. The roads to the Galilee from the coastal plain are narrow and twisting. They wind up steep slopes, clinging precariously to the sides of hills; the passes and defiles along the route offer excellent opportunities for ambushes. The hills to the east of the coastal plain are heavily populated by the Druse, an Arab people whose religion, an off-shoot of Islam, is deeply shrouded in mystery. The Druse, who live mainly in Syria, Lebanon, and northern Palestine, decided long ago that survival as a religious minority in this volatile region of religious passion and persecution dictated a pragmatic approach to politics. The Druse stay loyal to the national rulers and support them, even against the Druse of other countries, as long as they believe those rulers to be in control. When Dunkelman's forces secured the coastal plain, therefore, the Druse immediately to the east agreed to negotiate with the Israelis. On July 11, three villages were peacefully taken over by the Seventh Brigade which then established itself on a north-south defensive line in the foothills, far from the vital coastal road.[5] Fauzi al-Kaukji retaliated shortly afterwards with assaults on Jewish settlements at Nahariya and Sejera, but his forces were overextended and the assaults were beaten back.

Kaukji's headquarters were in Nazareth, an ancient city holy to Christianity, perched atop the hills of central Galilee. Nazareth held the key to four main roads—to Acre, Haifa, Tiberias, and Afula. An assault on Nazareth could come from one of two directions: from Afula, ten kilometres to the south; or from the Seventh Brigade positions twenty-five kilometres to the northwest. Afula was closer, but the road from there to Nazareth was steep and winding and could be easily defended from a Tegart fort on the south edge of the town. Nevertheless, a Seventh Brigade attack from the northwest would first have to conquer Shafa Amr, on the main road to Nazareth, as well as the smaller villages of Saffuriya, situated on a hilltop three kilometres north of the road, and Ilut, at the end of a dirt track two kilometres south of the road. Despite these obstacles, Dunkelman pressed Carmel to authorize a Seventh Brigade assault and Carmel agreed.

At Northern Command Headquarters in Afula, a plan was drawn up for a drive on Shafa Amr and Nazareth to be spearheaded by the 79th Armoured Battalion under the command of Joe Weiner. Carmel ordered Dunkelman to attack Shafa Amr, but insisted that he then wait until the flanks of his brigade were protected before moving on to Nazareth.[6] Carmel would not allow Dunkelman's troops to strike the full distance down the road in a single attack, passing through Arabheld territory, until he was certain the area around the road had been secured.[7] In his memoirs, Dunkelman presents no details of Carmel's plan to protect the flanks of the Seventh Brigade but, according to Weiner, it involved an infantry assault from Afula to capture Saffuriya and Ilut before the 79th spearhead attacked Nazareth.

Dunkelman was unhappy about the plan but was forced to agree.[8] When he presented it to his battalion commanders, Weiner immediately objected. He characterized it as an infantry assault backed by armour rather than a true armour attack, and claimed it would be a complete fiasco that would turn into another Latrun. He feared that the infantry would not be able to assault the two villages and then join the attack on Nazareth in the same night; this would necessitate a dangerous delay. In addition, he was certain that the different attack elements would not be able to communicate with each other because of the limited range of their Mark 9 radio sets in mountainous country. Dunkelman was furious and relieved Weiner of his command. When Weiner returned to his unit, his men were upset over the change, and Weiner was forced to reassure them by saying he would join the attack "as a private".[9]

Shafa Amr was a walled town populated by Moslem Arabs and Druse. The Druse promised to help the Israelis, and a plan was worked out whereby the 79th would attack the town from the Druse side, firing over the heads of the Druse defenders in a mock assault. The Moslems would hear the shooting and would be convinced that their Druse neighbours were fighting to defend their part of the town. In fact, however, the Druse would open the gates and allow the Israelis to enter. The plan worked. The armoured cars of the 79th were accompanied by two companies from the infantry battalion assigned from the Carmeli Brigade and supported by a small battery of mortars and jeeps with tandem machine guns mounted on them. They assaulted Shafa Amr after nightfall on July 13 and pushed rapidly through the Druse area. The Arabs were surprised from the rear and quickly defeated. By dawn, the entire town was occupied by the Seventh Brigade.[10]

While Dunkelman was laying plans for the assault on Nazareth, a unit of the Golani Brigade from Afula captured the small village of Ma'alul, eight kilometres west of Nazareth, and broke through to the encircled Jewish defenders of Kfar Hahoresh, three kilometres west of Nazareth. This apparently convinced Kaukji that the main assault on his headquarters would come from the south.

Late on July 14 a detachment of Israeli troops set out from Kfar Hahoresh to take up positions in the hills near Ilut, south of the main Shafa Amr-Nazareth road. By nightfall on July 15 the Seventh Brigade was ready for the final assault on Nazareth.

At 11:00 p.m., the main force, this time led by the 72nd Battalion, pushed off to attack the village of Saffuriya. This town was famous in Palestine as the former home of Sheikh Kasem, one of the most daring of the Arab guerrilla leaders during the 1936-39 revolt. However, the local defenders—villagers and a contingent of Arab Liberation Army troops—were caught by surprise and offered only feeble and sporadic resistance before fleeing. By 6:15 a.m., Saffuriya had fallen and the northern flank of the main Seventh Brigade attacking force was secured.[11] The southern flank was to have been protected by an assault on Ilut, south of the Shafa Amr-Nazareth road, mounted by a battalion from Afula, but the troops never arrived. Dunkelman was forced to dispatch patrols to take up positions on the dirt track leading to Ilut to ensure that Arab reinforcements did not move up the road while the assault on Nazareth was under way.

Although Joe Weiner was technically no longer in command of the 79th Armoured Battalion, he was the only man in the unit who had extensive experience in armoured warfare. His presence was crucial to the success of the Israeli attack, because the entrance to Nazareth was defended by a small but potentially deadly force of nine Arab Liberation Army armoured cars. Against this the 79th could muster only two real armoured cars captured from the Arab Legion at Latrun. Added to these were some homemade armoured cars with twin machine guns, some armed jeeps, and a half-track carrying a 20 mm Hispano-Suiza anti-tank/anti-aircraft gun.

At 4:30 p.m. on July 16 the attack on Nazareth began. As the 79th Battalion approached the town, Weiner saw two Arab armoured cars move down the road. He calculated that they would set up a roadblock over the crest of the next hill and try to hit the first Israeli vehicle as it cleared the top of the rise. This would block the way for the rest of the column, which could then be picked off at will. Even though he was technically not in command, he took charge and organized the assault that broke through the roadblock and opened the way into the city for the Jewish forces.

The 79th spearhead drove through the northern suburbs of Nazareth and halted at the main road junction on the northern edge of town. From there artillery shelled the known Arab Liberation Army positions inside Nazareth while the infantry fanned out through the narrow streets and alleyways, creeping forward cautiously to attack Arab Liberation Army strongholds. Except for a few sporadic shots, however, an eerie silence had settled over Nazareth. Kaukji and most of the Arab Liberation Army had gone into hiding.

At 6:15 p.m. a group of the town's leading citizens accompanied by Nazareth's Christian religious leaders approached the Israelis under a white flag and offered to surrender the town. They wanted the Israeli forces to treat Nazareth as an "open city". Dunkelman, who entered Nazareth after Weiner's breakthrough, accepted on condition that there was no further resistance. The group agreed and left to convince the remaining Arab Liberation Army troops inside the Tegart fort to surrender. When shots were fired from the fort, Dunkelman ordered his gunners to lob two shells at it, but both missed and exploded harmlessly inside the grounds of a monastery. The fort's defenders soon surrendered, however. When Israeli patrols moved in, they found the building empty. Later that night, Kaukji and the remnants of his Arab Liberation Army slipped away to the east.[12]

When Dunkelman and Laskov accepted the surrender of Nazareth, they pledged to do nothing to harm the city or its people. (The population of Nazareth had been swelled to about forty thousand by the arrival of refugees from other parts of Palestine.) However, the next day Dunkelman received orders to "evacuate" Nazareth's Arabs. He was shocked and notified his superiors that he would not comply. He reminded them of the promises that had been made to the town leaders and pointed out that the surrender document confirmed those pledges.

Within hours of his refusal, Dunkelman was replaced as military governor of the city by Avraham Yaffe, commander of the Golani 13th Battalion. Dunkelman was certain the replacement resulted from his refusal to carry out the evacuation order, and he extracted a promise from Yaffe that he would do nothing to harm or displace the Arab population of the city. Yaffe agreed. Dunkelman's resistance may have saved the Arabs of Nazareth, because no further "evacuation" orders were issued[13] and one observer even reported to the British Foreign Office in London that "stern measures were being taken to preserve the inhabitants' rights".[14]

Foreign volunteers, from Dunkelman and Weiner to the lowest ranks of the Seventh Brigade, were crucial to the capture of Nazareth. This is clear despite the considerable controversy—mentioned in Dunkelman's memoirs—that surrounds Dunkelman's role in Operation Dekel.[15] He claims responsiblity for much of the attack on Nazareth, including the over-all planning of the campaign and the negotiations with the Druse that led to the Seventh Brigade's initial successes.[16] He does not acknowledge Laskov as having been commander of the Dekel task group and describes him as having "a rather vaguely defined position supernumerary to establishment, as military governor of the western Galilee".[17] Dunkelman places himself at Nazareth during the final assault, even though Laskov and Weiner dispute this and assert he was in brigade headquarters at the time. Both claim they, not he, led the attack.[18]

It is clear from Laskov's own recollection that he was not in direct command of the Seventh Brigade during Operation Dekel and that Dunkelman was.[19] Since no proof has emerged to show that Dunkelman was not in control of his own command, it must be assumed that he made an important contribution to the victory through his planning, organization, and leadership at the brigade level. It is also safe to conclude that Dunkelman would not have been allowed to keep command of the Seventh Brigade until the end of the war if he had not acquitted himself well during the Nazareth campaign. He was, however, not the only volunteer to play a key role. Joe Weiner's experience and knowledge of armoured warfare—he had been discharged from the Royal Canadian Armoured Corps with the rank of captain—was crucial to the rapid defeat of Kaukji's armoured force at the gates of Nazareth. In the armoured cars, foreign volunteer drivers, loaders, and gunners kept the column moving and paced the rapid advance of the 79th Battalion. Since few Israelis had armoured experience, volunteer personnel gave the 79th much of its punch.

III

One of the Syrian army's objectives was to cut the north-south highway that ran a hundred metres or so to the west of Kibbutz Ayyelet HaShahar. If it could do so, Jewish settlements in the north, in the "finger" of the upper Galilee—including Metulla, the most northerly town in Israel—would be isolated. On the morning of July 10, five small tanks were sent across the fields near the kibbutz to seize control of the highway; there was nothing to stop them except Michael Landshut and his volunteer gun crews.

The two gun crews knew they were in trouble when Landshut ran back from the forward observation post to yell a warning that Syrian tanks were approaching. There was no chance to move the guns, because it took at least forty-five minutes to limber them up and attach them to the trucks. The gun crews could either abandon their artillery or stay and fight it out. One of the guns was out of action, and Landshut ordered the idle crew to grab its weapons and prepare to resist with machine guns and hand grenades while the other crew laid down a barrage against the advancing tanks. Although they all knew that five tanks would make short work of them, there was no panic. Arthur Goldberg remembered later that he felt strangely calm, with "no particular feeling of fear", and even took a moment or so to clean the spring of his Sten gun.[20] There was no armour-piercing ammunition, so the gun crew prepared its fuses to explode just over the advancing Syrian tanks. The gun fired, and fired again, as the crew lowered the elevation, walking the shell bursts nearer and nearer to the volunteers' own position. The low rise in front of the gun kept the Syrian tanks from view, but the men knew the tanks were very close when the barrel of the 75 mm was almost level with the top of the rise. Suddenly the tanks stopped and retreated to the Syrian lines.[21] The air bursts raining shrapnel on the tanks had caused no damage, but the Syrian tank crews, fearing the worst, had given up the attack.

Landshut's small battery was part of a larger Israeli force taking part in Operation Berosh. The object of Operation Berosh was to push the Syrians back across the Jordan River and recapture the area around Mishmar Hayarden that the Israelis had lost in the last days before the first truce. The Syrians had one infantry brigade at Mishmar Hayarden, backed by armoured units equipped with Renault light tanks and artillery, and supported by the Syrian Air Force, which mainly used Harvard training planes modified to carry bombs and machine guns. Against this the Israelis mustered the Carmeli Brigade, reinforced by units from the newly formed Oded (Ninth) Brigade and supported by a few 65 mm artillery pieces and the two 75 mm guns commanded by Michael Landshut.

The Landshut detachment had moved to northern Israel just before the truce expired. The small contingent drove north along the Rosh Pina-Metulla highway and pulled into a small ravine on the left side of the road about one kilometre south of Kibbutz Ayyelet HaShahar. The guns were pointed over a low rise towards the Syrian positions to the east, and were unlimbered and sighted-in[22] while a small observation post was set up several hundred metres to the west. Landshut had about 170 shells with time fuses. These were designed to explode in the air over enemy infantry, showering them with shrapnel, but were useless against hard targets such as pillboxes or tanks.[23]

As soon as the truce ended, fighting broke out. Israeli forces tried to attack the Syrian bridgehead from the rear by sending units to cross the Jordan River to the north of Mishmar Hayarden. At the same time, the Syrians were preparing to launch an attack to the southwest to capture the key road junction at Rosh Pina. Fighting continued throughout the night of July 9-10, and most of the Israeli troops were forced to withdraw with heavy losses. The handful of operational Avia

S-199 fighters were engaged in other sectors and the Syrians ruled the skies over the eastern Galilee. On the morning of July 10, Syrian Harvards bombed and strafed Israeli positions for several hours. After the softening up, the Syrians attacked westwards and captured the small settlement of Yarda and an Israeli outpost on Hill 243. Once these two positions had been taken, the five Syrian tanks were sent to cut the road to the north and were stopped dead by Landshut's guns. It was the closest Syria ever came to cutting off the Jewish settlements and villages to the north.

After ten days of fighting in the north, the Israelis were firmly in control of most of the Galilee from Haifa Bay to Lake Tiberias. Kaukji had survived to fight another day, but local resistance had been all but crushed and the Arab Liberation Army had been badly beaten. The Syrians, had not been dislodged, however. They were still as strongly entrenched around Mishmar Hayarden as they had been at the start of the truce in June. They continued to pose a major threat to the north-south road that linked Jewish settlements in the upper Galilee with the villages and agricultural settlements to the south and west of Lake Tiberias. The Lebanese stayed out of the fight completely and did not budge from the positions they had captured at Malkiya in the early days of the invasion.

IV

The Eighth Brigade, newly formed during the truce under the command of Yitzhak Sadeh, was intended to be an all-armoured formation using a motley collection of armoured vehicles that the Israelis had acquired since the start of the Arab invasion. Because few Israelis had any armoured experience, the brigade counted heavily upon the expertise of foreign volunteers.[24] The terrain chosen for its first operations was not suitable for tank warfare, however, and Israeli commanders did not know how to use the terrain. In its first days at war, the brigade did not exactly cover itself with glory.

The Eighth Brigade's total armoured complement included one Sherman tank (which was missing its main 75 mm cannon but which carried two machine guns), ten French-built light tanks, a number of homemade armoured cars, and two British-built Cromwell tanks.[25] Some of the French tanks had been spirited into Israel during the truce, others had been captured from the Syrians. The Cromwells had been stolen from a British depot near Haifa—where the last British troops were stationed in a small enclave after May 15—just before the final British withdrawal, by sergeants Michael Flanagan and Harry Macdonald, two deserters. The two men had started selling gasoline and other equipment to the Haganah in March 1948, and eventually agreed to desert and bring the tanks with them. Neither man was happy about being transferred back to Britain and both preferred to take their chances with the Israelis.[26] The two tanks, according to the American consul in Haifa, were in "excellent condition".[27]

The Eighth Brigade, assembled near Tel Litvinsky during the last days of the truce, included volunteers from Canada, South Africa, and Britain, as well as a large number of Russian immigrants who had had experience in the Red Army. It was part of a large force which launched attacks to the southeast of Tel Aviv on July 9. From a point just south of Petach Tikvah the brigade was ordered to attack in a southerly direction towards Ben Shemen, where it would meet other Israeli units attacking northwards. Once the link-up was complete, the small Arab cities of Lydda and Ramle and the Lydda airport would be isolated. This was the first phase of Operation Dani, which aimed to capture Latrun and strengthen the Israeli hold on the Jerusalem corridor.

The brigade ran into trouble from the start: the land was hilly and rocky and the infantry had not been trained to co-ordinate their movements with armour. The crews inside the tanks and armoured cars spoke several different languages, and few understood Hebrew; constant interpretation in Russian, English, and Yiddish was necessary.[28] The tank attack ground to a halt about half way to its objective, while an Israeli light commando group led by Moshe Dayan and using half tracks and machine-gun-bearing jeeps pressed ahead and completed the link-up.

This was not the only Eighth Brigade failure during Operation Dani. In an assault on Latrun launched a few days later, the Cromwells and the Sherman advanced on the police fort with one of the British-built tanks in the lead. The Cromwell began to fire, but was quickly put out of action when a round jammed in the main gun. The tank commander leaped out of his vehicle and told the driver of the second tank, in English, to continue the advance while his disabled tank returned to base at Lydda airport to have the shell extracted. The defenders inside the police fort had seen the advancing armour and were beginning to retreat but the driver of the second tank did not understand his instructions and thought he was being ordered to follow the first Cromwell back to base. The entire column returned to Lydda and the Transjordan Arab Legion kept control of the vital Latrun stronghold.[29]

If the volunteers had not already learned about the harsh face of war in Palestine, their experiences in Lydda and Ramle provided a grim education. On July 10, Israeli forces under Moshe Dayan smashed through the Lydda defences and halted on the outskirts of Ramle. The town leaders surrendered to Dayan's superior, Moshe Kelman, and promised to give up all fighting personnel and weapons within twenty-four hours. Towards noon on the next day, however, three Arab Legion armoured cars appeared briefly at the western edge of Lydda. When they discovered Israeli troops in the city they made a quick retreat but not before the Arab villagers concluded that the Legion was about to recapture their town. Within minutes a spontaneous revolt broke out directed at the 500 or so Israeli troops that had occupied the town after the surrender. Five Israelis standing guard near the main mosque were instantly killed and mutilated. Kelman's men were badly outnumbered. He ordered them to shoot at any target they could see. Within the next hour the Israelis killed several hundred Arabs and advanced on the main mosque, which was the centre of Arab resistance. Arab fighters were crowded inside the small building and, when the Israelis fired an anti-tank shell into it, most of those inside were blown to pieces.[30]

Although the brief revolt had been crushed, Kelman and his superiors feared further uprisings from behind the lines and were determined to maintain security in the rear areas. They arrived at a harsh decision. The Arabs of Lydda would not be given any further chance to revolt; they were ordered to leave for Arab Legion lines within three hours. The people of Ramle, in the words of Yitzhak Rabin, at that time commander of the Harel Brigade, "watched and learned the lesson". When their town surrendered the following day, their leaders "agreed to be evacuated voluntarily".[31] For South African doctor Lionel Melzer, the evacuation of Ramle was a human tragedy: "We found the Arab people bewildered. They were congregating on the square with their bundles and packets—women, children, and old men. They were beginning to walk the Lord knows where, and others were scrambling into buses. One could read tragedy on the women's faces and bewilderment on the faces of the children. The women were wondering where the babies would sleep and what they would eat. Dismay and helplessness. . . . I am terribly upset by all this."[32]

Melzer saw much to upset him during the fighting. He toured the battlefronts from the Negev to the north. He was caught in several air raids in Tel Aviv, including one on a house ninety metres away from him, which was bombed as he was about to enter army medical headquarters. He ran to the scene and found the mangled remains of two elderly people and two small boys. "I should be used to seeing dead people," he recorded in his diary, "but I must confess that today's experience upset me very much—they seemed to be so completely dead. . . . "[33] He and the other members of the South African medical team worked day and night during the fighting, visiting battlefields, performing emergency surgery, and setting up forward field hospitals. During one intense battle against the Egyptians near Iraq Suweidan on July 18 and 19, Dr. Stanley Levin performed a straight thirty-six hours of surgery, operating on twenty-eight wounded soldiers without a break.[34]

V

In the pre-dawn darkness of Sunday, July 11, 1948, a ramshackle B-17 took off from Tulsa Airport in Oklahoma with Swifty Schindler at the controls and headed northeast towards the Atlantic coast. Several hours later Schindler put the bomber down at a quiet suburban airport, used by private flyers, in Westchester, New York. Small, single-engine planes were parked around the field, so it was not surprising that a big four-engine bomber rolling down the runway at 6:00 a.m. should attract a great deal of attention.[35] On the flight from Oklahoma Schindler had noticed that his number-four engine was leaking oil and had decided to try to repair it before flying on across the Atlantic. A small group of volunteers recruited through Service Airways had been waiting to board the bomber, and they were pressed into service to help out. After several hours the engine appeared to be running properly. It was filled with oil while the wing tanks and two auxiliary tanks in the bomb bay were topped up with aviation gas. Schindler then took the bomber up for a few circuits of the field to make sure the engine was performing properly.[36]

The bomber's prolonged presence at the normally quiet suburban airport attracted considerable attention. Within a short time the newspapers were informed that something strange was going on and the New York *Herald Tribune* chartered a plane and sent three reporters and a photographer to see what was happening.[37] When the *Herald Tribune* plane landed at Westchester, the newspapermen kept a close watch on the bomber and tried to interview the crew, even though Schindler and his men refused to talk and continued to work on the plane until early afternoon. They then threw their gear aboard and climbed in. Schindler had filed a flight plan for California; without further ado, he ran up his engines, taxied to the end of the runway, and took off. The *Herald Tribune* plane followed in hot pursuit.[38]

Schindler's B-17 was the last of the four that had been purchased earlier by Schwimmer and was only one of a collection of bombers and transports scattered around the country awaiting crews to fly them to Israel. Schwimmer knew that the FBI was breathing down his neck and had planned a mass exodus of the planes for July 11; but before they could be flown out of the country, federal agents had swooped in and tried to seize the lot.[39] Somehow, they missed the B-17 and Schindler, who had been assigned to fly it, was determined to get it out of the country as quickly as possible. When he took off from Westchester on the afternoon of July 11, he headed northeast, planning to fly the great circle route to the Azores, passing south of Nova Scotia. As the bomber approached the Canadian coast, however, darkness began to fall and the weather started to deteriorate. The navigation equipment aboard the B-17 was in bad condition and Schindler worried that he would soon be lost over the ocean at night. He had little experience flying B-17s and he decided to head for Halifax.[40] He contacted the Royal Canadian Air Force station at Dartmouth for landing instructions, telling the RCAF that he was part of the "Overseas Air Training Corps" making a night flight over the Atlantic to brush up on stellar navigation, and received permission to land. The *Herald Tribune* plane was close behind.[41]

Although base personnel were at first confused about the bomber and its crew—Schindler and his men gave false names and continued to stick to the training story—the RCAF promptly informed Ottawa, which passed the word to the U.S. government. Less than a week before, Canada had agreed to inform Washington "of any activity by United States planes which [was] inconsistent with the intent of United Nations Security Council resolutions regarding the Palestine truce...".[42]

168

The State Department asked the Canadians to hold the B-17 "on one pretext or another" and, on the afternoon of July 12, Air Commodore Wait, Officer Commanding Eastern Air Command of the RCAF, received orders to detain the plane "even if it were necessary to run a truck across the runway to do so". By then Wait had concluded that Schindler and his crew were "on their way to join the Haganah in Palestine".[43] The American flyers were confined to the Halifax-Dartmouth area by the Royal Canadian Mounted Police, who kept them under constant observation. Their bomber was given a thorough inspection by the Collector of Customs and by representatives from the U.S. consulate. The inspectors found navigation charts of the Mediterranean area, enough food and the personal effects needed for a long flight, several pistols with a supply of ammunition, and cardboard boxes filled with bomb shackles.[44]

Although the Canadian government was just as interested in enforcing the U.N. embargo on arms shipments to Palestine as the government of the United States, it could clearly not hold the B-17 forever without reason. On July 14, the U.S. Ambassador in Ottawa was informed that, unless he made a formal request, by noon, to detain the plane, it would be released with just enough fuel to return to Westchester airport. Washington was in a bind. Such a request would take time to work out, and one State Department official concluded that, under the circumstances, "the best thing to do was to let the Canadians release the plane with a minimum amount of gas."[45] In preparation for this, the U.S. Consulate at Halifax warned United States Air Force bases at Argentia and Stephenville, Newfoundland, not to refuel the bomber should it land there, and Canadian authorities alerted all airports in eastern Canada to be on the lookout for the plane.[46]

The next morning Schindler and his crew were given permission to leave on condition that they return to the Westchester airport. (The *Herald Tribune* plane had already departed.) The bomb shackles, pistols, and ammunition were given back and a $100 fine was levied for "illegal entry into Canada". One thousand gallons of gasoline were taken from the bomber leaving, in the estimation of the officer in charge, 1200 or 1300 gallons—enough for a return trip with some margin of safety. At 4:50 p.m. the bomber took off, but returned to the field shortly after with engine trouble. Base personnel removed the batteries for the night, and the small arms and bomb shackles were also taken from the plane. At 4:30 p.m. the next day Schindler made another try. As the bomber roared down the runway, a United States Coast Guard plane circled the field waiting to escort it back to the United States. However, once again mechanical troubles intervened. One engine cowling flew off as the plane lifted into the air and two more cowlings tore loose as the B-17 came back to land. The Coast Guard plane returned to the United States and the bomber crew got busy making the necessary repairs. They were able to fix the two cowlings that had fallen off on landing, but the cover to the number-four engine had fallen into the sea.

At 8:20 p.m. the next evening, Schindler took off,[47] headed east, and kept low to avoid radar. Several hours out of Dartmouth the number-four engine began to heat up and Schindler was forced to shut it down and feather the prop: the B-17 continued on three engines. In the early morning hours of July 18, the plane landed in the Azores.[48] It will never by known for certain how Schindler was able to foil the best-laid plans of the RCAF and the U.S. State Department. One version of the story claims that members of the local Jewish community fuelled the plane at night, bringing gas on to the base in the back seats and trunks of their cars. Another asserts that the maintenance men at the base sympathized with the crew's objectives and refilled the fuel tanks. Either possibility could only have taken place if large numbers of base personnel had collaborated with Schindler, and this is highly unlikely.

After the B-17 had reached the Azores, the U.S. Consul at Halifax discovered to his chagrin that Schindler's bomber carried auxiliary fuel tanks. He further learned that the officer in charge of fuelling the B-17 had not been able to guess how much gas was in the tanks and had decided how much to put aboard the bomber only after Schindler had told him that the auxiliary tanks were "empty except for 20 gallons". This formed the basis for his decision to leave 1200 to 1300 gallons in the wing tanks of the B-17,[49] which probably gave Schindler enough gas, with careful flying and constant monitoring of his reserves, to reach the Azores, especially on three engines. It was, RCAF officials told the press, "a brilliant piece of flying".[50]

Schindler's daring availed him nothing. Teddy Kollek's organization in New York had tried to make arrangements to bribe local officials in the Azores to allow the plane to continue, but the plan fell apart when the crew decided to rest for a few hours before departure instead of refuelling immediately. The American consulate at Ponta Delgada flashed a message to Washington as soon as it discovered that the missing B-17 had made it across the ocean. The wheels of diplomacy began to grind and Schindler and his plane were caught.[51] The Portuguese detained the plane and crew, drained every drop of gasoline from the tanks, took out vital engine parts, and parked the bomber facing a hangar wall.[52] The plane was later returned to the United States by an American military crew, and Schindler and the others were flown directly back to the United States—aboard a commercial flight, and at their own expense—to face charges.[53]

VI

On July 14, a silver LAPSA C-46 landed at Zatec carrying several Air Transport Command pilots, navigators, and bombardiers, and a dozen or so South Africans with aerial gunnery experience. Heyman Shamir and Dov Judah, a South African working in Air Force headquarters, were also aboard. Shamir and Judah carried orders that the three bombers were to depart the next morning, bomb Cairo, Gaza, and El Arish, and proceed to Israel.[54] The planes had been equipped with a collection of Czech machine guns (there were still no turrets) fixed to fire from the tail, waist, dorsal, and nose positions. As well, a German bombsight had been fitted into the lead ship. This was the plane selected to hit Cairo and two men were picked to fly it: Bill Katz, an experienced B-17 pilot who had served with the Eighth Air Force during World War II piloted the craft, while Ray Kurtz, the mission commander, flew as co-pilot.[55] The other two planes were flown by Norman Moonitz and Al Raisen.

The three heavily laden B-17s struggled into the air on July 15 at 10:00 a.m. Each plane carried a full fuel load and twelve 500-pound bombs. The lead plane was stricken with mechanical difficulties from the start—two amplifiers had burnt out, the prop governor on one engine was frozen at 2400 rpm, the manifold pressure on another would not go above eighteen inches, and the artificial horizon was not working. A jerry-rigged oxygen system had been installed using cylinders of welders' oxygen that did not put out enough pressure to keep crew members breathing normally above 3048 metres.[56] Several of the men kept passing out on the long flight, and Katz was forced to stay as low as the security of the mission would allow.

The bombers stayed in loose formation as they flew south towards Austria, but separated on the long climb to clear the Alps. The peaks were shrouded in towering cumulus, and the bombers were forced to fly through the vicious air currents inside the clouds. The two pilots in the lead ship were severely handicapped by the lack of an artificial horizon and could barely keep the bomber right side up. However, the three bombers soon broke clear of the clouds, formed up again, and nosed into a shallow descent towards the Adriatic. They planned to follow the coastlines of Yugoslavia, Albania, and Greece to just west of Crete, at which point each plane would head for its assigned target. As the small formation flew past Albania, Katz was startled when several puffs of black smoke blossomed off the left side of his aircraft. He had not seen flak for several years but he quickly realized his plane was being fired on and made a course correction to take the group away from the anti-aircraft fire.[57]

The planes split up west of Crete and Katz headed towards the Libyan Plateau. He crossed the Egyptian coast near the Qattara Depression, turned due east towards Cairo, and climbed to 7620 metres. He intended to follow the route used by commercial aircraft to approach the Egyptian capital; his navigator tuned in on the Fayid Beacon and Cairo Radio to take navigational fixes. As the bomber drew near Cairo, Katz pointed the nose towards the centre of the city. The sun was setting and the lights of Cairo were blinking on as the bombardier aimed for King Farouk's palace and Katz opened the bomb bay doors. The entire load was released at once and Katz then nosed the bomber down and headed for Israel. The other two planes bombed Gaza, and Rafah instead of El Arish, which could not be found in the dark. Aside from a few rounds of anti-aircraft fire directed at one of the planes from a British base near Rafah, none of the bombers encountered any opposition.[58] Finally, after eleven and a half hours in the air, the B-17s touched down at Ekron, where they stayed overnight before flying on to their new base at Ramat David.

The bombers were pressed into service the next morning. Together they attacked El Arish on July 16th, Mishmar Hayarden on the 17th, and Majdal, Mishmar Hayarden, and Tulkarm on the 18th.[59] The missions were never long—the attack on Tulkarm, the farthest target from Ramat David, took only three hours from takeoff to landing—and the bombers encountered no fighter opposition at all and only scattered rounds of inaccurate flak. The planes were generally used to attack military targets, probably because they were far more accurate and could carry much heavier bombs than the bombchucking Dakotas. Attacks by B-17s on civilian targets were infrequent and were made in retaliation for Arab bombings of Tel Aviv and Haifa. In a July 17 attack on Tel Aviv, for example, Egyptian bombers struck a hospital and almshouse, killing sixty people;[60] the following day the B-17s hit Damascus killing fourteen.[61]

The bombchucking also continued, but with a new twist. C-46s bound for Zatec now often took a load of bombs aboard before leaving Israel and flew to attack Egyptian targets like Gaza, El Arish, Majdal, and Faluja before flying on to Europe. There they took aboard weapons and ammunition for the return flight to Israel. Dakotas were also used on bombing missions—usually flying from Ramat David and attacking Syrian targets—when they were not ferrying supplies to Israeli outposts and isolated settlements. On one night mission to Damascus, a bomb thrown out of the door of a Dakota hit its tail-control surfaces and the plane went into a sudden spiral dive. The pilot, a South African, panicked and crawled to the back, giving orders to bail out, but his co-pilot managed to grab the controls and pull the plane out of the dive. With the Dakota shuddering and groaning, he flew back to Ramat David and brought the plane in on its belly.[62]

VII

After fighting resumed on July 9 supplies of Czech arms were as vital to Israel as ever. Air Transport Command redoubled its efforts to continue the flow of weapons into the country. The French government continued to ignore the highly irregular landings at Ajaccio, but it was under increasing pressure from the United States to stop the traffic to Israel. It was clearly only a matter of time before the French would clamp down and the air bridge to Zatec would be dealt a serious blow. If the airborne flow of arms was to be ensured, an alternative to Ajaccio was needed.

Yugoslavia provided the answer. Israeli representatives obtained permission from the Belgrade government to use an abandoned airfield near the small town of Podgorica in Montenegro, on the Albanian border. The government placed a number of Yugoslav air force personnel at the disposal of the Israelis to help load the planes and guard the field; they also insisted on total secrecy. There was no food or aviation fuel available at the strip and everything had to be brought from Israel by ship to the nearby port of Kotor. Although the

173

Israelis slept in Podgorica, they were forbidden to buy supplies in town or to make any unnecessary contacts with the townspeople. The Israelis brought radio equipment from home to keep in touch with Prague and Tel Aviv and, shortly after they arrived at the field, the first planes began to land. When the French finally closed Ajaccio to Israel, Podgorica became the main stopping point from Zatec to Ekron.[63]

The Israeli Air Force continued to have difficulties with its Czech Avia fighters, although they were used constantly to provide cover for ground troops and launch strafing attacks against enemy strongpoints. The planes' inherent mechanical problems were a serious handicap and it was all too obvious that something better was needed. Again the air force turned to the Czechs. During World War II a large number of Czech pilots had made their way to England to fly in Czech-speaking squadrons of the Royal Air Force. They were provided with Mark IX Spitfire fighters and, when the war ended, they were permitted to take their planes back to Czechoslovakia.[64] By 1948 the planes were out of date. After the Communist takeover in February of that year, the Czech government was anxious to phase the Spitfires out and replace them with more up-to-date Russian equipment. The Israelis badly needed the British-built fighters and the Czechs agreed to sell them fifty-nine planes with spare parts for $23,000 apiece. The contract was signed on July 15.[65]

VIII

Within days after the resumption of hostilities, Israeli forces had pushed back Arab armies on two fronts but had failed to make significant headway on two others. In the far north, Syrian and Lebanese forces continued to hold positions on Israeli territory. The Israelis virtually ignored the Lebanese, the lesser of the two threats, and launched repeated attacks to dislodge the Syrians. At the same time, the Syrians were trying to break out of their salient at Mishmar Hayarden. There was heavy fighting but neither side could gain an advantage. To the southwest of the Syrian front the Israelis were more successful. Dunkelman's capture of Nazareth and the areas to the north and east of the town pushed Kaukji's Arab Liberation Army farther from Haifa and Acre and closer to the Lebanese frontier and strengthened the Jewish hold on the lower Galilee.

The major battles after the breakdown of the truce occurred in the central sector along the road to Jerusalem. Israelis were successful in strengthening their tenuous hold on the road from Tel Aviv to Jerusalem, pushing the Transjordan Arab Legion forces back north of Latrun and capturing Lydda, Ramle, and the important Lydda airport. Although the Legion continued to hold the Latrun police post, it was increasingly isolated and now stood at the end of a finger of Jordanian territory poking southwest into a widening Israeli corridor. An IDF attempt to re-take the old city of Jerusalem failed; thereafter, for the duration of the war, the Jordanian-Israeli front remained stable. King Abdullah had achieved his main war objectives of taking over the intended heartland of Arab Palestine in Judea and Samaria and the old city of Jerusalem. Israel, though it had lost the Jewish quarter of the old city, including the sacred Western Wall, had re-established communications with Jewish Jerusalem. Henceforth Israel's main efforts would be in the south where it would try to evict the Egyptians from the Negev. On that front Egyptian attacks to the northeast had made some progress before being halted by Israeli troops. Now, however, the IDF was having difficulty breaking through to the south to open lines of communication with the besieged settlements in the Negev.

As soon as the ceasefire ended, Count Bernadotte had intensified his efforts to bring an end to the fighting and to find a political solution to the Palestine question. Discussions with King Abdullah in Amman appeared to Bernadotte to offer hope that quick and resolute Security Council action to impose a ceasefire might provide the leeway necessary to break the political stalemate. Abdullah, in Bernadotte's opinion, "appeared not to be quite negative to the idea of a partition of Palestine" and even demanded "that in such a case certain exchanges of people should take place" so that the Jews would be in a clear majority in their part of Palestine while the Arabs would predominate in theirs. When Bernadotte arrived in New York he strove to convince the Security Council to order another ceasefire.

The Soviet Union and its allies attacked Bernadotte, but with British and American support he was able to line up the votes for a U.S. draft resolution that was adopted by the Security Council on July 15. That resolution ordered the governments and authorities concerned to cease fire on July 18 and threatened sanctions if they failed to comply. The Security Council also ordered "as a matter of special and urgent necessity" that fighting in Jerusalem be stopped within twenty-four hours. In contrast to the first truce, no time limit was set for the ceasefire.[66] The Israeli government announced acceptance the next day. The Arab League notified the United Nations of its acceptance of the Jerusalem ceasefire order on July 17; on July 18 it notified the United Nations that it would also comply with the general ceasefire order. At 7:00 p.m. on July 18, after ten days of fighting, a second truce took hold in Palestine.

9

"Truce Is Not Peace"

The small hilltop near Tamra, a village ten kilometres southeast of Acre, was held by an unknown number of Arab Liberation Army snipers who refused to observe the formalities of the U.N. truce. Just after dusk on September 7, Company B of the 72nd Battalion, an all-volunteer, English-speaking unit of Dunkelman's Seventh Brigade, was trucked to Tamra in preparation for an assault on the hill. The men crawled up the base of the hill and waited through the first hours of darkness. Israeli mortars opened up at 1:30 a.m. and shelled the hill for about thirty minutes. At 2:00 a.m. the order was passed along to move up, and Company B pushed its way to the hilltop, scattered the Arab defenders, and started to dig in. The men had no entrenching tools and instead used bayonets, helmets, and bare hands to scratch out defensive positions among the rocks.[1]

The Arab guerrillas returned with the dawn. They kept Company B pinned down with sniper fire as they worked their way around the slopes to surround the hilltop on three sides. Then platoon leader Aya Feldman gave the order to fix bayonets and the men of Company B rushed the Arabs and pushed them back off the hill. It was the only bayonet charge mounted by the Israeli army in the entire war.[2] The constant shooting took its toll: several men were badly wounded; three were killed. The medics, dodging bullets, worked all day to carry the dead and wounded down the steep slopes of the hill to Tamra where a temporary aid station had been set up. South African medic Locky Fainman wrote in his diary: ". . . I was covered in blood and filth. Even my cigarettes were soaked in blood. I was completely exhausted and found a bed in a house where I was only too happy to remove all my clothes and sleep until the next morning at six o'clock, when we were relieved."[3] This was the face of truce in northern Israel.

The U.N. truce of July 18 was imposed on both sides by threats of heavy economic sanctions. Bernadotte was determined to enforce the ceasefire, with its embargoes on the import of war materials and the arrival of reinforcements from abroad. Almost immediately he set about building a truce-supervisory establishment even larger than that used in the first truce. The Chief of Staff of the observer force was Swedish Air Force Major Age Lundstrom. From his Haifa headquarters, Lundstrom commanded more than three hundred officers from Sweden, France, Belgium, and the United States. Once again, the United States supplied the bulk of the necessary equipment—planes, ships, jeeps, and trucks—supplemented by contributions from France and Britain. The observer corps concentrated its truce-supervision efforts on Israel: 127 officers were stationed there, while 69 were placed in the Arab states, 40 in Arab Palestine, and 79 in Jerusalem.[4]

It is clear that Bernadotte intended to turn this ceasefire into a permanent peace. By the end of June he had worked out a set of proposals that, he believed, formed a good basis for a compromise settlement. Bernadotte's plan proposed the joining of Arab Palestine, the Negev, and Jerusalem to Transjordan, which would be united in an economic and political union with Israel. Haifa and Lydda were to become free zones, the western Galilee was to become part of Israel, and Jewish immigration would, after two years, come under the control of the United Nations Economic and Social Council. All Arab refugees were to be allowed to return to their homes and were to have their property restored.

Israel refused to accept the plan. Bernadotte's proposals would mean a loss of territory assigned to Israel by the partition plan, a major restriction on its sovereignty, including its rights to control its own immigration, and the forced repatriation of thousands of Arabs, many of whom had already demonstrated their implacable hostility to the new state. The Arabs condemned the plan because it still allowed a sovereign Jewish state, however truncated, to exist in the area. In addition, inter-Arab rivalry made any acceptance of the plan by Transjordan—its chief beneficiary—impossible.

For the next three months, in Sweden and on Rhodes, Bernadotte worked to modify his proposals into a form more acceptable to both sides and, more important, acceptable to the Great Powers at the United Nations. On September 16 he sent his revised peace plan to the

Security Council. This time he accepted the reality of Israeli existence as "a living, solidly entrenched and vigorous reality" and dropped the idea of a Transjordan-Israel union. Jerusalem was now proposed as an international zone under U.N. control. All of the Galilee was to be assigned to Israel, but the Negev was still to be joined to Transjordan, as were Ramle and Lydda, while the Arab refugees were to be repatriated.

Although Israel and the Arabs rejected this plan with no less vehemence than they had rejected the first, it appeared to find support in the U.S. State Department and the British Foreign Office. These two parties saw it as a basis for settlement between Arabs and Jews that would also allow the United States and Britain to patch up their differences over the Palestine question.[5]

Throughout the summer there had been a growing inclination in Israeli government circles to regard Bernadotte as a pro-Arab, pro-British agent and to mistrust the U.N. truce observers who worked for Bernadotte. In the ranks of the Lehi, this feeling soon hardened into a determination to destroy Bernadotte before his schemes won the support of the United States and United Nations and became the basis for the emergence of a truncated Israel. On September 17, one day after the proposals were placed before the United Nations in New York, Bernadotte was driving through the streets of Jewish Jerusalem on the way back to his headquarters in the city when his car was stopped and he was shot to death, along with an aide. The Israeli government expressed its shock and indignation and issued the necessary apologies. It undertook a mass arrest of Lehi members and ordered the dissolution of both the Lehi and the Irgun. However, no one was prosecuted for the killing, and those arrested were eventually released.[6]

II

On August 20, a tramp steamer slipped out of the port of Bari, Italy, and headed out to sea. It carried 8500 rifles destined for Syria. The rifles had been salvaged from the original 10,000 that had been sold to Syria by Czechoslovakia in the spring, and that were supposed to be shipped to the Syrians aboard the steamer *Lino*. The Haganah had uncovered this operation, and the *Lino*'s hull was blown open by a limpet mine. Much of the cargo was salvaged, however, and placed aboard a second ship, this time in the care of a Syrian officer. Israeli agents kept a close watch on the salvage operation and managed to place two of their number among the engine-room crew. When the ship sailed out past Italian territorial waters, the engines were shut down because of a "malfunction". The ship drifted until it was boarded by two "Syrian" officers from a fishing boat who turned out to be Israelis and who then directed the ship and cargo to Israel.[7]

Arabs and Israelis alike did their best to violate the U.N. embargo; Israelis did it better. Ironically, the Arab countries were now at a disadvantage in their efforts to cheat because their major source of supply for military equipment prior to May 30 had been Great Britain and the British were extremely reluctant to violate the embargo and have the Americans catch them at it. It was not that the British did not consider making "exceptions" under the embargo; it was simply that they felt the disapproving stare of the State Department scrutinizing their every action. This put Britain's Arab allies in a bind. Prior to May 30, they had not needed to develop clandestine arms-supply sources of their own—they received everything from Whitehall. Now they faced a shortage of replacements, spare parts, and ammunition.

On July 27, Transjordan Prime Minister Tewfig claimed, in an urgent message to British Foreign Secretary Ernest Bevin, that the Arab Legion was "desperate owing to the exhaustion of equipment and of ammunition both for artillery and small arms". If attacked by Israel, Tewfig declared, the Arab Legion was "defenceless" and would not be able to stay in Palestine "a single day". Tewfig implored Bevin to provide the Arab Legion "with the means of serving our joint interests in the Middle East" and demanded, at the very least, that "sufficient war material to enable [the Arab Legion] to repel the Jewish attacks" be made available at the Royal Air Force base at Amman.[8] Tewfig's assessment was confirmed by Arab Legion Commander Glubb, and his request for aid was supported by the British Ambassador in Amman.[9]

Iraq also approached London to request a resumption of arms shipments. It had been the biggest loser among the Arab states when the British cut off arms shipments at the end of May. The Iraqi government tried to strengthen its case by pointing to the growing Cold War tension between East and West over Berlin, claiming that it would be easy for the Russians to "make trouble" in Kurdistan. The British Ambassador in Baghdad cabled London that the Iraqis were "concerned at their shortage of weapons to suppress such trouble" and passed along the Iraqi prime minister's assurance that British arms would not be used in Palestine.[10]

The British military strongly favoured resuming arms shipments to Iraq and Transjordan. The Imperial General Staff pointed out that Israel had used the truce to build up its forces while the Arabs had been unable to rearm because the United Kingdom, their "only considerable source", had strictly observed the embargo. This body further claimed that the policy had led to a rapid growth of anti-British feeling in Transjordan, Iraq, and Egypt, and would have continuing repercussions on Arab-British relations as well as on the performance of the Arab armies.[11] What they did not mention was that, as late as August, Britain was still directly supporting the Transjordan war effort by continuing to subsidize the Arab Legion.[12]

The Imperial General Staff's forecasts of disaster were endorsed by Viscount Alexander, Britain's Minister of Defence. Alexander believed that an Israeli attack on the Transjordan Arab Legion "might mean disaster" and an almost total withdrawal of the Legion from Palestine. This would "almost certainly" lead to the destruction of Arab military control over the Arab portions of Palestine, which would be blamed on Britain and which would give Egypt an excuse to demand the removal of British forces there.[13] Alexander, after conferring with Lord Tedder, Chairman of the Chiefs of Staff Committee, urged Bevin to authorize the shipment of stores for the Transjordan and Iraqi forces to the RAF bases at Amman and Habbaniya "under the cover plan of ostensibly being for the security of British forces in both countries". Weapons could then be issued "against authority from London" if Israel broke the truce.[14]

The suggestion was taken up with the State Department in Washington, which responded almost immediately with the statement that it "did not care for the proposal" since reaction in the United States would be "strong and unfavorable". The British tried to convince the U.S. Ambassador in London that the arms shipments were necessary for the defence of British troops in the area. They asked him "what choice would the United States government make if the War Department found themselves in a similar situation?" but gave no evidence to show that an Israeli attack on British installations was imminent.[15] The State Department was willing to agree to any measures the British might take to protect their troops or installations, but pointed out to the Foreign Office in no uncertain terms that London must take "full responsibility for distinguishing between protection of British forces and installations and assistance to the Arabs in Palestine".[16] If the

British were asking the Americans to look the other way, the United States was clearly not prepared to do so.

The British were back where they had been in May and were still reluctant to fall foul of the United States. Bevin, therefore, put an end to the matter by telling Viscount Alexander that for the moment Britain should go no further than ensuring that supplies of ammunition could be flown to Transjordan "at a moment's notice should the integrity of Transjordan be threatened". "It would be better," Bevin believed, "not to run the risk of breaking the truce...and so, perhaps, of giving just the excuse which the Jewish extremists will want in order to take action on their side...."[17] The Arab countries were stuck.

III

On the first day of the truce, the small Panamanian steamer *Kefalos* began to take on cargo in the Mexican port of Tampico. The ship had tied up on June 24, but loaded nothing until July 19. Then thirty-seven carloads of surplus Mexican arms were placed aboard. The arms purchases had been arranged through the New York office of Teddy Kollek.

When the *Kefalos* sailed it carried 36 French-built 75 mm cannon, 17,000 shells, 2000 bombs, 500 machine guns, 7 million rounds of ammunition, and several thousand gallons of aviation gasoline. The entire cargo was topped off with 1400 tons of sugar to fool prying eyes should the *Kefalos* be stopped at sea.[18]

The ship was only one of several plying the sea lanes towards Palestine with arms for the Israeli forces. In late July the Panamanian steamer *Sorol* arrived at the port of Haifa with a cargo of "agricultural equipment" that included a deck load of half tracks.[19] On August 12, another ship of Panamanian registry, the *Enterprise*, arrived in Tel Aviv from New York and St. John, New Brunswick, with 3500 tons of cargo, including 48 jeeps, 6 trucks, and 24 tons of radio sets and parts.[20] In September the steamers *Borea*, *Resurrection*, and *Arsin* brought 30 discarded Sherman tanks to Israel; and in October a ship from Antwerp brought signalling equipment, batteries, aviation fuel, cars, motorcycles, trailers, and 50 jeeps that were later equipped with machine guns and sent to the Negev.[21]

During the ten days of fighting that preceded the truce, Israeli forces had started to turn the tide of battle. They had gone over to the offensive on every major front, even though they did not totally defeat any Arab army (with the exception of Kaukji's irregulars) and did not drive the Arabs out of the areas designated as part of the Jewish state by the United Nations in November 1947. The Israeli attitude towards the truce was moulded by the results of the ten days' fighting and the expectation that war would break out again sooner or later. The policy was "truce is not peace, be prepared."[22]

The struggles against the Syrians, Jordanians, and Egyptians had once again revealed the desperate need for modern military equipment; on every front battles had been lost and troops had died because tanks, planes, or artillery were not available to support assaults on the enemy's positions. This was true at Mishmar Hayarden, Latrun, and in the fighting against the Egyptian army in the northern Negev. It was clear that the Arabs were still better equipped than the Israelis. Israeli efforts to build up the army's striking power therefore continued throughout the truce.

The armed forces were also expanded and reorganized. At the start of the first truce in June, the Israeli forces included approximately forty-nine thousand troops; by October 15 this had grown to about ninety thousand men and women, larger than any of the Arab armies.[23] A large part of this increase came from internal recruitment and conscription, but some also resulted from the continuing arrival of *gahal* recruits from the displaced persons camps and *mahal* volunteers from abroad. Despite the best efforts of the U.N. truce observers to stem the flow of immigrants of military age, ships continued to dock at Tel Aviv and Haifa carrying Jewish refugees with volunteers mixed among them. The Israelis were anxious to empty the refugee camps in southern France as quickly as possible and increasing numbers of volunteers were flown directly to Israel from the Marseilles area aboard chartered aircraft. All were provided with false identity papers to enable them to escape the scrutiny of U.N. observers.

Many of the English-speaking arrivals were assigned to the 72nd Battalion of the Seventh Brigade, which soon became known as the "Anglo-Saxon" Battalion because of the three hundred or so foreign volunteers in its ranks from Canada, the United States, Great Britain, and South Africa.[24] Other volunteers sought duty in the navy and air force, while a growing number signed up with Palmach brigades in the south or the Jerusalem area. The Palmach had once been a small, elite strike force, but the necessities of war and the integration of the

183

Palmach into the new Israeli Army forced it to expand rapidly to approximately three times its pre-war size. It seemed to attract a large number of men and women who were drawn by the romance of the Palmach and welcomed the chance to become part of Hebrew-speaking units made up entirely of Israelis.[25] There was, in fact, some reluctance on the part of a number of English-speaking volunteers to join the Anglo-Saxon Battalion. These volunteers believed that they would not have an opportunity to learn much about the country or its people while serving primarily with those who shared the same basic background, cultural values, and language.

By contrast, French-speaking volunteers from France and North Africa had a strong desire to serve in an all-French unit. Such a group was formed in August under the leadership of Teddy Eytan, who had been commissioned as a major in the Israeli Army. Eytan was given the job of moulding 350 French-speaking volunteers into the 75th Battalion, but problems surfaced almost immediately. There were too few weapons, accommodation was poor, and no Israeli officers showed up to help integrate the French volunteers into the army. Moreover, the pay—two Israeli pounds a month—was five pounds less than that earned by English-speaking and Scandinavian volunteers, whose army pay was subsidized through contributions from Jewish communities abroad.[26]

Eytan was disappointed at the apparent lack of effort on the part of the high command to make the 75th a viable fighting unit. Discipline problems grew more severe with each passing day and desertions were increasing. Towards the end of August Eytan made his wishes known. He wanted the manpower branch of Army headquarters to allow French-speaking volunteers to join the 75th without interference. Up until then, many had been directed into other units, particularly the Palmach, even though they wanted to serve with Eytan. He asked for a raise in army pay, pointing out that two pounds a month was not sufficient for troops who had no family or relatives in the country to supply them with food or accommodation. He emphasized the need to motivate the French volunteers by creating a unit *esprit de corps* and by educating his men in the history and principles of the Zionist movement. Finally, he asked for the assignment to his unit of bilingual officers who could communicate with the troops and who understood their special needs.[27]

Despite Eytan's efforts, the 75th Battalion experiment ended in failure. There was a feeling in the high command that Eytan was working with poor material—soldiers with little motivation, some of whom were common criminals.[28] Eytan gave up and concentrated instead on the formation of a small, elite unit formed of French and North African volunteers which he named "Le Commando Français" and which was attached to the Negev Brigade of the Palmach.

IV

In mid-July two men in civilian clothes slipped past the U.N. personnel stationed at Lydda airport, climbed into a waiting car, and were whisked away to meet David Ben Gurion. One of the men was Cecil Margo, a former Lieutenant Colonel in the South African Air Force. Margo had flown more than one hundred operational missions as a bomber pilot in World War II and had been promoted to squadron commander in 1944. The other was Trevor Sussman, another veteran of the South African Air Force, who had come to aid Margo in his mission in Israel. Margo had been invited to the country by Ben Gurion to improve and reorganize the Israeli Air Force. At their first meeting, he was given *carte blanche* to examine all aspects of the air force and prepare a report for Ben Gurion. He set out almost immediately on a ten-day fact-finding mission that brought him to every air force installation and into contact with almost every important air force officer in the country.[29] Towards the end of July, he submitted his report.

Margo aimed to produce a small but highly efficient air force capable of getting the greatest use out of the smallest practical number of aircraft. He put great stress on the use of multi-mission fighter bombers that could attack and destroy enemy aircraft, perform close-support missions for the army, and fly long-range reconnaissance patrols. Such aircraft had to be capable of carrying additional fuel tanks and, ideally, should be armed with a variety of weapons, from bombs to machine guns and cannons. Margo suggested that the air force adopt the practice of overhauling aircraft and replacing components on a regularly scheduled basis. He outlined a basic structure of three fighter squadrons, one squadron of heavy bombers (the three B-17s), a squadron of Dakotas, and a reorganized Air Transport Command. He also suggested a list of priorities for the air force. These included: destroying the enemy air forces; aiding land and sea forces;

attacking the principal strategic targets of the enemy; organizing domestic and external transport; and training new air crews.

To accomplish these objectives, Margo outlined a rigorous training program to qualify pilots and air crew for instrument and night flying under all weather conditions. He pointed to the need to establish a proper air staff to undertake strategic planning, and, for its support, a well-run air-intelligence service. Margo suggested that Aharon Remez be confirmed as Commander-in-Chief of the air force with Heyman Shamir as his deputy, that Dov Judah, a South African, become Director of Operations, and that Smoky Simon, another South African, be made Chief of Air Operations.[30]

There was much wisdom in Margo's suggestions and, in fact, the modern Israeli Air Force has been built on the concept of maximum utilization of multi-purpose aircraft. But in the summer of 1948 there was little chance that his recommendations could be acted upon quickly. Cost—over £1.6 million—was one problem; but lack of time and the inability to acquire aircraft were also important obstacles. The air force that Margo found was a grab-bag affair because any and every plane that became available had been brought to Israel and pressed into service. Starting in early May 1948, in the short space of ten weeks, the air force had grown rapidly in both planes and manpower and it had not been possible to control or channel that growth effectively. Ben Gurion offered Margo command of the air force but the South African turned him down and left the country after little more than three weeks. Margo feared that the political structure of Israel would not allow him to develop his plans as he thought necessary and that he would be "wrecked on the rock of politics".[31]

V

Danny Cravitt, former bomber pilot with the United States Army Air Force, felt uneasy as he lifted his Dakota from the runway at Ramat David and headed south towards Nevatim. His new co-pilot, a recent addition to the squadron, had claimed extensive flying experience, but Cravitt was convinced after only a few minutes in the air that the man "had no idea what was going on, absolutely none". He seemed to know nothing about basic cockpit procedure. Cravitt knew that a Dakota could be flown by one man if necessary, but he also knew that it could be a difficult job and that planes approaching Nevatim were frequently

186

fired upon by the Arab forces surrounding the settlement. This night he had a full load, and he realized that without help he would have his hands full.

On the short flight the new man "talked a blue streak about his wartime experiences". Cravitt became more and more angry as he realized that his "co-pilot" was actually a fraud. By the time the plane was on final approach, tracer bullets were reaching up from the dark ground below, and Cravitt was swearing heavily as he barked instructions in preparation for landing. The landing was rough and the plane rolled off the edge of the runway into a mine field. As soon as the engine stopped, the other man tore off his harness, ran to the back of the plane, and prepared to jump to the ground. One of the men from the kibbutz who had opened the door shouted, "Don't move, you're in the middle of a minefield," and the ersatz co-pilot fainted and fell to the ground, missing the mines. It was his first and last mission.[32]

From the very start of the recruitment of foreign volunteers, glory-seeking liars had haunted Israeli recruiters and had managed to slip into the Israeli forces. But for every one of those there were many more like Danny Cravitt, skilled and conscientious flyers, who interrupted civilian careers to fly for Israel. During the second truce, large numbers poured into Israel and added considerably to the strength and depth of the air force, changing it from a shoestring, patchwork operation to a true air force. Although it still did not possess first-rate equipment, it could now carry out most of the necessary tasks of aerial warfare, from bomber and fighter operations to aerial reconnaissance and photography.

The number of squadrons was expanded and specialized roles were assigned to them, while more skilled personnel were either brought to the country or recruited from among foreign volunteers who were already in Israel. Canadian Yale Joffe, for example, had been a member of Landshut's gun crew but had been an experienced aerial photographer back home. He became one of a small number assigned to fly air force combat missions, recording the results of bombing raids and taking photographs of enemy positions. Skilled fighter pilots were also taken on. Among them were Canadian ace John McElroy, a former squadron leader with sixteen kills to his credit during World War II, and American Slick Goodlin. Goodlin had been a contract pilot for the Bell Aircraft Corporation and had test flown the Bell X-1 rocket plane prior to its first faster-than-sound flight in October 1947.

It is impossible to determine the exact ratio of foreign volunteers to Israelis in the air force, but it was high. From pilots and air crew to maintenance-crew chiefs, air-intelligence and reconnaissance specialists, and communications and radar personnel, almost everyone was a foreign volunteer. Remez and Shamir estimated at one point that volunteers made up the vast majority of pilots and air crew; 247 of these came from the United States, 143 from South Africa, 109 from Great Britain, and 60 from Canada.[33] The language of the air force was English, while command procedures were a mixture of American and British practice.

VI

Dave Panar, a Canadian aircraft engineer, surveyed the wreckage of the Egyptian Spitfire lying on the beach near Tel Aviv and slowly shook his head. The plane had been hit by rifle fire and the Egyptian pilot had made a wheels-up landing on the beach, damaging the propellor and tearing off a wing. There was no way to save it, Panar told the Israelis. They were undaunted. Panar was taken to several former RAF bases to see what seemed to be acres and acres of broken-up aircraft parts, air frames, and smashed engines, and tons of broken-up electronic gear, all lying out in the sun. Panar realized that working parts from one airfield might be mated with working parts from another. Within days a fuselage, wings, engine parts, and other components were brought to Herzliya to be constructed into a working Spitfire. The end product was a hybrid—the fuselage came from a photo-reconnaissance version of the Spitfire, while the wings were from a Mark IX fighter—but it performed beyond anyone's expectations. Much of the assembly was hit-or-miss; however, when the airplane took off on July 23, it flew as if it had come straight from the factory. It became Israel's first Spitfire to be used both for photographic reconnaissance missions and in combat. Later, a second Spitfire was constructed in much the same fashion.[34]

Although the Spitfire filled an immediate need, the air force still suffered from other important shortages. There were fighters, heavy bombers, light planes, and transports; but there were no attack bombers that could provide close, low-level support to ground troops. This type of aircraft was essential in the kind of war being fought in Palestine. In Britain, Freddy Fredkens came to the rescue and located four old Bristol Beaufighters—twin-engine attack bombers—which he purchased through Mayfair Air Services, a front company. A dummy

188

film-production corporation was then established to produce a screen drama about the exploits of New Zealand Beaufighter pilots during World War II, and the Beaufighters were leased to the corporation. On the morning of August 1, 1948, the four planes took off from Thames Airport in southern England, ostensibly to make several fly-pasts in front of the cameras. Instead, however, the pilots set course for the southeast and were next seen refuelling at Ajaccio, Corsica.[35]

The planes were in poor condition and were unarmed at first, until Israeli agents smuggled aircraft machine guns out of England in a chartered Halifax bomber, which crash-landed at Tel Aviv airport. The plane was a write-off, but cargo and crew were unscathed. The Beaufighters were then armed and three were kept in flying condition after the fourth had been cannibalized for parts.[36]

The Beaufighters were assigned to Ramat David airfield and became part of the newly formed 103 Squadron, which contained most of the twin-engine transports and bombers in the air force. The first two commanders of the squadron were Jimmy Blackwood and Danny Rosin, both South Africans. The majority of the air crews were also South Africans, with a handful of Americans and Canadians scattered among them.[37]

The squadron shared facilities at Ramat David with the B-17s, which were designated 69th Squadron. Ray Kurtz was the first commanding officer of the squadron, followed by Bill Katz.[38] To the south, at Ekron, another new squadron was formed during the truce using the Norseman aircraft that had been flown to Israel via Italy and Czechoslovakia. This was the 35th Squadron, which was first commanded by American Phil Marmelstein and later by Ted Gibson, a former pilot with the United States Navy and the son of a southern Baptist minister. The squadron's prime responsibility during the truce was to fly freight to the isolated settlements of the Negev, especially to the Palestine Potash Company works at Sdom, on the southern tip of the Dead Sea.

The trip to Sdom was one of the most unusual in Palestine. The supply aircraft took off from Ekron, headed southeast, and climbed to clear the hills of Judea just south of the ancient city of Hebron. The land near Hebron is about 900 metres above sea level, but Sdom, on the shores of the lowest body of water on earth, is almost 300 metres below sea level. The planes had to nose down after clearing the heights of the Judean hills and descend rapidly to the Dead Sea. All flights had to be made at night because the land below was occupied by the

189

Egyptian Army, and the descent in darkness, with the aircraft bobbing and lurching in the desert air currents, tried many a pilot's nerves. The landing strip at Sdom ran north-south on the western shore of the Dead Sea and had been laid out at the base of a cliff. The pilots were forced to fly over the Dead Sea, turn west, flick on their landing lights to pick out the bluffs that overhung the strip, and then turn sharply to the right just before touching down. The pilots and crews feared that forced landings en route would mean torture and mutilation by the Bedouins.[39]

While the 35th Squadron's prime responsibility was supplying Sdom, the Negev Squadron, based at Kibbutz Dorot, maintained a tenuous lifeline to the isolated Jewish settlements of the northern Negev. Most of these settlements had small, rough airstrips. The Negev Squadron consisted of a small number of single-engine light planes flown by a mixture of Americans and Israelis. It was commanded, during July, by Canadian Ralph Moster. The little fabric planes did triple duty—ferrying supplies, dropping small bombs, and bringing the sick and wounded to hospital. Shootings and small-scale clashes continued between Israelis and Egyptians during the ceasefire, and there was little let-up in pressure for the overworked fliers. Despite constant danger from Egyptian fighter planes, the squadron was often forced to fly in daylight on medical evacuation missions.[40]

VII

At the beginning of August, the State Department finally caught up with Operation Balak and Israel's Air Transport Command. The governments of the United States and Great Britain had known for some time that the Israelis were using the base at Zatec to ferry supplies to Israel in defiance of the U.N. embargo. Moreover, both clandestine ground observation and aerial reconnaissance confirmed that the Zatec base was as busy as ever at the start of the second truce. Because the Israelis feared the diplomatic pressure on the Czech government that was beginning to build, Balak flights were stepped up at the beginning of August. Eleven flights in one week, far more than the usual average, brought fifty tons of equipment—including the last batch of Avia fighters—to Israel. By the end of the first week in August the large stockpile of supplies that had been amassed at Zatec was beginning to dwindle.[41]

It was none too soon because, on August 11, Munya Mardor, Chief of Air Transport Command, received a warning cable from one of his representatives in Czechoslovakia. The U.S. government was about to make an official protest to the government of Czechoslovakia and the Czechs had issued instructions for the removal of all U.S. crews and aircraft from Zatec. The next day the Israelis were given twenty-four hours to clear out of Zatec. An immediate scramble began to collect crews from the two local hotels and pack everything that was still at the field aboard the remaining transports.[42] Everything was taken except Constellation RX 121, which had been damaged in a landing several weeks before. This was not the end of Czech military aid to Israel—flights continued on a sporadic basis until October[43]—but it marked the collapse of the regular air bridge that had brought hundreds of tons of arms and ammunition to the hard-pressed Jewish forces. After August 12 the continued presence of Israelis at Zatec—the airfield had effectively been an Israeli base in a foreign country—was ended when all ATC personnel were transferred to Ekron.

The final State Department blow to Air Transport Command came one month after the end of the Balak flights, when the United States finally convinced the government of Panama to revoke the registration of the LAPSA aircraft.[44] Henceforth, the C-46s were operated as part of the Israeli Air Force or were handed over to El Al, the new Israeli airline, which was formed in early 1949.

VIII

Despite the truce, killing continued on all fronts. In the north, Kaukji and his Arab Liberation Army refused to comply with the ceasefire order or to recognize the authority of the United Nations. Even though Israeli forces controlled the major towns and most of the roads of the central Galilee, Kaukji's irregulars continued to harass them from small villages and hilltop positions in the area west of Safed and north of Nazareth. The 72nd Battalion bore the brunt of the fighting, because the other two battalions of the Seventh Brigade had been withdrawn to the Nahariya area for rest, reorganization, and retraining.[45] This was a forgotten war of minor skirmishes in abandoned villages or on the rocky, terraced slopes of ancient hillsides. Even if the men of the 72nd thought that Kaukji was only an irritant and that his handful of guerrillas could no more endanger Israel or

191

change the course of the war than a swarm of desert flies, the wounds were no less painful and the deaths were no less sudden. The September 7 fight between Company B of the 72nd and Kaukji's ALA forces for the small hilltop near Tamra, ten kilometres southeast of Acre, was a short and brutal slugfest all too typical of the Galilee fighting.

On the Jerusalem front, Jordanians and Israelis settled into a deadly routine that usually began with a few scattered shots in the morning. This soon escalated to exchanges of machine-gun, mortar, and even artillery fire in the afternoon, then died out when U.N. truce observers intervened to arrange an end to the shooting.

These incidents were serious enough. However, it was the southern front that commanded Israel's primary attention. The July battles had ended in stalemate, with the Egyptians still in control of a band of territory from the coast north of Gaza across to the southern outskirts of Jerusalem. This meant that the Jewish settlements to the south were isolated. Both sides were forced to use a single road junction north of Huleiqat that was kept under constant U.N. supervision. For a number of hours each day the Egyptians would use the east-west road; the rest of the time, the Israelis would use the north-south road. At one point, just after the ceasefire, the Egyptians accused the Israelis of trying to widen their narrow road corridor and attacked several Israeli positions. The Israelis retaliated with attacks upon Egyptian positions. Although the attacks failed, the Israelis did succeed in pushing a large supply convoy through to their troops and settlers in the south.[46] The Israeli high command decided early in the truce that the next major effort in the war would be directed towards the total defeat of the Egyptian forces in central and southern Israel. The high command believed that King Abdullah's main objective—to annex Arab Palestine—had been achieved and that he would not order the Transjordan Arab Legion to aid the Egyptians. They further calculated that jealousies and rivalries would prompt Iraq, Syria, and Lebanon to tend to their own affairs. The Israelis planned, therefore, to concentrate the bulk of their forces against the Egyptians.

Planning for the offensive began in early August when Ben Gurion summoned Munya Mardor to a meeting along with several air force officers and military advisors, the Chief of Operations, Yigael Yadin, and the commander of the southern front, Yigal Allon. Ben Gurion told them that a campaign would soon begin against the Egyptians in the Negev and that it was essential both to transport at least 2000 tons

192

of supplies and equipment to the besieged settlements, and to replace the Negev Brigade with the Yiftah Brigade. A land operation was not feasible because it would be easily detected and would be subject to attack by Egyptian forces. Ben Gurion wanted to know what the Air Transport Command could do with its large C-46 aircraft, and Mardor told him that his main problem was the availability of fuel. Ben Gurion decided that fuel would somehow be found. He dismissed the confer-ence with the understanding that Air Transport Command would be responsible for the transfer of the troops and equipment. Thus was born Operation Dust.[47]

The isolated Negev setlements had been linked to each other and to the Jewish areas beyond the Egyptian lines by the planes of the Negev Squadron, which required only the most primitive dirt strips to land. However, a new landing area was needed for the heavy C-46s, so a relatively flat portion of desert was surveyed about half way between the settlements of Dorot and Ruhama, less than twenty kilometres south of the Huleiqat road junction. The Dorot and Ruhama settlers, aided by some Palmach troops and using a bulldozer and tractor, worked at night to ready a 1250 metre dirt runway lined with smudge pots, which were to be lit as planes approached in the dark. By August 18 all was ready, and a trial was conducted by Leo Gardner flying from Ekron. At dusk on August 23 the first operational flight began.[48]

Operation Dust, or Dustbowl as the Americans called it, was an incredible feat of flying, scheduling, and sheer determination on the part of air and ground crews alike. Each evening the first C-46 took off from Ekron in the fading light, spiralled up to 1525 metres and turned south for the twenty-minute flight to the Dorot/Ruhama airfield. Below, all was darkness: there were no radio beacons or other naviga-tional aids, and the flight was too short to allow for accurate celestial navigation. A crew could only hope that its compass, course, and air speed was accurate and that the correct signal would be flashed at them from the ground when they arrived over the desert airstrip.

Once over the airfield, the transports began a circling descent while ground crews raced up and down the sides of the runway with torches, lighting the kerosene-filled smudge pots. With flaps fully down, throttles cut back as much as safety allowed, and their landing lights piercing the dark, the big transports floated down to the runway, hit with a large puff of dust, and rolled to the end of the strip. Pilot and crew hurried to Dorot for something to eat while the ground crews unloaded supplies, fresh troops disembarked, and the exhausted soldiers of the Negev Brigade climbed aboard. The C-46 then took off for Ekron and, before long, the next transport was heard approaching, the signals were flashed, and the entire procedure began again.[49]

The pace was killing to air and ground crews alike. From five to eight planes worked each night with as many as nine crews. On September 7 they made the incredible total of thirteen trips between dusk and dawn and transported eighty-one tons of supplies. At the Dorot/Ruhama runway the dust was always thick and the danger of a night landing on a dark, rough, and uneven strip—there was even a slight curve in the middle—placed constant strains on the crew. Flyers and ground crew drank gallons of orange juice—there was little water—and prayed for dawn and sleep. For those who remained behind to direct landing and unloading operations, however, sunrise brought only heat and increased discomfort. "If you want to know what it's like out here," Canadian Bill Novick wrote home, "crawl into a blast furnace and you'll get a good idea."[50]

By September 9, 170 flights had been completed. The C-46s of Air Transport Command had carried more than 1000 tons of supplies and 621 passengers to the Negev and had taken 1764 people back to Ekron.[51] Mardor had pushed his crews hard and, now that the buildup was well along, there was a chance to slow the pace for a few weeks. Some of the crews had asked earlier for a temporary suspension of operations to allow the most exhausted to rest. However, Mardor had insisted that the frequency be maintained because of the urgent need to get troops into the Negev as soon as possible and he had convinced his men to carry on flying their overloaded planes with only a few hours' sleep each day.[52] Much had been accomplished and now the frequency of flights was temporarily reduced to about three each night.

IX

In late September Heyman Shamir stood in front of a packed room at the Bristol Hotel in Tel Aviv and waited for the talking to stop. The Air Transport Command had been paralysed. Disaffection among many of the flyers had been growing, and the difficulties of Operation Dust had been the last straw for many. A strike had been declared and the Air Transport Command had stopped flying. With the battles in the south about to begin, it was a serious situation, and Aharon Remez had sent the American-born Shamir to deal with it.

Shamir told the men that the strike was directly affecting Israel's efforts to prepare for the next round of fighting and urged them to return to their flying duties. He stressed that a strike was totally unnecessary because anyone who was unhappy with conditions in the ATC could leave the country, allowing the rest of the crews to continue with their operations. Al Schwimmer also spoke, making an impassioned plea for an immediate return to work. Ray Kurtz then told the meeting that, although he would support the strike if a majority were in favour, he wanted to keep flying. A vote was taken by a show of hands and the overwhelming majority of the men decided to end the walkout; a few returned to the United States.[53]

The short-lived ATC revolt was the most dramatic and potentially the most disruptive incident in a series of events that revealed growing morale problems among foreign volunteers in the ATC, the Israeli Air Force, and the Seventh Brigade. Some volunteers had been having difficulties accommodating themselves to service in the Israeli forces from the very beginning and morale problems had surfaced as early as April. For the most part, however, volunteers had been too busy fighting, learning new duties, preparing for the next round of fighting, and transferring to other units for these problems to grow to serious proportions. In the second truce, however, prolonged idleness, the rapid expansion of the forces, or, in the case of the ATC, a punishing schedule of operations brought morale problems to the fore. For ATC personnel a new irritant arose in the late summer. The Israelis gave notice that they intended to end the semi-autonomous status and special privileges of the ATC and integrate it into the air force as a combined heavy transport and bomber squadron. Some of the ATC flyers had come to Israel with the expectation that they would form the nucleus of a new Israeli airline, and they were bitterly disappointed to learn that this would not happen. Shortly after the first phase of Operation Dust ended, the revolt broke out.

In ATC, the brief revolt cleared the air. In Dunkelman's Seventh Brigade, however, there was no such catharsis to help re-unite Israelis and foreign volunteers. The Seventh Brigade troops suffered a long period of inactivity, broken by brief but vicious firefights—like the one at Tamra—and discipline and morale problems grew. At one point in early September Dunkelman was authorized to carry out a major operation to clear Kaukji's men from the north. However, when

Bernadotte was assassinated, the operation was quickly cancelled. This probably added to the disciplinary and morale problems that plagued the foreign volunteers in the "Anglo-Saxon Battalion".

The morale problems in the Seventh Brigade were typical of those that affected volunteers in other branches of the Israeli forces. The problems stemmed mainly from the half-in, half-out status of the volunteers in both the army and society. Volunteers had not been drafted for the duration, and few had signed up for a fixed term on a contract basis. Most of the volunteers were free to leave whenever they wished—sometimes without even having to inform their commanding officers. As a result, it could be difficult, as one observer commented, "to keep discipline in a battle unit made up of *mahal* men".[54] When volunteers were given leave they often arrived in Tel Aviv or other cities with no clear idea of where they could stay, and the system worked out by the army to create a centralized bureau of available rooms to distribute to soldiers often broke down. Also, few of the volunteers spoke Hebrew. This increased their isolation from Israeli society and made them feel rootless and friendless in the foreign country they had come to defend.[55]

Ever since the opening of the army's *mahal* office under Harold Jaffer, some efforts had been made to improve the lot of the foreign volunteers. For example, an attempt was made to add supplementary pay, funded by Jewish communities abroad, to the meagre stipend of the Israeli Army.[56] The additional cash was not much—an average of five pounds a month—but it did signify that someone was interested in the special problems of the foreign volunteers. Money, however, was only one part of the problem. This was recognized by the South African Zionist Federation whose office in Israel became a home away from home for South African volunteers. It provided a central mailing address, paid for cables to South Africa, and distributed additional pocket money.[57]

Neither the Americans nor the Canadians maintained an office in Israel that was the equivalent of the South African Zionist Federation. Supplementary pay to North Americans was distributed through the Tel Aviv head office of the Anglo-Palestine Bank, managed by Lee Harris. Harris, an American, had arrived in Palestine to take up a post with the Palestine Economic Corporation in February 1947. He was a former naval officer and took an interest in the plight of the foreign volunteers after they began to arrive in large numbers in the spring of

1948. Harris contacted Emmanuel Neumann of the American Zionist Federation and proposed that a joint arrangement be worked out to improve the lot of the volunteers. Contact was eventually also established with Canada and arrangements were completed to have Harris's bank distribute supplementary *mahal* pay. Harris soon reserved two rooms in the bank as a gathering place for volunteers and became unofficial father-confessor to many of those with grievances about their treatment in the army or in society.[58]

At the beginning of September, Lee Harris met D. Lou Harris from Canada. D. Lou Harris had come to Israel to look into some of the complaints that were filtering back to Canada with returning volunteers or in letters home. The Canadian spent close to four weeks visiting as many Canadians as possible in the front lines, in army camps and field hospitals, and in the hotels and bars of Tel Aviv. He questioned the Canadians closely on their situation, on the general state of volunteers in the Israeli forces, and on the "sometimes" unfriendly attitude of Israelis. He and Lee Harris then drew up a report for the army in which they recommended better recreational and accommodation facilities for those on leave, the institution of education and indoctrination programs, and the improvement of communication for the volunteers. Before he left Israel, D. Lou Harris told the Canadian volunteers he had discovered that "many [of their complaints] were fully justified" and that he had been assured by Ben Gurion and others that the recommendations in the report he had prepared with Lee Harris would be implemented.[59]

X

In Czechoslovakia the morale problems of the foreign volunteers in Israel seemed remote to Sam Pomerantz. He was working feverishly to choose the first shipment of used Spitfire fighters for Israel before the resumption of fighting on the southern front. Pomerantz was aided by Dave Panar and another volunteer. The three men inspected Spitfires at as many as three different airfields in Czechoslovakia in order to be able to choose those in the best operating condition and with the least number of hours on engines and airframes. The men were particularly interested in the state of tires and propellers, since these could not be repaired and replacements for them were not readily available.[60] The Czechs allowed Pomerantz and the others to take the best of the lot.

197

The planes were then flown to a factory at Kunovic (400 kilometres from Prague) for refurbishing before being handed over to Israel. All spare parts, armaments, and ground-maintenance equipment were also to be collected and packed at Kunovic prior to being shipped out of the country.

The exacting job of picking the fifty best Spitfires was made more difficult by a noticeable cooling of official Czech attitudes towards Israel in the late summer. The change could be seen in the fact that administrative obstacles, restrictions on travel and on contact with Czechs, and, on one occasion, threats to arrest Pomerantz for espionage now began to plague the Israeli representatives.[61] The new attitude appeared to be linked to Moscow's growing hostility towards the Jewish state, which showed no signs of joining the Communist camp. There was minimal participation by the Israeli Communist Party in the Provisional Government of Israel. Moreover, the new state also appeared to be serving as a rallying point for nascent Zionist sympathies among Soviet Jews. It was soon quite plain to the Israelis that the Czechs were anxious to get the Spitfires out of the country as soon as possible but were not prepared to allow Israel to mount another airlift patterned after the Balak flights to bring the fighters out.[62]

The alternative to an airlift appeared to be shipment by land to the closest port and then by sea to Israel. However, this would take months, and would also deny Israel the use of the precious fighters at the start of operations against Egypt. Pomerantz came up with a daring alternative. He proposed to strip the fighters of all non-essential equipment, including radio compasses, and to install in them auxiliary fuel systems consisting of two extra gas tanks slung under the wings, a German-designed fuel pump, and a complicated network of fuel lines to bring gas from the wing tanks into the main tank inside the fuselage. Pomerantz could not hope to get Spitfire wing tanks, so he designed a modification for the Messerschmitt tanks that were available in abundance in Czechoslovakia.[63]

The object of these alterations was to extend the range of the fighters to 2250 kilometres. Pomerantz believed that the extra range would allow the Spitfires to be flown to Yugoslavia (a distance of about 800 kilometres) on a first leg, refuelled, and then, guided by a C-54 mother aircraft to provide navigation, taken the entire distance to Israel. The Yugoslavs were reluctant to allow their airfield at Podgorica to be used, but agreed on condition that the Spitfires carry no national markings and that the C-54 used to guide the Spitfires carry the Red Star on its side. The orders came directly from Tito, who was having difficulties with Moscow and who did not wish to add fuel to the fire by allowing planes with Panamanian or U.S. markings to land in his country.[64]

By late September the first batch of six Spitfires was ready for ferrying to Israel. A small group of fighter pilots were flown from Israel to Podgorica in the C-54 and then continued to Kunovic in two Norseman aircraft to pick up the fighters. After some discussion it was decided that Sam Pomerantz would fly one of the planes. The others would be piloted by another American, Jack Cohen; three South Africans, Boris Senior, Syd Cohen, Tuxie Blau; and Modi Alon, commander of 101 Squadron. The men bore a double burden: successful passage to Israel would mean the delivery of six much-needed fighters; it would also convince the sceptical Czechs that Pomerantz's scheme was feasible. The Czechs had made it clear that they would cancel further flights if the planes were forced to land en route and or if the pilots divulged their starting point.[65]

The six fighters took off on the morning of September 22 and headed almost due south across Hungary to Podgorica. Pomerantz instructed the other pilots to keep a close watch on their fuel consumption as a measure of how well the planes would perform on the much longer flight from Podgorica to Ekron. The trip was without incident until the last few minutes. At that point, Blau's undercarriage failed to extend and he was forced to do a wheels-up landing which damaged his fighter beyond repair.[66] At Podgorica a route was laid out that would take the C-54 and the five remaining fighters south over the Adriatic and Mediterranean and then west to Israel, to avoid flying over most of Greece. Greece was in the throes of a civil war between royalists and communists and could not be expected to welcome strange fighters in its air space. After a delay of several days caused by Yugoslav government indecision, permission was finally granted for the planes to continue and, on September 30, the C-54 took off followed by the five fighters.

The small formation kept radio silence as it started on its journey. The fighter pilots stayed close enough to the C-54 to be able to follow course changes easily, but not so close as to risk collision with it or with each other. It was a long, cold, and uncomfortable flight for the pilots cooped up in the cramped confines of their fighter cockpits.[67] The little formation skirted the Albanian coast, flew over the Peloponnesus, and headed towards Israel, passing just south of Rhodes.

They were almost half way between Rhodes and Cyprus when Senior called the C-54 to report that his tanks were almost empty and to ask for advice. The lead navigator did some quick calculations and determined that Senior could not reach Israel but would be able to land in Turkey or return to Rhodes. Rhodes was the best choice and Senior nosed down and turned back to certain internment and the seizure of his fighter. Minutes after Senior left the group Alon called to report the same problem and was also told to go to Rhodes. This left three Spitfires to continue to Israel.[68]

Pomerantz and the others received a joyous greeting from political and military leaders as they touched down at Ekron. Alon and Senior were greeted far differently on landing at Maritza airfield on Rhodes. As they descended towards the air field, they ditched as many documents as possible and agreed to tell the Greeks they were Israeli pilots forced down on a long-range patrol mission. However, police picked up fragments of maps they had dumped over the side just before landing, and these clearly showed that the fighters had come from Czechoslovakia. Also, both Senior and Alon had kept their passports, which contained Czech visa and entry stamps.

The two pilots were separated and closely questioned, but they stuck to their story. When asked to prove their military status they answered that they had forgotten their air force papers. When questioned about the lack of national markings on their fighters they replied that Israel had not yet determined what markings to paint on its aircraft.[69] It was not until the two men were taken to Athens for further questioning that Greek authorities discovered that they had flown out of Czechoslovakia.[70] The Greeks reported the incident to the United Nations, seized the two Spitfires, and kept Senior and Alon in the country for several weeks before finally releasing them.

The arrival of the Spitfires in Israel coincided with an increase in the number of nightly airlift flights of Operation Dust. On September 28 a new airstrip was opened near the Jewish settlement of Urim not more than four kilometres from Egyptian emplacements at Tel Fara. New planes were added to the airlift as flights continued to Dorot/Ruhama and more flights were made to Sdom. In this second phase of the airlift, several thousand tons of supplies and about 9000 passengers were ferried into and out of the Negev in preparation for the coming offensive.[71]

By mid-October the Israeli forces—three brigades north of the main Egyptian positions and one behind Egyptian lines in the Negev, ready to attack from the south—were in place. The air force was poised for an opening strike against Egyptian air bases in the Sinai. On October 15 the Egyptians opened fire on a U.N.-authorized convoy bringing supplies to Israeli settlements and provided the pretext the Israelis needed to attack.[72]

10

"We Fight Till We're Dead"

Danny Rosin and Len Fitchett sat in the cockpits of their twin-engine Bristol Beaufighters at Ramat David air base in north-central Israel and completed their pre-flight check before taxiing onto the long, wide, main runway. It was late afternoon on October 20, 1948, and the sun was beginning to cast long shadows, throwing the hangars, revetments, and buildings of the former Royal Air Force base into sharp relief. Fitchett was a former night fighter pilot in the Royal Canadian Air Force and Rosin had flown twin-engine Blenheim bombers in North Africa for the South African Air Force during World War II. In the rear cupola of Fitchett's plane, Dov Sugarman from England sat facing the tail, manning the machine gun that gave the Beaufighter some protection against enemy fighter attacks from the rear. Crouched in between was Stanley Andrews, from California. Andrews often hitched rides on combat missions aboard the normally two-place attack bombers. Rosin's rear gunner was Syd Kentridge, also a veteran of the South African Air Force.

With a final check of his instrument panel, Fitchett gunned his engines and swung onto the main runway. He held the control column steady, keeping his plane lined up with the centre of the runway as he gathered speed. Within seconds the tail lifted off the ground and Fitchett pulled the yoke back to claw for altitude. Behind him, Rosin's Beaufighter was also climbing away from Ramat David. Together the two aircraft headed west towards the Mediterranean, on the first leg of their mission to attack the Egyptian-held police fort at Iraq Suweidan, a formidable thick-walled structure, bristling with anti-aircraft guns, that had resisted repeated Israeli assaults. The Israeli soldiers had called it "the monster on the hill".

The two planes were to be part of a combined air and ground assault that was due to begin at nightfall.[1] Each plane carried two 500-pound bombs armed with delayed-action fuses. The planes were to come in low from the sea, with the setting sun behind them, skip over the walls of the fort, and dump their bombs inside; the delayed-action fuses would protect the attackers from damage from their own bombs. The air attack was to be the signal for a concentrated barrage from field guns, light artillery, and a small battery of homemade mortars, as a prelude to an infantry assault. Both pilots were under strict orders not to try a second pass. Surprise would be with them on their first bombing run but, once alerted, the Egyptians in the fort would throw up a deadly barrage of anti-aircraft fire.[2] As the sun neared the western horizon, the two Beaufighters—with Fitchett in the lead and Rosin close behind and to the right—cleared the Israeli coast near Haifa and turned south. They maintained strict radio silence as they flew.

When the two aircraft neared the point on the coast where they planned to turn eastward, they dropped low and headed for their target. Fitchett and Rosin strained to pick up familiar landmarks in the gathering gloom and took care to avoid the Egyptian anti-aircraft position at Majdal. They streaked over the main highway from Gaza to Tel Aviv and over the now-severed rail line that had once connected Egypt with Lebanon, and bore in on the fort at Iraq Suweidan. The bombers skimmed the ground and came in fast. Surprise was almost complete; anti-aircraft fire was light. As they rose to clear the fortress walls, Fitchett and Rosin fired their forward machine guns and released their bombs, but Rosin's guns jammed almost immediately. With full power on and still in tight formation, the Beaufighters turned round to the south and Rosin glanced back over the wing to catch a glimpse of explosions at the wall of the police fort. He knew his guns were jammed and thought his bombs were gone: there was nothing left to do but return to Ramat David.

Fitchett, however, kept turning to the right, heading back to the fort. Rosin was puzzled; the fort's defenders were now fully alert and were putting up a storm of anti-aircraft fire. Rosin broke to the left, climbed up to 500 metres and circled, looking for Fitchett. The sky over the fort was black with anti-aircraft fire and Fitchett had disappeared. For about a quarter of an hour, Rosin circled, but saw no sign of Fitchett. As the darkness came on he reluctantly headed back to Ramat David.[3]

In the operations room of the air base, the word had spread quickly—one of the Beaufighters was missing. Dov Sugarman's wife was a clerk in the operations room and, when Rosin walked through the doors, she knew that Fitchett's Beaufighter had gone down with her husband aboard. For Rosin the tragic loss was compounded when an inspection of his plane revealed that his bomb-release mechanism had jammed and the bombs meant for the police fort were still hanging under the Beaufighter.[4]

A small, twin-engine Rapide was sent out to look for the missing bomber. Zvi Treuherz, Maurice Mann, and Smoky Simon, all South Africans, flew over the Egyptian lines carrying Sten guns and ammunition for Fitchett, Andrews, and Sugarman. At 6:35 p.m., about thirty minutes after the attack, they spotted the wreckage of Fitchett's bomber burning furiously in the dark. It had come down near the coast, about sixteen kilometres northwest of the police fort. The Rapide dropped down to thirty metres and made a pass over the burning fighter. Two Egyptian army trucks close by opened fire but Treuherz, who was flying the aircraft, went back for two or three more passes until it was completely dark. There was no sign of life, and the Rapide returned to base.[5]

I

For David Ben Gurion, Israel's future lay in the Negev, a triangle of semi-arid and desert land that thrust like a dagger into the space between Transjordan and Egypt. The region was thinly populated by wandering Bedouins and dotted with small Arab villages spread over a wide area. The important town was Beersheba, where Abraham had watered his flocks in biblical times.

Although the Negev had very few natural resources, it did have one thing that was sorely lacking in the rest of Israel—space for expansion. Ben Gurion and others believed that, with proper irrigation, the semi-arid soil could one day be farmed as it had been by the Nabateans almost two millennia before. This would give Israel a place for the settlement of the millions of Jews who would some day come to live there. The Negev's small stretch of beach on the Gulf of Aqaba, where King Solomon's ships had once sailed to Africa from the biblical port of Etzion Geber, would also give Israel a southern coast.

The Arabs, who also coveted the Negev, were supported in their desires by the British. Transjordan and Egypt knew that a Negev in Jewish hands would interrupt the geographical contiguity of the Arab world, literally splitting it in two. The British wanted the Negev in Arab hands for strategic purposes. Britain needed free access to the Negev in order to maintain the defensive structure that supported the British military establishment in the Suez Canal zone. Given the bad blood that marred British-Jewish relations, the new Jewish state could not be counted on to give Britain that access. This was a key reason why Britain was eager to see the implementation of the second Bernadotte Plan. Since the emergence of Israel could no longer be blocked, Britain would at least salvage something if the Negev could be kept in Arab hands.

By late summer it was clear that time was running out for Israel in the Negev. During the July fighting, Israeli forces had failed to dislodge Egyptian troops in the northern Negev, and Egypt continued to hold a wide band of territory from the Gaza area to the southern outskirts of Jerusalem. Bernadotte's plan, submitted to the United Nations on September 16, had advocated the transfer of the Negev to the Arabs. Even after Bernadotte's assassination, that plan formed the basis of British and American views about the eventual shape of a peace settlement. Diplomatic pressures had been building in the United Nations for an imposed peace. If British and American ideas were accepted, Israel would lose the Negev. It was clear that possession would be nine-tenths of the law; if Israel could decisively defeat Egypt in the south and regain control of the Negev, no diplomatic forces on earth would dislodge it. In addition, there was always the possibility that Egypt would withdraw from the fighting if it was expelled from the Negev, effectively ending the war.[6] These were the major considerations governing Israeli strategy in the October offensive that began with an Israeli air strike at Egyptian air bases in the Sinai peninsula.

II

On the evening of October 15, three 101 Squadron Spitfires, laden with bombs, headed out to sea, flew down the coast, and turned towards Sinai. They dropped low before roaring over the Egyptian air base at El Arish and attacking lines of parked fighters with cannon, machine guns, and bombs. As the three were wreaking havoc on the Egyptian Air Force, other Israeli planes were bombing Majdal, Bet

Hanun, Gaza, and Beersheba.[7] At Gaza the intense, radar-directed flak seemed more concentrated than at many a German target during World War II. Through the night, the C-47s of 103 Squadron flew south from Ramat David with bombs hung under their wings in makeshift racks, and the C-46s of 106 Squadron (formerly ATC), doors off in classic bombchucking style, dumped tons of bombs on Faluja and Gubrin and returned to bomb Majdal, Bet Hanun, and Gaza also. It was by far the most intensive air attack launched by either side since the start of the war.[8]

The Israeli Air Force was out to win undisputed control of the skies over the battlefield, and it pressed home the attack despite inferior numbers and second-rate equipment. To help overcome Egyptian numerical superiority, maintenance men worked round the clock to keep planes in the air. The greater skill and combat experience of the largely volunteer Israeli pilots took their toll in Egyptian planes and crews again and again. Egyptian fighters usually broke formation and ran at the first sight of Israelis, even when the Israelis were outnumbered two and three to one. An encounter on October 21 was typical. Jack Doyle and Rudy Augarten were patrolling in Spitfires in the area west of Beersheba when they spotted four Egyptian fighters. They dived to the attack, but were spotted almost immediately by one Egyptian pilot, who pulled back his stick and soared up into a high loop to come back down on the tails of his attackers. Doyle and Augarten shook him off and bore in on the other three, flying through cloud banks, and firing bursts at the fleeing Egyptians. When the brief battle ended, one Egyptian fighter lay burning on the desert floor and two more had been damaged. This was one of the few dogfights in which an Egyptian pilot showed any aggressiveness at all.[9]

The assault on the ground was mounted by four brigades. Three were situated north of the Egyptian positions, which stretched like an arc from Majdal through Beersheba to the vicinity of Hebron; the fourth was located behind Egyptian lines in the northern Negev. The three northern brigades attacked southwards in an effort to link up with the isolated Jewish-controlled area in the northern Negev and simultaneously to cut off the Egyptian forces to the east. The southern brigade attacked westwards towards the sea. The Egyptians had a fortified position at Iraq El Manshieh, on the east-west highway from Majdal to Hebron. This had to be captured by the Israelis if the highway was to be cut and an Israeli corridor opened into the Negev. At dawn on October 16, the Eighth Brigade, headed by volunteer tank crews, launched the assault on Iraq El Manshieh.

The artillery opened up at 6:20 a.m. and shelled Egyptian lines for forty minutes before the tanks, accompanied by infantry, headed out. Things began to go wrong almost from the start. The tanks moved too quickly for the infantry to keep pace, and the advancing troops were mowed down by accurate Egyptian shell fire, which wiped out at least one third of an attacking infantry company within minutes. One tank overturned in an anti-tank ditch, a second was immobilized by mechanical trouble, a third was diverted to the rescue of the second tank, and a fourth ran out of ammunition.[10]

Inside the tanks, crews were too busy to be scared. The rattle of the tracks, the noise of the gun, the smell of the cordite, and the incessant squawking of the radio added to the tumult of battle. Drivers peered through periscopes trying to steer around obstacles, avoid other tanks, and stay clear of running men. Gunners were fully occupied keeping their weapons trained on target as the tanks bounced and jolted across the rough terrain. Loaders pulled shells from ammunition racks and shoved them into gun breeches, all the time struggling to keep their footing among the jumble of empty shell casings that littered the floor of the tiny compartments.[11]

By 9:00 a.m. it was clear that the attack had failed. Casualties were heavy, several of the tanks had been knocked out of action, and reserves arrived too late to change the course of battle. Dead and wounded littered the battlefield and medics and stretcher-bearers bent to the task of evacuating those who could be saved. The attack had been foiled by Egyptian artillery from the vicinity of Faluja, three and a half kilometres up the road. However, confusion in Israeli ranks and the failure either to concentrate the tanks into one armoured fist or to co-ordinate them properly with the advancing infantry had given the Egyptian gunners both time and opportunity to find their targets.

Following the failure at Iraq El Manshieh, Yigal Allon, the commander on the southern front, decided to shift the main assault effort farther west to the vicinity north of Huleiqat. The attack began in the early morning of October 17, when Israeli troops overran Egyptian positions north of the vital road junction on the Majdal-Hebron highway. The junction was soon in Israeli hands. Even though the village of Huleiqat, several kilometres to the south, was controlled by the Egyptians, the Majdal-Hebron highway had been cut and the

Egyptian forces to the east—in the Iraq Suweidan police fort, at Faluja, and at Iraq El Manshieh—were cut off from the main concentration of Egyptian troops on the coast. They were soon further isolated when Israeli troops captured Bet Hanun eight kilometres north of Gaza on the coast highway. This forced the Egyptians to the north to begin a hurried withdrawal on a makeshift road quickly prepared along the beach by army engineers.

The four thousand Egyptians in the Faluja vicinity were rapidly being encircled. However, as long as they held the Iraq Suweidan police fortress, they could not be completely isolated since the Israeli force was not nearly large enough to contain them. Thus, at nightfall on October 19, a massive artillery barrage and an infantry assault were directed against the fort. The Egyptians held firm. The lead Israeli platoon ran into heavy grenade and machine-gun fire as it neared the walls of the fort. By dawn, it had managed only to breach two fences and destroy a bunker.[12] The Israelis withdrew and immediately began preparations for another attack, scheduled to start at twilight. This attack was to open with air force bombing, followed by another artillery and mortar barrage, and then an infantry advance. Danny Rosin and Len Fitchett were to pilot the two bombers. This was the mission that was to end so tragically for Fitchett and his crew, and so frustratingly for Rosin.

At 6:00 p.m. on October 20 the two Beaufighters piloted by Rosin and Fitchett swept in from the sea, dropped down, and headed for the Egyptian positions. The defenders were taken by surprise and failed to bring their anti-aircraft guns to bear before the two planes passed over the wall. Moments later, the Israeli ground attack began.[13] Under intense Egyptian fire the Israelis managed to penetrate to the western entrance door, place explosive charges, and blow their way into the post. When the smoke cleared, however, only four men managed to attack, and only one, the platoon leader, made it inside the walls. After killing several Egyptians, he was wounded and was forced to retreat with the remainder of his men. Once again daylight forced the Israelis to cut off their attack and Iraq Suweidan remained firmly in Egyptian hands.

Despite the failures at Iraq Suweidan, Israeli troops had managed to capture Huleiqat and, by October 20, the road to the northern Negev was totally under Israeli control. Then, mindful of an October 19 Security Council resolution calling on the warring parties to re-impose a ceasefire in the area, the high command turned its attention to the capture of Beersheba. The Security Council resolution was a mild one and did not order an end to the fighting, but Israeli military planners believed it was only a matter of time before their offensive would have to be halted. In the meantime, they were determined to take as much territory as possible, in order to complete the encirclement of the Egyptian troops in what was now known as the "Faluja pocket".

The attack on Beersheba was mounted by the Eighth Brigade reinforced by several weapons battalions and units from the Negev Brigade. It was spearheaded by Teddy Eytan's Commando Français. The assault began at 4:00 a.m. on October 21. Within several hours, Eytan's men had advanced to the central town square, which was bordered by a police fort and a mosque and located near the old Turkish railway station that served as headquarters for the Egyptian defenders.[14] Reinforcements that were supposed to support Eytan's commandos failed to arrive on time. When dawn broke, the French-men found themselves in the centre of the town, virtually surrounded, facing about 500 Egyptian troops only a few metres away. "What do we do now?" one commando asked Eytan. "Simple," the commander replied, "we fight till we're dead...."[15]

Reinforcements soon arrived, however, and the Egyptians began to pull back, convinced they had no chance to survive the Israeli onslaught; Israeli blocking units outside Beersheba reported running into fleeing Egyptians. An Israeli anti-tank gun was then set up to fire at the police fort that dominated the town square and, after four rounds, the defenders raised the white flag and Egyptian resistance in Beersheba collapsed. By 10:00 a.m. the town was occupied and the Eighth Brigade withdrew to join in attacks elsewhere on the southern front.

For the next twenty-four hours Israeli units continued to advance in the area north of Beersheba, consolidating their hold on the southern portions of the Judean foothills and continuing to put pressure on the Egyptians inside the Faluja pocket. The Israelis had succeeded in pushing a corridor through to the northern Negev, ending the isola-tion of Jewish soldiers and settlers that had begun with the Egyptian invasion in May. They had driven the Egyptians down the coast, almost as far as Gaza. However, when a ceasefire again took hold on the afternoon of October 22, they had still not swept the Egyptians from Israel.

The Israelis were able to concentrate as many as 15,000 troops against the Egyptians in the south because they did not believe their other major adversaries—Syria, Transjordan, Iraq, and Lebanon— would take advantage of the fighting in the south to launch major attacks against Israeli positions on the central, Jerusalem, and northern fronts. With one exception, their forecast proved accurate. On October 22, Fauzi al-Kaukji and his Arab Liberation Army tried to take advantage of the Israeli preoccupation with Egypt by launching a raid southwards from Lebanese-held territory into the upper Galilee. This move gave Israel the excuse it needed to finish Kaukji off.

III

Dunkelman and the men of the Seventh Brigade had waited in Safed for a chance to attack Kaukji since September; on October 28 the opportunity finally came. After dark, engineers and sappers moved quietly out onto the main road leading west and worked quickly to clear roadblocks and to bridge culverts and wadis in preparation for a 79th Battalion assault on the village of Jish, where Kaukji had his headquarters. By 3:30 a.m. they reported the last obstacle removed. The infantry chased Arab fighters from villages along the road, while the brigade sped towards Jish, which was situated atop a high hill. With guns blazing in the night the mobile column raced up the hill and the battle for Jish was joined. The fight was intense though brief. The Arab Liberation Army defence was bolstered by a Syrian contingent of about four hundred men who had driven into Jish only hours before, but by daybreak the Seventh Brigade had succeeded in pushing Kaukji's troops out of the town. A final infantry assault, which swarmed around a fiercely burning ammunition truck, completed the takeover. Israeli troops then fanned out to take up defensive positions along the flanks of the road and on the approach to Jish.[16]

The assault on Jish was the opening phase of Operation Hiram, a plan to expel Kaukji from the Galilee in a lightning campaign, to be completed before the Syrians or Lebanese could come to his rescue. Operation Hiram called for the co-ordinated action of four brigades to capture Sasa, a town that lay astride the junction of the four main roads in northern Israel. The Oded Brigade, with elements from the 79th Battalion, would mount a diversionary attack, from Nahariya on the coast, through Tarshiha, towards Sasa. The main assault would be mounted by the remainder of the Seventh Brigade attacking from Safed. The Golani Brigade would mount diversionary attacks towards the south to prevent the Iraqis from moving north to support Kaukji; and the Carmeli Brigade would exert pressure on the Syrians to secure the rear of the Seventh Brigade from a possible attack from Mishmar Hayarden.[17]

The Seventh Brigade quickly achieved its immediate objective at Jish. However, to the west other Israeli forces ran into serious difficulties when the Oded Brigade's attack on Tarshiha bogged down. The road leading to the town was heavily mined, so that despite the best efforts of the Israeli engineers the advance was slow and nerve-wracking. At one point an armoured car hit a mine and blew up, blocking the road. Although the crew escaped unhurt, the column was forced to halt until the wreck could be towed out of the way. Later, an Israeli sapper was badly wounded when a mine he was dismantling exploded; he was forced to lie in a culvert, screaming in pain, for most of the night. At daybreak the road was still blocked by mines; the sun rose to reveal the Israeli column stretched out and completely exposed. Within minutes Arab mortar fire began to range in on the vehicles. The column was forced to retreat but the single-lane road gave no room for vehicles to pass each other. The rear armoured cars were forced to turn around and head back, followed by the next in line, until the entire column had withdrawn.[18]

While the armoured column was stalled in its advance on Tarshiha, a company of Israelis and Druse captured the village of Yanuach, three kilometres southwest of Tarshiha. When the main attack on Tarshiha failed, however, Kaukji's forces rallied and re-captured Yanuach. The town's Druse population, apparently wishing to win Kaukji's goodwill, fell upon the mixed force of Israelis and Druse and killed many of them. Emboldened by the Arab Liberation Army defence of Tarshiha, Kaukji next threw a small armoured-car force down the road from Sasa to Jish to attack the newly established Seventh Brigade positions there. But the 79th Battalion had ranged its guns on the road and the Arab Liberation Army thrust was turned back. At the same time Seventh Brigade infantry attacked along the flank of Mount Atzmon and cleared the way into Sasa.[19] By mid-day Israeli troops were in possession of this key road junction and Kaukji's forces were in retreat towards the Lebanese border. When Kaukji's troops disappeared to the north, Tarshiha surrendered after a brief artillery barrage.

The Seventh Brigade troops and their commanders had had almost no sleep since the morning of October 28. Dunkelman held a staff conference after dark on October 29 in which he and his officers stayed on their feet to help themselves keep awake.[20] In the armoured cars and trucks, drivers' heads nodded over steering wheels, and eyes heavy with sleep peered into the gloom to negotiate the sharp mountain curves where steep drops awaited the unwary. The advance to the north continued, however, as the brigade forced its way past the Sasa junction and sped up the road toward Malkiya and Beni Yusha; Kaukji was allowed no rest and no opportunity to regroup. The Lebanese at Malkiya were not prepared for an attack from the south and put up little opposition. As Kaukji's forces melted away, the siege of the Metulla-Tiberias road ended and the Jewish settlements at Eilon and Manara were relieved.[21] By nightfall on October 30 the Lebanese Army and the Arab Liberation Army had been routed from the upper Galilee, never to return, and Israeli forces stood at the Lebanese frontier. A South African volunteer recorded the arrival of the first troops at the Israel-Lebanon border:

> ...we descended from our vehicle and approached a...blockhouse which marked the border of Israel and Lebanon. We entered the building without resistance and found that the enemy had destroyed the roof. . . . we packed huge rocks to close half the doorway. . . mounted our guards in all directions and tried to sleep the night. It was extremely cold and uncomfortable but we all managed a few hours sleep on and off.[22]

The following day forward elements of the brigade pushed several kilometres into Lebanon and halted at the Litani River for a few days before withdrawing inside the Israeli border.

IV

The Seventh Brigade played the major part in securing the Galilee for Israel but, with Operation Hiram completed, it was forced to return once again to the humdrum routine of garrison duty and the daily chores of military life.[23] Morale problems among the foreign volunteers in the 72nd Battalion grew and eventually blossomed into a minor revolt, which brought on a full-scale army inquiry. The situation was so tense for a time that army high command considered reducing the number of volunteers in the battalion by scattering them throughout other battalions and brigades. The difficulties stemmed partly from the general condition and status of volunteers in Israel, and partly from particular problems inside the unit.

As early as August there was some feeling among enlisted men that the high command of the brigade was not sensitive to the needs and requirements of the volunteers. One Canadian complained that he and his fellow volunteers had been "railroaded" to their particular units: "No matter how good the unit is," he wrote home, "we still feel that we have been tricked."[24] It is impossible to determine how widespread this feeling was, but on October 21, about a week before Operation Hiram was due to begin, eleven soldiers from Company B staged a "sit-down strike" in front of the company headquarters and were carted away to prison.[25] Despite this incident there is no evidence that these morale problems directly affected the fighting ability of the volunteers in the fighting that followed.

The commanding officer of the 72nd, Jackie Nursella, had served in the British Army, though he was American-born. Nursella was considered a "spit and polish" officer by Akiva Skidel, a member of Kibbutz Kfar Blum who had served in the U.S. Army during World War II and was with the Seventh Brigade as a welfare officer. However competent Nursella may have been in combat, he was not temperamentally suited to dealing with restless volunteers who had come to fight but who were forced to spend much of their time sitting around. These men were not likely to knuckle under to "spit and polish" discipline and, in Skidel's opinion, their unit "was a source of trouble because there were several hundred and they felt strong and had all kinds of trouble makers among them." At one point several of the volunteers were removed from the 72nd Battalion and sent home when they tried to instigate a rebellion against Nursella's leadership.[26]

In February 1949, a General Headquarters inquiry committee was established to investigate the problems of the Seventh Brigade. The committee concluded that the volunteers had been handled badly from the very start, in that promises had been made to them when they enlisted that could not be kept. Many had not been classified properly during their assignment to the battalion, and the fact that so many volunteers were concentrated in the 72nd interfered with their integration into the army and enhanced their feeling of isolation. There were all-too-few cultural and educational activities to keep the soldiers occupied and to bring them into closer contact with Israeli society. There was also a strong feeling among the volunteers that Nursella and his vice-commander were discriminating against them. Although the committee of inquiry concluded that this was not true, they did point out that Nursella had not helped the volunteers integrate into the unit and had not built a comprehensive system for Hebrew-language education. The committee also decried both the lack of a clear high-command policy towards volunteers and its tendency to treat them differently from other soldiers.[27] These conclusions reinforced the belief that additional efforts were needed to make the volunteers feel more at home and, perhaps, convince more to settle in Israel when the war was over.

By the autumn of 1948 many volunteers had become disaffected with Harold Jaffer's work in the *mahal* department of the army and were personally angry at him for what they alleged was a failure to act in their best interest; he was, at times, physically threatened.[28] In November he was replaced as head of the department by Akiva Skidel who was given the rank of major in the Israeli army. Skidel had excellent qualifications for the job. He had a strong background of Zionist involvement since the late 1930s. Although born in Poland, he had immigrated to Canada in 1931 and attended the University of Toronto before settling in the United States in 1937. As head of the *mahal* department Skidel was responsible for planning and operating welfare and cultural activities, working on legal problems for foreign volunteers worried about losing their citizenship, and interceding with officers when volunteer-related problems arose in the units. It was also his duty to distribute special embarkation bonuses to volunteers returning to their home country.[29] He was, in Lee Harris's opinion, an immediate improvement over Jaffer.[30]

Skidel's task in working to improve volunteer morale was somewhat eased by the start-up of a number of national *mahal* committees in Israel dedicated to the distribution to volunteers of extra pay, clothing, food parcels, and other items, mostly of a recreational nature. Prominent members of the Zionist organizations in countries like the United States, Great Britain, Holland, and Canada usually took on the job of raising money and overseeing its distribution to the committees for *mahal* welfare in Israel. By November these committees often met together and worked with Skidel, and with Harris, who had been appointed civilian advisor to the army on *mahal* matters. The committees helped establish a special *mahal* club in Tel Aviv to cater to the recreational needs of the volunteers.[31]

Although Israelis usually pointed to a lack of motivation and discipline among the volunteers as a prime cause of low morale, Israeli attitudes towards *mahal* were equally at fault, and Lee Harris, Skidel, and others found this to be a major obstacle to their efforts. There was a belief in some Israeli circles that "a Jew was... a Jew first and that his loyalties and duties were therefore owed to the Jewish state first, regardless of his nationality or passport."[32] This belief was buttressed by a strong conviction in Israeli society that Jews from western countries—particularly from Canada, the United States, Great Britain, and South Africa—were only fooling themselves about being secure in their native lands: sooner or later they, too, would be marched away to the death camps. There was, therefore, no reason to treat foreign volunteers any differently from the displaced persons of Europe, since the volunteers were only the vanguard of what would eventually become a forced migration to Israel from the western countries.[33]

This attitude caused bitter feelings among the volunteers. It could also create practical problems. Some volunteers had difficulty getting exit visas for themselves or for Israeli girls they had married during their stay.[34] It even affected the dead. In one instance, volunteers wanted to ship the body of a Canadian home, but were thwarted by Israeli officials who insisted he be buried in Israel. A small group threatened to place the coffin on the steps of a hotel that housed a number of *mahal* offices and to parade in the streets of Tel Aviv to bring the case to the attention of foreign newspaper correspondents, but eventually Lee Harris succeeded in calming them down.[35]

Despite these difficulties, morale began to improve by December.[36] An English-language newspaper, *Frontline*, patterned after *Stars and Stripes* and other World War II service newspapers, began to publish in November. The *mahal* club opened its doors, food parcels and recreational equipment began to arrive, and, perhaps most important, the army began to acknowledge both the presence and the contribution to the war effort of the volunteers. Though grudging, this recognition was enough to satisfy most of the volunteers. They were not malcontents or troublemakers; they had simply had legitimate grievances about the manner and method of their integration, or lack of it, into the army and society.

215

V

On the night of October 24-25, an Israeli Dakota, flown by Canadian Wilfred Canter, took off from Ramat David on a supply mission to Sdom. Canter, as usual, planned to land at Ekron, take on supplies, and then continue to the Dead Sea. Two other Canadians, William Fisher and Fred Stevenson, were aboard. Canter had led a charmed life during World War II. He had been shot down twice while serving with Bomber Command. The first time, he had escaped with the help of the French underground; the second time he had been taken prisoner by the Germans. At roughly midnight on October 24, his luck ran out. As the plane approached Ekron, its landing lights on, a lick of flame appeared from the starboard engine, grew in the slipsteam, and engulfed the right wing, which exploded. The Dakota fluttered to the ground in flames and subsequent investigation by the chief mechanic of 103 Squadron revealed that a cracked manifold had caused the fatal engine fire.[37]

The truce in the south was honoured more in the breach than in the observance and the air force continued to fly reconnaissance missions, fighter sweeps, and bombing attacks on Egyptian positions. Particular attention was paid to the Egyptians trapped in the Faluja pocket; they were pounded daily, sometimes on an around-the-clock basis. The dive bombers arrived first, early in the day. These were Harvard trainers smuggled in crates from Canada and the United States, reassembled in Israel, and fitted with bomb racks and machine guns. They were assigned to 35 Squadron which put aside its Norseman transports for several weeks in the autumn and winter of 1948 to take on the dive-bombing responsibilities.[38] Pilots with Harvard experience from other squadrons were loaned to 35 Squadron, which placed as many as six Harvards in the air at any given time.

After the dive bombers, the B-17s arrived. Wheeling in from the sea in a wide arc at high altitude, escorted by 101 Squadron fighters, the three bombers dropped full loads of 500-pound bombs on Egyptian troop concentrations in the Faluja pocket before heading back to Ramat David for the night. After dark the Dakotas of 103 Squadron and the C-46s of 106 Squadron droned over Faluja for hours (keeping the soldiers below awake and on edge) as they dropped their loads from the makeshift racks on the Dakotas or from the open doors of the C-46s. Precise schedules were worked out to ensure that the two squadrons did not arrive over the target at the same time; on one occasion, however, a mix-up almost ended in disaster. On one night-bombing run, Danny Rosin looked down from his Dakota and noticed the flashes of bomb explosions below. He realized, to his horror, that a C-46 was somewhere above him dropping bombs that could blow him and his plane to bits,[39] and wasted no time diving away from the danger zone. The Egyptian commanding officer in the Faluja pocket noted in his diary on November 17: "Enemy planes attack daily. . . . The sight of the three Flying Fortresses has become a regular feature every day at 5:00 p.m." One day later he added: "The night before was the hardest and cruelest Faluja has witnessed. The enemy's air activity continued for twelve hours without interruption. . . . "[40]

Despite the air bombardment of Faluja, the 4000 trapped Egyptian troops held out. From their position at Iraq Suweidan, they continued to harass Israeli traffic passing over the Isdud-Huleiqat road. On November 9, after a massive artillery and mortar bombardment that stunned the defenders, the Eighth Brigade launched yet another assault on the police post. Yitzhak Sadeh, brigade commander, reasoned that past attacks had failed because they had counted on the element of surprise, even though surprise in an operation of this sort was clearly not possible. His new tactic was virtually to pound the fort into submission before sending in his troops. He was dramatically proved correct when the attack succeeded in capturing the fort with no losses to the main assault troops (there were casualties in a diversionary action). With the fall of the fort the Faluja pocket shrank, and additional pressure was placed on the Egyptians trapped within it. The Israelis refused to allow U.N.-sanctioned food or supply convoys to enter the pocket and opened negotiations with the Egyptian commander to attempt to convince him to surrender. They did not succeed; although continuous pressure was placed on Faluja, the Egyptians held out.

By mid-November the strength of the Israeli Air Force was no longer a secret, since it had been closely monitored by the Royal Air Force in a regular series of high-altitude reconnaissance flights, which had been started before the British withdrawal in May. No ministerial authority was obtained for these flights, since it did not appear to RAF commanders to be legally necessary as long as the British maintained an official presence in Palestine. After the withdrawal the flights were continued in order to provide British forces with up-to-date information on the strength and disposition of the Israeli army and air force.[41]

217

This was done despite an order issued by the Provisional Government of Israel in August requiring any "British Subject" to seek permission for overflights of Israeli territory at least twenty-four hours beforehand.[42] As far as the British Minister of Defence was concerned, there could be no legal objection to the passage of RAF aircraft over Israel, since Palestine was "technically *res nullius*" after the British departure.[43] The RAF used a specially equipped Mosquito fighter, which flew from north to south over northern and central Israel and then turned out to sea. The intruder—the Israelis thought it Syrian or Iraqi—appeared regularly, always following the same route, and was a constant source of frustration to the pilots of 101 Squadron, who watched the contrail of the high, fast plane knowing they did not have time to climb to meet it with the few minutes' warning they had received.

They got lucky on November 20. An American, Wayne Peake, was aloft on an operational training flight in a Spitfire when he received word from squadron headquarters that the unknown intruder was approaching rapidly. Peake pulled the Spitfire into a climb to get above the oncoming Mosquito. He was in a good position for an attack, but he had no oxygen and he began to feel light-headed as he closed with the twin-engine fighter.

Far below, at Qastina, the pilots of 101 Squadron saw the two contrails merge and heard the faraway rattle of gunfire. Suddenly Peake's voice crackled in frustration over the squadron loudspeaker: "My fucking guns are jammed." Those watching below felt a surge of disappointment as they saw the intruder begin to make a wide turn out to sea. They were sure Peake had failed, but within moments the Mosquito's contrail began to thicken, and then to turn black, as the entire aircraft became one large burning mass and then exploded. Two fighter pilots jumped into a light plane while the wreckage was still falling and flew out to sea to examine the scene—the last pieces of the Mosquito were still fluttering down when they arrived.[44] The following day the Israeli government issued a press release that mentioned the destruction of an "enemy Mosquito" over Israel.[45] The Israelis were not to learn for some months that the aircraft had been an RAF fighter.

By early December, southern-front commander Yigal Allon began to complete preparations for the final campaign—to be launched before the end of the month—to bring about the total defeat of the Egyptian Army. The air force was a party to these plans and was anxious to bring more Spitfires from Czechoslovakia to use in the attack. However, a setback followed the September landings of the two Spitfires at Rhodes when the government of Yugoslavia refused to allow the Israelis to use Podgorica as a refuelling stop. For a brief time Sam Pomerantz experimented with fitting the fighters with additional fuel tanks inside the fuselage to provide the range needed for a non-stop trip. However, the flying qualities of the planes were drastically affected by the extra weight and Pomerantz was not certain the landing gear would support the fighters when all gas tanks were full. When experimental flights confirmed his fears, the scheme was abandoned.[46]

In Belgrade Israeli efforts to convince the Yugoslav government to change its mind eventually proved successful. Grudging permission to continue to use Podgorica was given provided a number of conditions were met: there could be no more than six fighters in each flight; the Israelis would have to stay at the airfield and were prohibited from entering the nearby town; they would have to provide all the fuel, food, and other necessary supplies; and all aircraft would have to bear Yugoslav markings. On December 18, Pomerantz and five others took advantage of a clearing in the heavy winter weather over the Alps and took off from Czechoslovakia for Podgorica. Several hours later watchers anxiously scanning the skies at the Yugoslav base made out four Spitfires approaching for a landing. Two of the fighters had crashed and one pilot—Sam Pomerantz—had been killed. On the following day twelve more fighters arrived in two groups, this time without mishap. One of these planes was eventually abandoned at the field because of mechanical problems. Even so, by December 22, fifteen Spitfires had joined 101 Squadron.[47] The aircraft that remained in Czechoslovakia were eventually crated up and shipped by sea, arriving months later.

VI

On December 22 Israel informed the United Nations that since Egypt had refused to comply with a U.N. demand to begin negotiations with Israel, it was free to resume military operations to expel the Egyptians from within its borders. The offensive began almost immediately with the main body of Yigal Allon's forces concentrated in the Beersheba area for an attack designed to outflank the Egyptian troop concentrations at El Arish, Rafah, and Gaza. Allon hoped to mount diversionary attacks against enemy positions on the coast to convince the Egyptians that the main Israeli assault would come there. Meanwhile, his troops would thrust south from Beersheba to El Auja and then swing north-west towards El Arish.[48] Once again the air force was called on to attack the El Arish air base and to conduct bombing and strafing runs against the Egyptians. Many Egyptian planes were destroyed on the ground, but the remainder rose to meet the Israelis in the air and to attack Israeli positions: for the first and last time in the war, Israeli pilots returned almost daily from escort missions or fighter sweeps with reports of dogfights, damage inflicted on Egyptian aircraft, and Egyptian fighters left burning in the desert. Israeli fighters and attack bombers swooped low over the roads and tracks of the Negev and Sinai to shoot up lines of fleeing Egyptian trucks and armour. Just as regularly, the Egyptians sent their fighters to harass the Israeli advance.

The volunteers in the Commando Français, the Negev Brigade, and the tank companies of the Eighth Brigade were swept up in the thickening tide of battle. Three Israeli columns pushed south from Beersheba, laid siege to Bir Asluj and then pushed on to El Auja on the Israeli-Egypt border. At one battle at the T'mille Hills on the Beersheba-El Auja road the Commando Français found themselves under Egyptian counterattack at 1:00 a.m. Christmas morning and were forced to retreat, leaving a number of wounded behind. When the hill was recaptured soon afterwards, the wounded men were found dead— their bellies had been slit open by the Egyptian attackers.[49]

At nearby El Auja Hafir two companies of the Eighth Brigade with a large contingent of American and South African volunteers ran into murderous fire and suffered many casualties within minutes. A lone charge towards the Egyptian positions by a wounded Rhodesian helped save the day and allowed the Israelis to regroup for a second, successful try at storming the enemy strongpoint.[50] The Egyptian positions at El Auja were quickly surrounded and placed under siege. Fighting was heavy and the Eighth Brigade again ran into difficulties, although the Egyptians eventually surrendered shortly after noon on December 27.

From El Auja Israeli units advanced into Sinai and raced towards Abu Ageila. Several captured Egyptian trucks were pressed into the fast-moving column and this attracted the attention of Israeli fighters roaming over the battlefront searching for targets. For a few tense moments Israeli Spitfires strafed the Israeli column until one pilot noticed Israeli markings on a jeep and broke off the attack. He had not expected to find friendly vehicles so far to the west.[51]

On December 29 the United Nations Security Council ordered yet another ceasefire and called upon the warring parties to return to the positions they had held when the truce had broken down. The Israelis, however, had finally defeated the Egyptian Army and put it to flight, ensuring Israeli control over the Negev. They were not about to accede to such a demand. The next day, December 30, Britain intervened directly by invoking the 1936 Anglo-Egyptian treaty and warning Israel that failure to pull out of the Sinai would lead to British military involvement. Although Ben Gurion assured the British through Washington (Britain still did not recognize Israel) that the entry into Sinai was a tactical manoeuvre only, he also issued orders to Allon to begin an immediate withdrawal from the El Arish area. Israeli troops began to pull back along the coast to the northeast, towards Rafah, in preparation for an assault on that town, which lay just east of the Israeli-Egyptian border. If Rafah was captured, Egyptian positions in Gaza would become untenable.

The campaign to capture Rafah reached a climax on January 6. By then the town was completely surrounded. Israeli columns that had fought their way from Beersheba through Abu Ageila to the coast arrived to reinforce other units that had moved on Rafah from the east. Allon prepared to launch a heavy attack on the night of January 6 when he received word that Egypt had requested an armistice and that the Israeli government had immediately agreed to open discussions. The attack was called off and a ceasefire was arranged to begin at 2:00 p.m. the following day.[52]

VII

Despite the impending ceasefire, January 7 started off like every other day of the fighting for the Israeli Air Force. The planes took to the air at the crack of dawn: fighters escorted B-17s on a bombing mission to Khan Yunis, and Harvards to Deir El Balah and then roamed over the battle area seeking any opportune target. When gas and ammunition were exhausted, the planes returned to base to rearm, refuel, and get back into action. On one mission Jack Doyle, flying a Mustang that had been smuggled to Israel from the United States, and an Israeli in another plane, were flying escort when Doyle spotted eight enemy fighters strafing Israeli troops. Expecting to be covered by his wing-man, Doyle dived to the attack, but the second pilot failed to follow him down. The Egyptians were flying in a loose line-abreast formation and Doyle snapped out a burst at the last enemy fighter as he roared up to them. The Egyptian rolled over and crashed. Doyle then throttled back, turned into the next fighter and opened fire, hitting the wings, engine, and body before turning to a third fighter, which he sprayed until he ran out of ammunition. Right on the deck and going fast, he flew straight across an Egyptian army camp before heading out to sea to turn back to base.[53]

At about the time that Doyle was returning home, four Royal Air Force Spitfire MK-18s took off from the RAF base at Deversoir, Egypt, and headed for the battle zone. The planes carried long-range drop tanks and loaded guns:[54] the pilots had been instructed "to look over the battle area; avoid all aircraft and not to make any hostile move with regard to other aircraft."[55] This was not the first time RAF fighters had flown over the battle zone: similar reconnaissance flights had been carried out twice on December 30 by a combined group of RAF and Egyptian fighters; observation flights by RAF planes alone had followed in the first days of January. The RAF "on occasion" passed photo-graphic information from these missions to Egyptian officers "because of the difficulty of obtaining positive identification of Jewish ground forces in Egyptian territory".[56] The RAF was surely aware that Egyptian fighters, with similar camouflage and of similar make, had flown almost daily attack missions against Israeli troops in the area.

The four RAF fighters approached the battle zone, two at 150 metres altitude and the other two slightly higher at 600 metres, and began their observation of the ground fighting. They flew along the main highway from Ismailia to Abu Ageila, then turned north at Abu Ageila, flying towards Rafah, staying over Egyptian territory. They intended to turn back to Deversoir when they reached an Israeli roadblock in the Rafah vicinity; at some point before reaching their objective they jettisoned their drop tanks. As the two lower Spitfires arrived over the roadblock they turned westwards and were immediately engulfed in a storm of Israeli anti-aircraft fire. One pilot bailed out as his aircraft plummeted to the desert below. The flight leader, Flying Officer T.J. McElhaw, flying at 600 metres, pulled around in a tight turn to the left to keep the parachute in sight but while still in his turn, he heard his wingman call, "Break, there is an aircraft on your tail."[57]

From above, Slick Goodlin and John McElroy of 101 Squadron were closing fast. It is impossible to determine whether they saw the RAF markings on the aircraft swelling in their gunsights, though they later claimed they did not. But here were four non-Israeli fighters flying low over an Israeli column in an area that was frequently visited by the Egyptians on strafing attacks. It appeared to Goodlin and McElroy that these four fighters were doing more of the same, while Israeli troops manning anti-aircraft guns on the ground might have seen the falling drop tanks and mistaken them for bombs. There was no time for second thoughts. Goodlin and McElroy opened fire and the three remaining RAF fighters crashed and burned.[58] One RAF flyer was killed; McElhaw and his wingman survived and made their way on foot to Egyptian lines. The first pilot, shot down by groundfire, was taken prisoner and later released.

When the four Spitfires failed to return, the RAF base commander at Deversoir dispatched a large force of four Spitfire reconnaissance aircraft escorted by fifteen Tempest fighters. Approximately three kilometres southwest of Rafah this formation was jumped by five Israeli Spitfires and one Tempest was shot down.[59] Within the space of three hours, the RAF had lost five fighters to Israeli guns. Ironically, these were the last aircraft shot down in the war.

VIII

By sundown on January 7 the shooting in the south had stopped. The ceasefire took hold, and the final campaign of the first Arab-Israeli war was over. Israeli victory was complete. The Egyptians still held the small piece of territory in Palestine soon to be known as the Gaza Strip, but had been totally chased out of the Negev. The four thousand men trapped in the Faluja pocket were allowed to return to Egypt and armistice negotiations soon began, under Dr. Ralph Bunche's auspices, on the island of Rhodes. There were brief fears in Israel and Washington that Britain would take retaliatory action for the destruction of the five aircraft on January 7, and Britain did indeed rush troops to southern Jordan. However, the uproar in Britain over the secret dispatch of British airmen to the battle zone drowned out those voices calling for revenge. The incident pointed up the folly and unreality of Britain's continuing refusal to recognize Israel and brought recognition much closer.

Around Jerusalem, on central and northern fronts, along the Sinai border, and near the Gaza Strip, Arabs and Israelis dug in while attitudes hardened, hates deepened, and fears and suspicions grew. The hopes of Israelis that victory would mean acceptance, recognition, and eventually peace were quickly dashed. For a brief time in late 1949 and early 1950 there was a strong possibility that Israel would conclude a peace treaty with King Abdullah, who had annexed those portions of Arab Palestine that his Arab Legion held at the close of hostilities. (Abdullah had then proclaimed himself ruler of the Hashemite Kingdom of Jordan, which included lands on both sides of the Jordan River.) However, the King was assassinated in Jerusalem by a follower of the Mufti and the peace agreement was never concluded. The Arab-Israeli war of 1948, therefore, "resolved the question of Israeli independence", as an American military historian has written, but "did not resolve the issues which led to that independence."[60] It is the continuing tragedy of the people of the Middle East that the issues are unresolved still.

11

"We Fought for a Jewish State"

Thirty-five years later, at the sprawling Israeli Air Force base of Ramat David, the roar of turbo jets pushed to full throttle suddenly overwhelms the everyday routine sounds of maintenance vehicles, repair shops, and taxiing aircraft. Two camouflaged fighters bearing the blue Star of David begin to roll on the main runway. Within seconds the wave of sound floods the landscape as the fighters gather speed, climb steeply away towards the Mediterranean, and dwindle to small specks trailing thin wisps of black smoke in the blue. The base has changed during the years since Leonard Fitchett, Stanley Andrews, and Dov Sugarman took off on their last mission. Nevertheless, signs of the past—the concrete bomber revetments built by the British, the now-abandoned shacks that volunteer pilots slept in on hot nights, even the old RAF control tower—are still there. The Israeli Air Force has also changed. Its aircraft are no longer flying wrecks salvaged from surplus yards around the world but modern and highly sophisticated craft some of which have been designed and built by the Israelis themselves. The pilots, too, are different. They are all young Israelis, a carefully selected and highly trained elite that is, without question, among the best in the world. But despite the dramatic changes, the air force has its roots in the past. Nowhere is this more apparent than in the small, wood-panelled room at Ramat David that contains, mounted on the walls and filling large books on the tables, the names of all those pilots and crew members from Ramat David who have been killed in the defence of Israel. In one of those books, Fitchett, Andrews, and Sugarman are memorialized.

There are other signs of the passage of the foreign volunteers. In a forest near the Harel Interchange on the modern busy superhighway that links Tel Aviv with Jerusalem, a small plaque placed by the American Veterans of Israel lists the names of eighty men and women, Canadians and Americans, who were killed in action in the Israeli War of Independence. In a large military cemetery beneath the heights of Mount Carmel on the southern outskirts of Haifa, a small marked-off section contains, among others, the remains of Fitchett, Beurling, Fred Stevenson, and Wayne Peake. Peake returned to the United States after the war, but never forgot Israel: when he was dying of cancer in 1979, he insisted that he be buried in the land for which he had fought thirty years before.

I

A few volunteers remained to settle in Israel. Australian Michael Landshut, who commanded the all-volunteer gun crew in the fighting against the Syrians, converted to Judaism, settled in Israel, and married. Eventually, he became a travel agent. Canadians Lionel Druker and Arthur Goldberg, who had been Zionists to begin with, saw a future in tourism and, with the help of backers in Canada, started a small self-drive car service that eventually became the largest privately owned tour bus company in Israel. Al Schwimmer went back to the United States to face charges arising out of his aircraft-smuggling activities and then after an unsuccessful attempt to start a small airline, returned to Israel to head Israel Aircraft Industries. Some of the men who served with ATC or the 69th Bomber Squadron went to work at El Al Israel Airlines, which began operations early in 1949 and then quickly expanded its air routes to America, Europe, and Africa. Bill Katz, from the United States, eventually became El Al's chief pilot. Sam Lewis also flew for El Al for a while, before taking a job flying the private jet of a wealthy Israeli industralist. Danny Rosin returned to South Africa for a short time, but the crockery business was no substitute for flying, and within a few months he and his wife returned to Israel where he served with Training Command in the air force before joining El Al.

Other volunteers who left Israel drifted back many years later. South African Syd Cohen—who commanded 101 Fighter Squadron after Modi Alon was killed in action in October 1948—was one such. Cohen returned home to become a doctor, but came back to Israel to offer his medical talents to the army in the 1956 and 1967 wars. After this he decided to come back to Israel for good. Smoky and Myra Simon, who had been with the first group of South African volunteers to leave for Palestine, returned to South Africa just after the war, where Smoky resumed civilian life as an accountant. In the early 1960s, however, they returned to Israel. Jules Cuburnek, from Chicago, was another volunteer who returned home only to move back to Israel (where he became an English teacher) in later years.

Most volunteers, however, left and never returned. They came back from Israel in 1949 and 1950, like most World War II veterans before them, to become ordinary citizens. Few achieved great wealth or prominence in their communities. They became taxi drivers, mechanics, insurance salesmen; they could not contribute more than a small percentage of the vast sums raised every year for Israel in a myriad of Jewish campaigns and appeals. These volunteers had laid their lives on the line, but they were quickly forgotten by those who valued money above raw courage in the continuing efforts of Jews outside Israel to aid their people in the re-born Jewish commonwealth.

The Israeli government showed some interest in making a special effort to attract *mahal* settlers, but not much. Despite repeated pleas from Lee Harris and Skidel, the government insisted that its first priority was to care for the hundreds of thousands of European displaced persons pouring into the country from Europe and Cyprus and the other hundreds of thousands that were beginning to seek refuge from the Arab countries, particularly from Iraq, Syria, Yemen, and Morocco. Israel was, after all, a small country recovering from a devastating war. It had suffered approximately six thousand dead, fully 1 per cent of its Jewish population, a far higher percentage than in any subsequent war. It had few resources, little money, and a major absorption task facing it. It is probable, however, that most volunteers would have returned to their homes in any case. Few, after all, had come to Israel out of Zionist conviction, and some of those who did were disillusioned by what they had found.

II

The basic differences in thinking that separated volunteer from Israeli had created the morale problems that began to show up as early as April, grew more serious during the first truce, and eventually, by the autumn of 1948, threatened to impede the operational ability of the

227

Seventh Brigade's 72nd Battalion and the Air Transport Command. This morale problem has blemished the record of the foreign volunteers. Many Israelis who were associated with volunteers during the war came away with an impression that they were chronic complainers, who were not worth the trouble they caused and who contributed little to the victory. Volunteers, on the other hand, came to view Israelis as arrogant, impatient, and even callous in their view of Diaspora Jews. The morale problem had a marked impact on reducing the chances that large numbers of volunteers would settle in Israel after the war. It also clouded the historical judgment of many Israelis about the importance of the volunteers to their victory.

The morale problem was not really caused by bad food, low pay, or complaints about command. It arose when, for the first time, large numbers of Diaspora Jews met large numbers of Israelis. Each group had expectations that the other could not possibly fulfil. The foreign volunteers' views had undoubtedly been coloured by the legend of the noble, tanned pioneers labouring in the Palestine sun. Instead they found a tough, independent, self-reliant community that was confident of its own abilities and demanded, as a matter of course, the support and assistance of foreign Jews. The Israelis had been led to believe that Diaspora Jews were soft, complacent, and timid. Instead, they found these veterans as tough and unyielding as themselves. In the highly charged atmosphere of a war situation, clashes of personality, of will, and of expectation were bound to occur.

Most volunteers had disrupted their lives and left families and friends to come to Palestine because they wanted to do their part to avoid a second Holocaust so soon after the first. But the Israelis they met often believed that these same volunteers were coming because they had no choice, because anti-semitism was so rife around the world that these volunteers were only the vanguard of a forced Jewish migration that would follow very soon. This then led to another problem: should the volunteers be treated the same as all other Israeli troops or should they have special status? This problem was never really resolved.

III

Israelis, for the most part, have failed to keep alive the memory of the *mahal*; the volunteers have been all but forgotten. Israel gave them

228

little recognition during the war and little afterwards. At first, in the spring of 1948, there was a definite military need to keep the existence of the volunteers secret both from the Arab enemy and from countries like the United States and Great Britain that were doing all in their power to maintain an embargo on the supply of weapons and the flow of men of military age to the area. There was also a need to protect the men themselves in cases where their participation in a foreign war and army placed their citizenship in jeopardy. After the war, although there was no longer any military need to hide the contribution of the volunteers, other motives took over. National pride probably played a major role. Perhaps Israeli leaders believed that it was better for the people of Israel, and particularly its young people, to think that Israel had won its battles without outside help. Perhaps it was easier to point with pride to the build-up of a modern and efficient armed force—the best in the Middle East—if they could believe that they had done it all from scratch, from nothing, by themselves.

To the Israelis the War of Independence was just the beginning of a long and costly military struggle for existence. There is, unfortunately, nothing unique about fighting and dying for survival in Israel. Most of the volunteers left Israel soon after the war to resume their lives in a dozen countries throughout the world while the Israelis—and a handful of volunteers—stayed to continue the battle. Thus most Israelis find it difficult to understand why they should pay special attention to the contribution of foreign volunteers, while the volunteers find it difficult to understand why so little attention is paid to them.

IV

Foreign volunteers—including those who stayed at home but helped collect and ship arms and other war material—played a vital role in Israel's victory. It is true that Czechoslovakia sold war-surplus equipment directly to Israel, and countries like Mexico, Nicaragua, Panama, Italy, and Yugoslavia aided the Jews by allowing Israeli agents to use their soil for transshipment. However, this alone would not have been sufficient to enable Israel to equip its forces to face and defeat the Arab invasion. Throughout the months of the war, Britain and the United States did everything in their power to stop the flow of weapons to Israel. In addition, Britain sold and shipped weapons to the Arabs, continued to subsidize the Arab Legion, and provided air-reconnaissance information to the Egyptians. Britain's intervention kept the Gaza Strip in Egyptian hands. Neither the West, in the accepted sense of that word, nor the United Nations brought about the military victory that allowed Israel to be born. That victory was forged by Israel, with the help of Diaspora Jews, especially the foreign volunteers and a small number of non-Jewish volunteers, and with the aid of a handful of small countries. There was certainly no American or British "complicity".

Diaspora Jewry became Israel's most trustworthy ally. No one among the Jewish people who thought of himself or herself as a Jew—as part of a larger people—was going to allow more Jew-killing while Hitler's ovens were still warm. It took two thousand years and the slaughter of one third of the Jews of the world before the Jewish people recognized the realities of being powerless sheep in a world of wolves. After 1945 the lesson had been learned. The Jews of Palestine would fight, Golda Meir told American audiences in the spring of 1948. They would not run up the white flag for the Mufti. The Jews of the United States, Canada, South Africa, and other countries, along with non-Jewish friends, listened quietly and firmly resolved that they too would fight, each in his or her own way. For more than 5000 people, this meant going off to war for the second time in a decade.

These volunteers contributed much to the outcome of that war. No conventional war has been won in the modern era without air superiority. The volunteer pilots, air crews, air-intelligence personnel, and ground-maintenance staff of the air force gave Israel control of the skies over the battlefield. The volunteers did not aid the Israeli Air Force, they *were* the Israeli Air Force. They were also the Air Transport Command, which brought the Czech arms and fighter planes that were so vitally needed. The air force and its transport squadrons played an increasingly important part in the fighting in the autumn and winter of 1948. They struck deep into Egyptian territory, provided close support to the advancing troops, mounted around-the-clock bombing of the Egyptians trapped in the Faluja pocket, and provided fresh aerial reconnaissance of enemy troop movements. They airlifted thousands of tired troops out of the blockaded Negev and brought in thousands of fresh troops. They provided air cover over Israeli cities and stemmed the Arab bombing offensive. Their expertise, their knowledge of tactics, their ability to improvise, and their previous training in the Allied air forces of World War II provided a solid foundation upon which the future Israeli Air Force was built.

The foreign volunteers did not add much to the ground forces by way of numbers, but they did bring experience in conventional warfare that was invaluable at many levels—from military medicine to the use of armour, artillery, mortars, and modern communications equipment. Their experience, when added to the training that some Israelis had received in the British army in World War II, helped transform the underground Haganah into an efficient conventional army. No one wishes to, or should, downplay the brilliance of native Israeli commanders. Those like Yigal Allon, especially, with previous experience only in the underground Haganah, nevertheless quickly grasped the essentials of commanding large bodies of troops in open battle and utilized the existing strengths of the Haganah—flexibility, informality, the ability to fight at night, knowledge of the terrain—to build a formidable army remarkably quickly. But their task was undoubtedly made easier by the presence of foreign volunteers who already possessed the necessary skills.

In one theatre—the north—volunteers made up a large part of the command and approximately 10 per cent of the manpower of the Seventh Brigade. This brigade, it will be recalled, cleared Kaukji and the Lebanese from northern Israel in two actions. The morale problems that afflicted the brigade and the controversy surrounding the question of who was in command, and when, should not detract from the swift victories scored by the brigade in the taking of Nazareth or in the drive to the Litani River. Kaukji was not nearly as formidable a foe as the Syrian or Egyptian forces. Nevertheless, control of the Galilee was vitally important to securing a Jewish hold on the coastal plain and re-establishing territorial contiguity between the Jewish-held areas in the finger of the northern Galilee and those to the south and west. Seventh Brigade successes literally filled out the map of north-central Israel.

The volunteers made yet another contribution to the Jewish war effort. Their presence was visible and dramatic proof that Israel was not alone in its struggle for survival. There were thousands around the world—most of them Jewish but a significant number non-Jewish—who were prepared to undergo hardships and to risk jail sentences, torture, and even death to help re-establish the Jewish state. Whatever their motives, they were not fickle allies.

Perhaps the most important impact of the volunteers was that their knowledge and expertise, recorded in Israel's first training manuals and regulations of military procedures, allowed the Israelis to construct a post-war modern army much more quickly than they might otherwise have done. Israel did not need foreign experts as many developing countries do; they had the volunteers. The Israeli armed forces that emerged by the early 1950s had learned much about military medicine, air operations, the use of artillery, mortars, and tanks, and proper maintenance procedures from the volunteers. Thus the army, one of the most important institutions in Israeli society, was helped in its initial development by these volunteers from abroad. That army has been the shield keeping Israel alive for more than three and a half decades. It remains vitally important to Israel as long as peace is still mostly a dream.

V

Israel's re-birth in the War of Independence revitalized the Jewish people after the terrible agony of the Holocaust and gave them new hope of a renaissance in their historic homeland. Israel has become the focus for those Jews who care about their survival as a people. It also stands as a beacon to people around the world who care about the survival of democratic institutions in an increasingly hostile environment. Israel is not perfect—what country is?—but the survival of democracy there despite the country's continuing struggle for survival is more of a miracle than Israel's survival itself. The world has been preoccupied with the growing Arab economic power, and the democratic and self-governing nations of western Europe and North America have progressively abandoned Israel in their pursuit of Arab markets and to slake their thirst for Arab oil. Nevertheless an essential fact remains clear. The Jewish people by dint of sweat and blood have established their right to emerge from centuries of oppression as a sovereign nation.

Israel's rebirth has changed the power balance of the Middle East. Israel is a factor to be reckoned with, not only because of its military prowess but because of the example of its achievement. It has faced the challenge of the ingathering of millions of homeless and destitute Jews from around the world and, with few resources, has created a modern society. The Israeli people have sent deep roots into their ancient soil. It is those roots, not military expertise, that have enabled them to

232

overcome the awesome challenges to their existence. This achievement sent shock waves through the world of power politics and it is because of it that the contributions of the foreign volunteers are so important. They played a vital role in the victory that allowed the process of building and ingathering to continue.

Although the foreign volunteers who fought in the Israeli War of Independence remain forgotten heroes, they themselves have not forgotten and their brief moment of glory will remain with them always. The importance of their role is well stated by Ben Ocopnik, of Canada: "We fought for the re-establishment, after nearly 2000 years, of a Jewish state. I am sure that when I die the last thing that will pass through my mind will be what I and others did in Israel then."

Notes

Chapter 1

1. Yigal Allon, *Shield of David: The Story of Israel's Armed Forces* (New York, 1970), pp. 67-68.
2. The story of Herzl's efforts is in Amos Elon, *Herzl* (New York, 1975), pp. 187-200, 330-59.
3. Howard M. Sachar, *A History of Israel: From the Rise of Zionism to Our Time* (New York, 1976), pp. 107-10.
4. George Antonius, *The Arab Awakening* (New York, 1965), pp. 267-75.
5. *Ibid.*, pp. 419-20.
6. *Ibid.*, pp. 285-86, 437-39.
7. *Ibid.*, p. 441.
8. Sachar, *A History of Israel*, pp. 199-201.
9. *Ibid.*, pp. 222-26.
10. Allon, *Shield of David*, p. 81.
11. On Sadeh see *Ibid.*, pp. 86-88. For Wingate see Edward Luttwack and Dan Horowitz, *The Israeli Army* (New York, 1975), pp. 14-16.
12. Luttwack and Horowitz, *The Israeli Army*, p. 17.
13. Allon, *Shield of David*, p. 114.
14. Encyclopedia Judaica, vol. 16 (New York, 1972), p. 306.
15. Nicholas Bethell, *The Palestine Triangle: The Struggle Between the British, the Jews and the Arabs, 1935-1948* (London, 1979), pp. 185-86.
16. Sachar, *A History of Israel*, p. 250.
17. See Yehuda Bauer, *The Jewish Emergence from Powerlessness* (Toronto, 1979) for a development of this theme. This issue is also covered in Walter Laquer, "Hitler's Holocaust: Who Knew What, When & How?", *Encounter*, July 1980, pp. 6-25.

18. Zvi Ganin, *Truman, American Jewry and Israel, 1945-1948* (New York, 1979), p. xiii.

Chapter 2

1. Netanel Lorch, *The Edge of the Sword: Israel's War of Independence* (Jerusalem, 1961), pp. 46-48.
2. Bethell, *The Palestine Triangle*, pp. 288-315.
3. Sachar, *A History of Israel*, pp. 249-76.
4. Trygve Lie, *In the Cause of Peace* (New York, 1954), pp. 160-61.
5. Sachar, *A History of Israel*, p. 292.
6. National Archives, Washington (NAW), General Records of the Department of State, RG 59, 867N.01/10-847, American Legation, Beirut, to Secretary of State, October 8, 1947. (Henceforth State Department Records.)
7. Larry Collins and Dominique Lapierre, *O Jerusalem* (New York, 1973), pp. 164-67.
8. State Department Records, 501.BB Palestine/10-1847, Memminger to Secretary of State, October 18, 1947.
9. Lorch, *The Edge of the Sword*, pp. 20-21.
10. Trevor H. Dupuy, *Elusive Victory: The Arab Israeli Wars, 1947-1974* (New York, 1978), pp. 11-19.
11. Lorch, *The Edge of the Sword*, p. 26.
12. Ben Gurion Diary, August 15, 1947.
13. Jon and David Kimche, *Both Sides of the Hill: Britain and the Palestine War* (London, 1960), p. 67.
14. *Ibid.*, pp. 76-77.
15. Dupuy, *Elusive Victory*, p. 117.
16. Murray Rubenstein and Richard Goldman, *Shield of David: An Illustrated History of the Israeli Air Force* (Englewood Cliffs, N.J., 1978), pp. 12-14.
17. Leonard Slater, *The Pledge* (New York, 1972), pp. 11-19.
18. Allon, *Shield of David*, pp. 156-60; Munya Mardor, *Haganah (Strictly Illegal)* (New York, 1964), pp. 106-09, 220-21.
19. Moshe Pearlman and David Ben Gurion, *Ben Gurion Looks Back in Talks with Moshe Pearlman* (London, 1965), pp. 139-40; Slater, *The Pledge*, pp. 19-94.
20. Slater, *The Pledge*, pp. 119-20.
21. Ehud Avriel, *Open the Gates! The Dramatic Personal Story of 'Illegal' Immigration to Israel* (London, 1975), pp. 330-31.

22. Interview with Aharon Remez, Jerusalem, November 1979.
23. M. Hadar and Y. Ofer, eds., *Heyl Ha'avir* (Tel Aviv, 1971), p. 25.
24. Benjamin Kagan, *The Secret Battle for Israel* (New York, 1966), pp. 34-36.
25. Public Records Office (PRO) Foreign Office Records, FO 371/68646/E1044, Ministry of Defence to H.Q. British Troops, Palestine, January 28. 1948. (Henceforth Foreign Office Records.)
26. *Foreign Relations of the United States*, 1948, Vol. V, Part 2 p. 562. (Henceforth FRUS.)
27. *Ibid.*
28. Foreign Office Records, FO 371/68402, Stapleton to Burrows, January 16, 1948, with attachments; 68410/E 1461, Top Secret Memorandum of January 27, 1948.
29. Foreign Office Records, FO 371/68414, Baghdad to Foreign Office, August 2, 1948; 68410/E 1983, Barker to Sargent, February 9, 1948, with attachments; 68410/E 1792, Eastern Department to Chancery, February 21, 1948, with attachments. Other arms shipments are reported in FO 371/68411, Foreign Office to Baghdad, February 25, 1948; Cairo to Foreign Office, February 25, 1948; and 68412, Bryers to Walker, March 15, 1948; BMEO (British Middle East Office) to Foreign Office, March 23, 1948; Battye to Beeley, April 2, 1948.
30. Foreign Office Records, FO 371/68635, Cunningham to Secretary of State for the Colonies, January 2, 1948.
31. Slater, *The Pledge*, pp. 124-25.
32. Foreign Office Records, FO 371/68410/E1105, Washington to Foreign Office, January 16, 1948; State Department Records, 867N.01/1-2648, Marshall to London, January 26, 1948.
33. Foreign Office Records, FO 371/68410/E1461, Top Secret Memorandum of January 27, 1948.
34. Shlomo Slonim, "The 1948 American Embargo on Arms to Palestine", *Political Science Quarterly*, Vol. 94, No. 3, p. 499.
35. Israel State Archives, Foreign Relations Files, RG 93.03, File 21, Box 2268, "M.S." to "F.D.R., Jr.", December 24, 1947. (Henceforth Israel Foreign Relations Files.)
36. State Department Records, 867N.01/1-1648, Magnuson to Marshall, January 16, 1948.
37. *Ibid.*, Bullen to Magnuson, January 23, 1948.
38. FRUS, p. 580.

Chapter 3

1. Avriel, *Open the Gates!*, pp. 331-33; Arnold Krammer, *The Forgotten Friendship: Israel and the Soviet Bloc, 1947-1953* (Urbana, 1974), pp. 59-60.
2. Avriel, *Open the Gates!*, pp. 333-36; Krammer, *The Forgotten Friendship*, pp. 60-62.
3. Krammer discusses these, *Ibid.*, pp. 66-82.
4. State Department Records, 501.BB Palestine/6-2148, Steinhardt to Secretary of State, June 22, 1948.
5. Krammer, *The Forgotten Friendship*, pp. 62-63; Mardor, *Haganah*, p. 237.
6. Collins and Lapierre, *O Jerusalem*, pp. 237-40.
7. Lorch, *The Edge of the Sword*, pp. 51-63.
8. *FRUS*, pp. 742-43.
9. State Department Records 711.00111 Armament Control/7-2348 contains many U.S. government reports, correspondence, and memos, including information gained by Customs and FBI agents, bearing on the operations of Service Airways, Schwimmer Aviation, and the Jewish Agency. It was collected in connection with a suit brought by the Justice Department after an attempt to export illegally 42 aircraft engines. Documents in the file are copies of the originals. (Henceforth "United States *v.* 42 Combat Aircraft Engines".) Arazi's contact with Schwimmer described in "Anticipated Attempt to Export Military Aircraft without License", May 27, 1948.
10. Interview with Teddy Kollek, November 1979.
11. Teddy and Amos Kollek, *For Jerusalem: A Life by Teddy Kollek* (New York, 1978), p. 68.
12. Teddy Kollek Interview; Slater, *The Pledge*, pp. 173-78.
13. Interview with Wellesley Aron, November 1979.
14. Slater, *The Pledge*, pp. 178-93.
15. "United States *v.* 42 Combat Aircraft Engines", and "Anticipated Attempt...without License", May 27, 1948; Slater, *The Pledge*, pp. 136-37.
16. *Ibid.*
17. Slater, *The Pledge*, p. 138.
18. Robert Herron, "The Miami Connection", *Miami Pictorial*, March 1973.
19. Interview with Sam Lewis, November 1979.

20. "United States v. 42 Combat Aircraft Engines", Gwinn to U.S. Attorney, Los Angeles, June 24, 1948.
21. Ibid., Wyatt to E.J. Shamhart, March 25, 1948.
22. Slater, The Pledge, pp. 145-58.
23. State Department Records, 867N.01/1-1548, Tuck to Secretary of State, January 15, 1948.
24. See, for example, "United States v. 42 Combat Aircraft Engines", "W" To the Customs Agent in Charge, Philadelphia, March 17, 1948.
25. Slater, The Pledge, pp. 221-33; State Department Records, 711.00111 Armament Control/3-3148 CS/A, Neal to Bell, March 31, 1948.
26. "United States v. 42 Combat Aircraft Engines", "Hearing in Connection with the Exportation...", Irvin R. Schindler, witness.
27. Interview with Boris Senior, November 1979; Henry Katzew, South Africa's 800: The Story of Volunteers in Israel's War of Birth (unpublished manuscript), Chapter 2, Part 1, pp. 24-25.
28. Interview with Harry (Smoky) Simon, September 1979.
29. Katzew, South Africa's 800, Chapter 2, Part 1, p. 7.
30. Ibid., p. 16.
31. Ibid., pp. 21 ff.
32. Boris Senior Interview; Ezer Weizman, On Eagle's Wings: The Personal Story of the Leading Commander of the Israeli Air Force (New York, 1976), pp. 48-49.
33. Boris Senior Interview.
34. Interview with Joseph N. Frank, February 1979.
35. Public Archives of Canada (PAC), Privy Council Office Records, RG 2/18/Vol. 86, File M.30.2, "Export of Armaments (Including Ammunitions and Implements of War) to Foreign Governments", March 7 and April 2, 1947. (Henceforth, Canada Privy Council Records.)
36. Slater, The Pledge, pp. 56-68.
37. Joseph N. Frank Interview; Interview with Joe Baumholz, June 1979.
38. PAC, Frank Papers, Vol. 5, Loewenson to Sherman, July 6, 1948.
39. Department of External Affairs Files (DEA), File 8903-E-40, Vol. I, Crowe to Watkins, May 24, 1948. (Henceforth Canada External Affairs Files.)

40. Joe Baumholz Interview.
41. Israel Foreign Relations Files, RG 93.03, File 16, Box 69, Zacks to Lourie, October 19, 1948.
42. Interview with Moe Appel, June 1979.
43. Joe Baumholz Interview.
44. Department of National Defence, Directorate of History, Aircraft Record Cards. I am grateful to Brereton Greenhous for this source.
45. Moe Appel Interview.
46. Joe Baumholz Interview. Invoices and shipping lists can be found in Baumholz's personal possession.

Chapter 4
1. Interview with Jules Cuburnek, November 1979.
2. Haganah Archives, Ben Gurion Diaries, May 27, 1947.
3. Kimche, *Both Sides of the Hill*, pp. 68-69
4. *Ibid.*
5. Israel Foreign Relations Files, RG 93.03, File 21, "M.S." to "F.D.R., Jr.", December 24, 1947.
6. Evan M. Wilson, *Decision on Palestine* (Stanford, 1979), p. 116.
7. Israel Foreign Relations Files, RG 93.03, File 21, "M.S." to "F.D.R., Jr.", December 24, 1947.
8. Slater, *The Pledge*, pp. 92-93; Jay Mallin and Robert K. Brown, *Merc: American Soldiers of Fortune* (New York, 1979), pp. 32-33.
9. Israel Defence Forces Archive, Mahal File, "The Committee for Overseas Mobilization, Instructions for Mobilization in Foreign Lands, in Accordance with the Resolutions of Jewish Agency Board, January 25, 1948". (Henceforth, Mahal File.)
10. Central Zionist Archives, File K14A/110, Marcus to Hammer, April 29, 1948. (Henceforth Zionist Papers.)
11. Israel Foreign Relations Files, RG 93.03, Box 126, Comay to Lourie, May 18, 1948.
12. Marcus is discussed in M. Pail, *The Emergence of Zahal* (Tel Aviv 1979).
13. Haganah Archives, Ben Gurion Diary, March 3, 1948.
14. Wellesley Aron Interview.
15. *Ibid.*
16. *Ibid.*; see also Slater, *The Pledge*, pp. 207-15, and Kollek, *For Jerusalem*, p. 64.

17. Aharon Remez Interview.
18. Teddy Kollek Interview.
19. Sam Lewis Interview. See also Slater, *The Pledge*, pp. 229-33.
20. State Department Records, 867N.01/5-1548, Yingling to Flynn, June 25, 1948.
21. This is discussed in Slater, *The Pledge*, p. 206.
22. Wellesley Aron Interview.
23. State Department Records, 867N.01/1-748, Bohlen to Kilday, February 27, 1948.
24. Slater, *The Pledge*, pp. 210-11.
25. Wellesley Aron Interview.
26. State Department Records, 867N.01/4-2148, Wasson to Secretary of State, May 14, 1948.
27. Taken from "Important Notice to Passengers" in possession of Sydney P. Cadloff.
28. Interview with A. J. Siegel, July 1979.
29. *Canadian Jews in World War Two*, Vol. I, pp. 2-4.
30. Ben Dunkelman, *Dual Allegiance* (Toronto, 1979), pp. 152-53.
31. *Ibid.*, pp. 47-48.
32. *Ibid.*, p. 157.
33. Mahal File, Tamkin to Zadok, April 9, 1948.
34. Teddy Kollek Interview.
35. Canadian Jewish Congress, *Inter Office Information*, April 29, 1947, p. 3.
36. Interview with Arthur Goldberg, September 1979.
37. Interview with Harold Freeman, April 1979; Interview with John and Lee Secter, April 1979.
38. Dunkelman, *Dual Allegiance*, p. 155, mentions some of the members of his committee but not all.
39. Zionist Papers, File K14A/110, Harris to Zacks, June 13, 1948.
40. Harold Freeman Interview; Interview with Lionel Druker, October 1979; Interview with Ralph Hamovitch, April 1979.
41. Zionist Papers, File K14A/110. See pencilled notation in D. Lou Harris's handwriting on Kollek to Harris, June 8, 1948; Harold Freeman Interview; John Secter Interview.
42. Zionist Papers, *ibid.*
43. *Ottawa Journal*, April 3, 1948.
44. Canada External Affairs Files, File 9693.A-40C, RCMP to G. G. Crean, April 19, 1948.

45. Mahal File, Tamkin to Zadok, April 9, 1948.
46. Canada External Affairs Files, File 9693.A-40C, "Application of Foreign Enlistment Act to Palestine", Memo of February 17, 1948, written by G. C. Langille.
47. Ibid., File 10013-40, RCMP to Pearson, May 27, 1948.
48. Katzew, South Africa's 800, Chapter 2, Part 3, pp. 1-4.
49. Ibid., Chapter 2, Part 1, pp. 27-30.
50. Ibid., Chapter 2, Part 2, pp. 1-3.
51. Ibid., Chapter 2, Part 3, p. 1.
52. Ibid., pp. 2-3.
53. Lorch, The Edge of the Sword, pp. 388-92.
54. Katzew, South Africa's 800, Chapter 2, Part 3, p. 1.
55. Interview with Danny Rosin, October 1979.
56. Katzew, South Africa's 800, Chapter 2, Part 3, p. 11.
57. Teddy Eytan, Neguev—L'Héroique Naissance de l'Etat d'Israel (Paris, 1949), pp. 20, 32, 59.
58. Judah Ben David, Sword in Foreign Lands: The Haganah in Europe, 1945-1948 (Tel Aviv, 1978), pp. 248-56.
59. Motive is discussed in a variety of works by others who have studied this topic. One of the most exhaustive discussions, based on surveys of volunteers, is in Avigdor Shahan, The Wings of Victory (Tel Aviv, 1966), pp. 300-06. My observations are based on Shahan and other sources such as Slater, The Pledge, and R. Silverberg, If I Forget Thee O Jerusalem (New York, 1972), as well as my own interviews. See also Efraim Talmi, Israel's Campaigns (Tel Aviv, 1972), pp. 344-45.
60. State Department Records, 867N.01/1-1748, Macatee to Secretary of State, January 17, 1948.
61. Jewish Historical Society (Ottawa), Shaffer Papers, Harris to Shaffer, January 17, 1948.
62. Mahal File, Tamkin to Zadok, April 14, 1948.
63. Yehuda Slutzki, The History of the Haganah, Vol. III (Tel Aviv, 1973), p. 1469.
64. Interview with Norman Levi, April 1979.
65. Interview with Harry (Smoky) Simon, October 1979.
66. Interview with Harlow Geberer, August 1980.
67. Interview with Harry Eisner, August 1980.
68. Interview with Len Hyman, April 1979.
69. Interview with Joe Weiner, January 1979.

70. *Maclean's Magazine*, May 15, 1948.
71. Interview with Sydney Shulemson, June 1979.
72. *The Globe and Mail* (Toronto), May 28, 1948.
73. Sydney Shulemson Interview.
74. *Maclean's Magazine*, May 15, 1948.
75. Lorch, *The Edge of the Sword*, pp. 89-96.
76. *Ibid.*, pp. 93-94.
77. Israel Foreign Relations Files, RG 93.03, File 15, Box 66, Bidmead to A/A.I.G., C.I.D., April 16, 1948.
78. Interview with Sydney P. Cadloff, June 1979.
79. Ben David, *Sword in Foreign Lands*, p. 267; Mahal File, Tamkin to Yo'ash, April 14, 1948.
80. Departure date and time for *Marine Falcon* passenger ticket in possession of Sydney P. Cadloff.
81. Mahal File, Yaski to Tamkin, April 13, 1948.
82. *Ibid.*; Ben David, *Sword in Foreign Lands*, pp. 267-68.

Chapter 5
1. Interview with Jack Goldstein, June 1979.
2. *Ibid.*
3. State Department Records, 711.00111 Armament Control/5-648, "Report by American Consulate General, Milan...", April 27, 1948.
4. *Ibid.*, 711.00111 Armament Control/5-648, American Embassy, Rome, to Department of State, May 6, 1948; Kagan, *The Secret Battle for Israel*, pp. 46-47.
5. *Ibid.*, 711.00111 Armament Control/5-648, Schindler to Societa Aeronautica Italiana, February 26, 1948.
6. "United States v. 42 Combat Aircraft Engines", Vogoilo to Service Airways, March 4, 1948.
7. "United States v. 42 Combat Aircraft Engines", Rogers to Customs Agent in Charge, Philadelphia, April 2, 1948.
8. State Department Records, 711.00111 Armament Control/1-2148, Cummins to White, February 6, 1948.
9. "United States v. 42 Combat Aircraft Engines", "Hearing in Connection with the Exportation of a Constellation...", March 25, 1948.
10. Slater, *The Pledge*, pp. 238-39.
11. Kagan, *The Secret Battle for Israel*, pp. 49-50.

12. *Ibid.*
13. "United States *v.* 42 Combat Aircraft Engines", Wyatt Memorandum of February 10, 1948.
14. *Ibid.*, Wyatt to Shamhart, March 29, 1948.
15. *Ibid.*, "Hearing in Connection with the Exportation of a Constellation...", March 25, 1948.
16. Slater, *The Pledge*, pp. 233-34.
17. "United States *v.* 42 Combat Aircraft Engines", Wyatt to Shamhart, March 25, 1948.
18. *Ibid.*, Moore to Supervising Customs Agent, New York, March 23, 1948.
19. Slater, *The Pledge*, pp. 248-51.
20. "United States *v.* 42 Combat Aircraft Engines", "Statement of John L. Westland...", May 14, 1948.
21. Slater, *The Pledge*, pp. 252-53; Sam Lewis Interview.
22. Sam Lewis Interview.
23. State Department Records, 867N.01/4-1948, Rankin to Secretary of State, April 19, 1948.
24. *Ibid.*, 867N.01/4-2448, Rankin to Secretary of State, April 24, 1948.
25. *Ibid.*, 867N.01/5-548, Rankin to Secretary of State, May 5, 1948.
26. Slater, *The Pledge*, p. 124; Aharon Remez Interview.
27. State Department Records, 867N.01/4-1948, Rankin to Secretary of State, April 20, 1948.
28. *Ibid.*, 867N.01/12-2048, Patterson to Secretary of State, December 20, 1948.
29. Aharon Remez Interview.
30. Foreign Office Records, FO 371/68648/E 7128, Rome to Foreign Office, May 28, 1948.
31. State Department Records, 501.BB Palestine/6-948, Dunn to Secretary of State, June 9, 1948.
32. *Ibid.*, 711.00111 Armament Control/5-1149, "Letter Received from London by British Embassy, Washington", May 11, 1949.
33. *Ibid.*, 867N.01/4-1648, Rankin to Secretary of State, April 16, 1948.
34. *Ibid.*, 711.00111 Armament Control/2-2849, Powell to Barringer, February 28, 1949.
35. *Ibid.*, 711.00111 Armament Control/2-2849 and /10-1848, Pomeroy to Cummins, October 18, 1948.

36. Slater, *The Pledge*, p. 262.
37. State Department Records, 711.00111 Armament Control/2-2849, Powell to Barringer, February 28, 1949.
38. *Ibid.*, 711.00111 Armament Control/12-948, Barringer to Cummins, December 9, 1948.
39. Katzew, *South Africa's 800*, Chapter 4, pp. 1-4.
40. *Ibid.*, Chapter 3, pp. 1-2; Boris Senior Interview.
41. *Ibid.*, Chapter 3, pp. 13-15.
42. *Ibid.*, Chapter 3, pp. 2-3; Boris Senior Interview.
43. Slater, *The Pledge*, pp. 267-69.
44. Jules Cuburnek Interview.
45. "Operations Schedule for Wednesday, May 5, 1948", in possession of Bill Katz.
46. Slater, *The Pledge*, pp. 273-74. All dates of departure and arrival of Raab's C-46 (RX 138) and elapsed times in air taken from Jules Cuburnek's flight log book in possession of Jules Cuburnek.
47. State Department Records, 867N.01/6-948, Robertson to Secretary of State, June 9, 1948.
48. Jules Cuburnek Interview; Interview with Eddy Chinsky, October 1979. This story is also in Slater, *The Pledge*, p. 274.
49. Jules Cuburnek Interview.
50. *Ibid.*; Slater, *The Pledge*, p. 283.
51. Jules Cuburnek Interview.
52. Eddy Chinsky Interview.
53. Jules Cuburnek Interview.
54. Dunkelman, *Dual Allegiance*, pp. 164-66.
55. Mahal File, Tamkin to Zadok, April 14, 1948.
56. Dunkelman, *Dual Allegiance*, pp. 167-69.
57. *Haganah Speaks*, September 3, 1948.
58. Harry Eisner Interview.
59. Katzew, *South Africa's 800*, Chapter 3, pp. 6-7.
60. *Ibid.*, pp. 8-11.
61. State Department Records, 867N.01/12-347, Lovett to American Embassy, Cairo, December 10, 1947.
62. Mahal File, "Statement by Canadian Group from Toronto", May 4, 1948.
63. Luttwack and Horowitz, *The Israeli Army*, p. 34.
64. *Ma'arachot*, pp. 263-64, June 1978.
65. Avraham Ayalon, *Givati Brigade During the War of Independence* (Ma'arachot, 1959), pp. 534-35.

66. *Ibid.*, p. 538.
67. Lionel Druker Interview.
68. Ayalon, *Givati Brigade*, pp. 536-37.
69. *Ibid.*
70. Interview with Murray Cappell, July 1979; Interview with Irving Kaplansky, August 1980.
71. Sydney Cadloff Interview.
72. Murray Cappell Interview; Irving Kaplansky Interview.
73. *Ibid.*; Lionel Druker Interview; Ayalon, *Givati Brigade*, p. 537.
74. Ayalon, *ibid.*, p. 538 ff.
75. Letter in possession of Sydney P. Cadloff.
76. Irving Kaplansky Interview.
77. Events at the United Nations are recounted in Zeef Sharef, *Three Days* (New York, 1962).

Chapter 6
1. Jules Cuburnek Interview.
2. Dupuy, *Elusive Victory*, pp. 41-59, contains a concise summary of the initial invasion objectives and actual achievements. Other sources are Luttwack and Horowitz, *The Israeli Army*, and Lorch, *The Edge of the Sword*.
3. Dupuy, *Elusive Victory*, pp. 41-59.
4. Dan Kurtzman, *Genesis 1948: The First Arab-Israeli War* (New York, 1970), p. 500.
5. Katzew, *South Africa's 800*, Chapter 3, pp. 15-18.
6. State Department Records, 711.00111 Armament Control/8-1148, McNiece to Secretary of State, August 11, 1948.
7. Jules Cuburnek Interview.
8. Shahan, *The Wings of Victory*, pp. 315-16; Slater, *The Pledge*, p. 289.
9. *L'Unita*, May 21, 1948; *Il Messagero*, May 21, 1948.
10. Haganah Archives, Intelligence Files. "The Death of Beurling and L. Cohen", n.d.
11. State Department Records, 867N.01/5-2048, Pinkerton to Secretary of State, May 20, 1948.
12. Zionist Papers, File Z5/1291, Merriam to American Zionist Emergency Council, December 4, 1946.
13. *Marine Carp* confidential interview; Harlow Geberer Interview. Ownership data is from State Department Records, 867N.01/5-

2448, American Consulate, Alexandria, to Secretary of State, May 25, 1948.

14. State Department Records, 867N.01/5-1948, Pinkerton to Secretary of State, May 19, 1948; /5-2048, Pinkerton to Secretary of State, May 20, 1948; Foreign Office Records, FO 371/68493/E 6645, Beirut to Foreign Office, May 20, 1948.

15. Confidential interview with *Marine Carp* detainee, July 1979.

16. Foreign Office Records, FO 371/68493/E 7050, Beirut to Foreign Office, May 26, 1948.

17. State Department Records, 867N.01/5-2948, Marshall to American Legation, Beirut, May 20, 1948.

18. *Ibid.*; 867N.01/5-2248, Pinkerton to Secretary of State, May 22, 1948.

19. Foreign Office Records, FO 371/68493/E 7050, Beirut to Foreign Office, May 26, 1948.

20. State Department Records, 867N.01/5-2448, Pinkerton to Secretary of State, May 24, 1948.

21. *Ibid.*, /5-2248, Gross to Secretary of State, May 26, 1948; Secretary of State to American Legation, Beirut, May 26, 1948.

22. *Ibid.*, 867N.01/5-2748, Pinkerton to Secretary of State, May 27, 1948.

23. Canada External Affairs Files, 10013-40, Secretary of State for External Affairs to the High Commissioner for Canada in the United Kingdom, May 29, 1948.

24. *Marine Carp* confidential interview.

25. Lorch, *The Edge of the Sword*, pp. 247-50.

26. Krammer, *The Forgotten Friendship*, pp. 88-90. Krammer quotes $40,000 per fighter which, according to most sources is not correct. The figure is clearly low.

27. "Israel's First Fighters", *Flying Review International*, Vol. 22, No. 12, August 1967, pp. 809-11.

28. Slater, *The Pledge*, pp. 293-96; Kagan, *The Secret Battle for Israel*, pp. 76-77.

29. Sam Lewis Interview.

30. State Department Records, 501.BB Palestine/6-1048, Marshall to American Embassy, Panama, June 10, 1948.

31. Mardor, *Haganah*, pp. 263-65.

32. *Ibid.*, p. 267.

33. Flight details taken from Jack Goldstein Interview; Interview

with Morris Beck, June 1979; Jules Cuburnek Interview; Cuburnek Flight Log; State Department Records, 867N.01/12-2048, Patterson to Secretary of State, December 20, 1948.

34. Weizman, *On Eagle's Wings*, p. 67.
35. Robert Jackson, *The Israeli Air Force Story* (London, 1970), p. 34.
36. Ben Gurion Diary, June 1, 1948; Lorch, *The Edge of the Sword*, p. 268.
37. Collins and Lapierre, *O Jerusalem*, pp. 548 ff.
38. Lorch, *The Edge of the Sword*, pp. 205 ff.
39. *Ibid.*, p. 222.
40. Dunkelman, *Dual Allegiance*, pp. 216-18.
41. Canada External Affairs Files, File 47B(S), Clutterbuck to St. Laurent, May 19, 1948.
42. *FRUS*, p. 1016.
43. *Ibid.*, pp. 1019-20.
44. *Ibid.*, pp. 1021-22.
45. *Ibid.*, pp. 1027-28.
46. *Ibid.*, pp. 1047-50.
47. *Ibid.*, p. 1064.
48. Foreign Office Records, FO 371/68413/E 7602, War Office to Commander in Chief, Middle East Land Forces, Cairo, May 31, 1948.
49. Dupuy, *Elusive Victory*, p. 67.
50. Smoky Simon Interview; Katzew, *South Africa's 800*, Chapter 5, pp. 19-20; Lorch, *The Edge of the Sword*, p. 269.
51. Lorch, *The Edge of the Sword*, p. 228.

Chapter 7
1. State Department Records, 501.BB Palestine/6-1748, Marshall to American Consulate, Jerusalem.
2. Kagan, *The Secret Battle for Israel*, p. 98; State Department Records, 501.BB Palestine/7-948, Burrows to Secretary of State, July 9, 1948.
3. Interview with W. H. Novick, June 1979.
4. State Department Records, 501.BB Palestine/6-3048, Saltzman to Lovett, June 30, 1948.
5. Mike Minnich, "The Queen's Last Battle: The Story of Israel's Three Bomber, B-17 Air Force!", *Wings*, February 1981, p. 21.
6. State Department Records, RG 559, 711.00111 Armament Con-

trol/8-1248, Marshall to American Consulate, Marseilles, August 12, 1948.

7. Ibid., 501.BB Palestine/7-1048, Dunn to Secretary of State, July 10, 1948.

8. Slater, The Pledge, pp. 255-57.

9. State Department Records, 501.BB Palestine/7-1048, Dunn to Secretary of State, July 10, 1948.

10. Danny Rosin Interview.

11. National Archives Washington, Records of the Army General Staff, Plans and Operations Division, RG 319, Palestine, Section I, Case I, Box 93, "Intelligence Estimate Palestine Dated 16 March 1948". Updated June 9, 1948.

12. Sune O. Persson, Mediation and Assassination: Count Bernadotte's Mission to Palestine in 1948 (London, 1979), pp. 128-29; 134-35.

13. Ibid., pp. 122-23.

14. State Department Records, 501.BB Palestine/6-1648, Lie to Secretary of State, June 16, 1948.

15. Canada External Affairs Files, File 47 B(S), Canadian Permanent Delegate to the United Nations to Secretary of State for External Affairs, June 14, 1948.

16. Foreign Office Records, FO 371/68632/E 15352, "Entry into Palestine of Men of Military Age", Balfour Minute, November 28, 1948.

17. Canada External Affairs Files, File 47 B(S), Canadian Permanent Delegate to the United Nations to Secretary of State for External Affairs, June 14, 1948.

18. State Department Records, 501.BB Palestine/6-1648, Radius to Smith, June 16, 1948.

19. Ibid., 501.BB Palestine/6-1648, Douglas to Secretary of State.

20. Foreign Office Records, FO 371/68413, Foreign Office to Amman, June 12, 1948.

21. Ibid., FO 371/68412, Foreign Office to Baghdad, June 10, 1948.

22. State Department Records, 867N.01/6-1248, Davis to Secretary of State, June 12, 1948.

23. Ibid., 501.BB Palestine/7-1048, American Embassy, Panama, to State Department, July 10, 1948.

24. Ibid., 501.BB Palestine/6-848, Marshall to American Embassy, Rome, June 8, 1948.

25. Ibid., 501.BB Palestine/8-1648, "Greek Cabinet Decision Imple-

menting Security Council Decisions on Palestine Truce", August 16, 1948.

26. *Ibid.*, 501.BB Palestine/6-1748, Marshall to American Embassy, Prague, June 17, 1948.

27. Foreign Office Records, FO 371/68637/E 12195, Prague to Foreign Office, June 21, 1948.

28. State Department Records, Rusk Book, Box 4, Caffery to Secretary of State, June 22, 1948.

29. *Ibid.*, June 30, 1948.

30. *Ibid.*, 711.00111 Armament Control/5-1149, "Letter Received from London by British Embassy, Washington", May 11, 1949.

31. *Ibid.*, 501.BB Palestine/6-2348, Steinhardt to Secretary of State, June 23, 1948.

32. United Nations Archives, Mediators Files, DAG 13/3.30, Box 14, "Report on Four Week Truce", Part III.

33. Weizman, *On Eagle's Wings*, pp. 71-74.

34. *Daily Express* (London), July 15, 1948.

35. Katzew, *South Africa's 800*, Chapter 3, p. 34.

36. Krammer, *The Forgotten Friendship*, pp. 92-93.

37. "Israel's First Fighters", *Flying Review International*, August 1967, p. 810.

38. McGunigal Interview with Giddy Lichtman.

39. McGunigal Interviews with Harold Kates and Stan Miller.

40. Katzew, *South Africa's 800*, Chapter 6, pp. 7-8.

41. *Ibid.*, Chapter 3, pp. 4-6.

42. *Ibid.*, Chapter 5, p. 25.

43. Israel Foreign Relations Files, RG 93.03, File 3, Box 126, Comay to Adler, July 7, 1948.

44. Katzew, *South Africa's 800*, Chapter 5, pp. 31-33.

45. Israel Foreign Relations Files, RG 93.03, File 3, Box 126, "Memorandum for B. Gering on Medical Unit", July 25, 1948.

46. Katzew, *South Africa's 800*, Chapter 3, pp. 22-26.

47. Lorch, *The Edge of the Sword*, pp. 295-98.

48. Shahan, *The Wings of Victory*, p. 306.

49. (Munya) Meir Mardor, *A Secret Mission: Special Operations in Haganah Campaigns* (Tel Aviv, 1965), p. 292 (Hebrew).

50. Shahan, *The Wings of Victory*, pp. 315-16.

51. *Frontline*, December 12, 1948.

52. Irving Kaplansky Interview.

53. Mahal File, Tal to Dunkelman, May 25, 1948.
54. State Department Records, Palestine Reference File of Robert McClintock, Box 11, Gray to Secretary of State, June 16, 1948. (Henceforth McClintock File.)
55. Arthur Goldberg Interview; Interview with Sam Wasser, July 1979; Interview with Harold Lennett, April 1979; Interview with Len Waldman, August 1979.
56. State Department Records, 867N.01/4-548, Hart to Secretary of State, April 5, 1948.
57. Robert St. John, *Shalom Means Peace* (New York, 1949), pp. 34-37.
58. *Ibid.*, pp. 38-40; State Department Records, 501.BB Palestine/6-1448, Marshall to American Consulate, Marseilles, June 14, 1948.
59. Sachar, *A History of Israel*, p. 329.
60. Interview with Ben Ocopnik, May 1979; Irving Kaplansky Interview.
61. St. John, *Shalom Means Peace*, pp. 39-40.
62. *Ibid.*, pp. 44-45.
63. Ben Ocopnik Interview.
64. *Ibid.*
65. Mediators Files, DAG 13/3.3.0, Box 7, "Altalena" Incident, "Conversation between Captain Virully and the Captain of the S.S. Altalena", n.d.
66. *Ibid.*, "Verbal Report by Col. Bonde on the incident, involving the Irgun and the Haganah, which took place on the shore of Nathaya [sic] and Tel Aviv on June 21st and 22nd"; Luttwack and Horowitz, *The Israeli Army*, p. 382.
67. State Department Records, United States Mission to the United Nations Records, RG 84, Box 87, Eban to Ross, June 24, 1948.
68. Interview with Yale Joffe, March 1979; Luttwack and Horowitz, *The Israeli Army*, p. 39.
69. Yale Joffe, Arthur Goldberg, and Harold Lennett Interviews; Interview with Harvey Sirlin, June 1979.
70. Yale Joffe Interview.
71. Dupuy, *Elusive Victory*, pp. 72-73.
72. Joe Weiner Interview.
73. Dunkelman, *Dual Allegiance*, pp. 236-41.

Chapter 8

1. Joe Weiner Interview.
2. *Ibid.*, Interview with Haim Laskov, September 1979.
3. Haim Laskov Interview.
4. Dunkelman, *Dual Allegiance*, pp. 244-45.
5. *Ibid.*, pp. 249-55; Lorch, *The Edge of the Sword*, p. 323.
6. Haim Laskov Interview.
7. Dunkelman, *Dual Allegiance*, pp. 257-58.
8. Joe Weiner Interview.
9. *Ibid.*
10. *Ibid.*; Dunkelman, *Dual Allegiance*, pp. 259-61.
11. Moshe Carmel, *The Northern Campaigns* (Tel Aviv, 1949), p. 207.
12. Dunkelman, *Dual Allegiance*, pp. 267-68; Lorch, *The Edge of the Sword*, p. 326.
13. *Ha Olam Hazeh*, July 9, 1980, pp. 34-35.
14. Foreign Office Records, FO 371/78511, Haifa to Foreign Office, July 18, 1948.
15. Dunkelman, *Dual Allegiance*, pp. 327-29.
16. *Ibid.*, pp. 249-55, 257-58.
17. *Ibid.*, p. 247.
18. Haim Laskov Interview; Joe Weiner Interview.
19. Haim Laskov Interview.
20. Arthur Goldberg Interview.
21. Harvey Sirlin Interview.
22. Arthur Goldberg Interview.
23. Katzew, *South Africa's 800*, Chapter 7, Part 1, p. 18.
24. Lionel Druker Interview.
25. Dupuy, *Elusive Victory*, p. 76.
26. Kurtzman, *Genesis 1948*, pp. 144-46.
27. State Department Records, 501.BB Palestine/7-1348, Lippincott to Secretary of State, July 13, 1948.
28. Lorch, *The Edge of the Sword*, p. 337.
29. Kurtzman, *Genesis 1948*, pp. 599-600.
30. *Ibid.*, pp. 577-79.
31. *Jerusalem Post*, October 24, 1979.
32. Katzew, *South Africa's 800*, Chapter 7, Part 1, p. 11.
33. *Ibid.*, pp. 10-11.
34. "Acts of Heroism Performed by Mahal Soldiers", *D'var Hashavua*, No. 18, 12/5/49, p. 8.

35. Kagan, *The Secret Battle for Israel*, p. 101.
36. Interview with H. P. Marks, October 1979.
37. Slater, *The Pledge*, p. 313.
38. H. P. Marks Interview.
39. State Department Records, 711.00111 Armament Control/3-2849, Emerick to Commissioner of Customs, March 25, 1948; /7-2748, Neal to Cummins, July 27, 1948; /7-2248, Neal to Cummins, July 22, 1948.
40. H. P. Marks Interview.
41. W. A. B. Douglas to author, December 14, 1979. Douglas quotes Diary of RCAF Station Dartmouth.
42. State Department Records, 501.BB Palestine/7-748, Atherton to Secretary of State, July 7, 1948.
43. *Ibid.*, 711.00111 Armament Control/7-1248, Klieforth to Secretary of State, July 12, 1948.
44. *Ibid.*, 711.00111 Armament Control/7-2848, Azores to Secretary of State, July 29, 1948.
45. *Ibid.*, 711.00111 Armament Control/7-1448, Foster Memorandum, July 14, 1948.
46. *Ibid.*, 711.00111 Armament Control/7-1948, Klieforth to Secretary of State, July 19, 1948.
47. *Ibid.*
48. H. P. Marks Interview.
49. State Department Records, 711.00111 Armament Control/7-1948, Klieforth to Secretary of State, July 19, 1948.
50. *Ibid.*, 711.00111 Armament Control/7-2248, Neal to Cummins, July 27, 1948.
51. *Ibid.*, 711.00111 Armament Control/7-1848, Marshall to American Consul, Ponta Delgada, July 19, 1948.
52. *Ibid.*, 711.00111 Armament Control/7-2448, Macveagh to Secretary of State, July 24, 1948.
53. *Ibid.*, 711.00111 Armament Control/8-3048, Hickerson to Anderson, August 30, 1948.
54. Katzew, *South Africa's 8oo*, Chapter 7, Part 2, p. 4.
55. Interview with Bill Katz, October 1979.
56. Minnich, "The Queen's Last Battle...", p. 23.
57. *Ibid.*; Mardor, *Haganah*, pp. 268-70.
58. Mardor, *Haganah*, pp. 268-70; Bill Katz Interview.
59. Jules Cuburnek Flight Log.

60. Foreign Office Records, FO 371/68511, Haifa to Foreign Office, July 18, 1948.
61. Ibid., FQ 371/68813/E 9714, Damascus to Foreign Office, July 18, 1948.
62. Katzew, South Africa's 800, Chapter 7, Part 2, pp. 1-2; Interview with Eddy Kaplansky, October 1979.
63. Krammer, The Forgotten Friendship, pp. 97-98.
64. Foreign Office Records, FO 371/68638/13371, Plant to Balfour, November 30, 1948.
65. Krammer, The Forgotten Friendship, p. 99.
66. Persson, Mediation and Assassination, pp. 158-67.

Chapter 9
1. "Diary of Locky Fainman".
2. Ibid.; Dunkelman, Dual Allegiance, p. 272.
3. Fainman Diary.
4. Persson, Mediation and Assassination, pp. 168-70.
5. Sachar, A History of Israel, pp. 336-39.
6. Dupuy, Elusive Victory, pp. 90-91; Kurtzman, Genesis 1948, pp. 621 ff.
7. Lorch, The Edge of the Sword, pp. 396-97.
8. Foreign Office Records, FO 371/68414/E 10178, Amman to Foreign Office, July 27, 1948.
9. Ibid., FO 371/68414/E 10150, Amman to Foreign Office, July 28, 1948.
10. Ibid., FO 371/68414/E 10342, Baghdad to Foreign Office, August 2, 1948.
11. State Department Records, 867N.01/11-148, Holmes to Secretary of State, November 1, 1948, Enclosure Three.
12. Foreign Office Records, FO 371/68414/E 10342, Baghdad to Foreign Office, August 2, 1948.
13. Ibid., FO 371/68419/E 10895, Alexander to Bevin, August 4, 1948.
14. Ibid., FO 371/68419/E 10614, Alexander to Bevin, August 6, 1948.
15. Ibid., FO 371/68419/E 11154, Foreign Office to Washington, August 19, 1948.
16. Ibid., FO 371/68419/E 11154, Foreign Office to Washington, August 21, 1948.
17. Ibid., FO 371/68419/E 11184, Bevin to Alexander, August 25, 1948.
18. Slater, The Pledge, p. 308; State Department Records, 711.00111

Armament Control/7-2148, Quarton to Secretary of State, July 21, 1948.

19. State Department Records, 501.BB Palestine/7-3148, Roberts to Secretary of State, August 2, 1948.

20. Mediators Files, DAG 13/3.3.0, Box 6, "Embargo on War Materials", Lundstrom to Vigier, September 8, 1948.

21. Lorch, The Edge of the Sword, p. 395.

22. Ibid., p. 385.

23. Ibid., p. 387.

24. Ibid., p. 390.

25. Interview with A. D. Gelmon, March 1979; Harvey Sirlin Interview.

26. Mahal File, "Report of Captain Jean Schiffer...", August 20, 1948.

27. Ibid., "R. Feigin Meeting with T. Eytan", August 26, 1948.

28. Ibid., "Confidential Report About T. Eytan", September 8, 1948.

29. Katzew, South Africa's 800, Chapter 10, pp. 2, 7-13.

30. David Ben Gurion, The Restored State of Israel (Tel Aviv, 1969), pp. 205-06.

31. Smoky Simon Interview.

32. Interview with Danny Cravitt, November 1979.

33. Shahan, The Wings of Victory, pp. 295-96.

34. McGunigal Interview with Dave Panar.

35. Foreign Office Records, FO 371/68638/E 14202, Plant to Balfour, November 2, 1948; and E 12671, Secretary of State, Colonies, to Lord Winster, September 18, 1948; Kagan, The Secret Battle for Israel, pp. 110-11; Robert Jackson, The Israeli Air Force Story: The Struggle for Middle East Aircraft Supremacy Since 1948 (London, 1970), pp. 38-39.

36. Foreign Office Records, FO 371/68638/E 12671, signature unreadable to Vile, September 23, 1948; State Department Records, 711.00111 Armament Control/5-1149, "Letter Received from London by British Embassy, Washington", May 11, 1949; Kagan, The Secret Battle for Israel, pp. 114-15.

37. Danny Rosin Interview.

38. Bill Katz Interview.

39. Danny Cravitt Interview; Katzew, South Africa's 800, Chapter 11.

40. McGunigal Interview with Hyman Goldstein.

41. Kagan, The Secret Battle for Israel, pp. 116-17.

42. Mardor, *Haganah*, pp. 270-71; Krammer, *The Forgotten Friendship*, pp. 119-20.
43. State Department Records, McClintock File, Box 12, Erhardt to Secretary of State, October 11, 1948.
44. State Department Records, 711.00111 Armament Control/9-1348, Confidential memorandum on "Lineas Aereas de Panama, S.A. Clandestine Operations", September 13, 1948.
45. Dunkelman, *Dual Allegiance*, p. 271.
46. Dupuy, *Elusive Victory*, pp. 88-89.
47. Mardor, *Haganah*, pp. 272-73.
48. *Ibid.*, pp. 273-74.
49. Interview with Jack Doyle, June 1979; Eddy Kaplansky Interview; Morris Beck Interview; Danny Cravitt Interview; W. H. Novick Interview.
50. "Bill to Akie", August 26, 1948, in possession of W. H. Novick.
51. Mardor, *Haganah*, p. 277.
52. *Ibid.*, pp. 276-77.
53. Aharon Remez Interview; Jules Cuburnek Interview; Sam Lewis Interview.
54. Katzew, *South Africa's 800*, Chapter 8, p. 7.
55. *Ibid.*, Chapter 13, pp. 8-10; Shahan, *The Wings of Victory*, pp. 310-12.
56. Mahal File, Mahal Special Fund Payment Records, July 31, 1948.
57. Katzew, *South Africa's 800*, Chapter 12, p. 8.
58. Interview with Lee Harris, December 1979.
59. Mahal File, D. Lou Harris to Canadian Troops, September 28, 1948.
60. Dave Panar Interview.
61. Krammer, *The Forgotten Friendship*, pp. 99-100; Kagan, *The Secret Battle for Israel*, pp. 122-24.
62. Krammer, *ibid.*, pp. 100-02; Kagan, *ibid.*, p. 124.
63. Krammer, *ibid.*, p. 102; Dave Panar Interview.
64. Krammer, *ibid.*, p. 103; Morris Beck Interview.
65. Krammer, *ibid.*, pp. 102-03; Kagan, *The Secret Battle for Israel*, p. 125.
66. Katzew, *South Africa's 800*, Chapter 12, pp. 25-26.
67. Interview with Sydney Cohen, October 1979.
68. Boris Senior Interview.
69. Mediator's Files, DAG 13/3.3.0, Box 15, Spitfires–Rhodes, Part III, Bunche to Riley, October 3, 1948.

70. Foreign Office Records, FO 371/68638, Hoyland to Tahourdin, October 5, 1948.
71. Mardor, *Haganah*, pp. 179-281.
72. Luttwack and Horowitz, *The Israeli Army*, pp. 46-47. A different version of these events is given in Sachar, *A History of Israel*, p. 340: "In fact, undetected by United Nations observers, the Israelis themselves had dynamited the trucks." He cites no source for this.

Chapter 10
1. Lorch, *The Edge of the Sword*, pp. 424-25.
2. Smoky Simon Interview; Danny Rosin Interview; Lorch, *The Edge of the Sword*, pp. 424-25.
3. Danny Rosin Interview.
4. *Ibid.*
5. Smoky Simon Interview.
6. Sachar, *A History of Israel*, pp. 271-72, 339 ff.
7. Lorch, *The Edge of the Sword*, pp. 441-42.
8. Katzew, *South Africa's 800*, Chapter 14, pp. 1-7; Mardor, *Haganah*, pp. 280-81.
9. McGunigal Interview with Rudy Augarten.
10. Lorch, *The Edge of the Sword*, pp. 413-15.
11. Norman Levi Interview.
12. Lorch, *The Edge of the Sword*, pp. 424-26.
13. Danny Rosin Interview.
14. Lorch, *The Edge of the Sword*, pp. 426-29.
15. Kurtzman, *Genesis 1948*, pp. 670-71.
16. The account is from Carmel, *The Northern Campaigns*, pp. 268-70; Dunkelman, *Dual Allegiance*, pp. 294-95; and Lorch, *The Edge of the Sword*, pp. 451-52.
17. Dupuy, *Elusive Victory*, p. 101.
18. Sam Wasser Interview.
19. Dunkelman, *Dual Allegiance*, p. 295.
20. *Ibid.*, pp. 295-96.
21. Lorch, *The Edge of the Sword*, pp. 454-55.
22. Fainman Diary.
23. See *Frontline*, December 12, 1948, for an example of these types of problems.
24. Zacks Papers, Vol. 2, File A, Olyan to Appel, October 7, 1948.

25. Fainman Diary.
26. Interview with Akiva Skidel, October 1979. Dunkelman, *Dual Allegiance*, p. 311, mentions an incident, but conveys the incorrect impression that all was solved by a Nursella pep talk to his troops.
27. Mahal File, "Inquiry Committee of Israel General Headquarters concerning the problems in the 72nd Battalion of the 7th Brigade".
28. Lee Harris Interview; Akiva Skidel Interview.
29. Akiva Skidel Interview.
30. Lee Harris Interview.
31. *Ibid.; Frontline*, May 15, 1949.
32. State Department Records, Rusk Book, Box 4, Lippincott to Secretary of State, June 23, 1948.
33. Lee Harris Interview.
34. Mahal File, Lee Harris to D. Lou Harris, December 8, 1948.
35. Lee Harris Interview.
36. Mahal File, D. Lou Harris to Lee Harris, December 13, 1948.
37. Danny Rosin Interview.
38. Eddy Kaplansky Interview.
39. Danny Rosin Interview.
40. Minnich, "The Queen's Last Battle...", p. 49.
41. Foreign Office Records, FO 371/68639, Alexander to Attlee, December 23, 1948.
42. *Ibid.*, FO 371/68582/E 11057, Haifa to Foreign Office, August 31, 1948.
43. *Ibid.*, FO 371/68639, Alexander to Attlee, December 23, 1948.
44. Sydney Cohen Interview.
45. Foreign Office Records, FO 371/68639/E 15621, Foreign Office to New York, December 15, 1948.
46. Krammer, *The Forgotten Friendship*, p. 105.
47. Kagan, *The Secret Battle for Israel*, pp. 133-38.
48. Dupuy, *Elusive Victory*, p. 109.
49. Kurtzman, *Genesis 1948*, pp. 727-29.
50. Katzew, *South Africa's 800*, Chapter 16, pp. 5-8.
51. *Ibid.*, p. 9.
52. Dupuy, *Elusive Victory*, p. 112.
53. McGunigal Interview with Jack Doyle.
54. Foreign Office Records, FO 371/75147/E 3286, Draft of State-

ment prepared for House of Commons. The portion of the draft mentioning the drop tanks was deleted in the final statement.

55. *Ibid.*, FO 371/75247/E 7667, Millet to Bunche, January 15, 1949.
56. Canada External Affairs Files, File 47B(S), Ford to Secretary of State for External Affairs, January 27, 1949.
57. Foreign Office Records, FO 371/75247/E 7667, Millet to Bunche, January 15, 1949.
58. McGunigal Interview with J. McElroy.
59. Mediator's Files, DAG 13/3.3.0, Box 23, "RAF Planes—Rhodes, January to June", "Secret and Personal" Report of January 8, 1949.
60. Dupuy, *Elusive Victory* p. 123.

Bibliography

I State Papers and Government Records
1. Canada
Public Archives of Canada
   Department of External Affairs Records
   Department of Transport Records
   Privy Council Office Records
Department of External Affairs
   Department of External Affairs Files
2. Great Britain
Public Records Office
   Records of the Colonial Office
   Records of the Foreign Office
3. Israel
Military (Israel Defence Forces) and Defence Establishment Archives
   Mahal File
Israel State Archives
   Foreign Relations Files
Haganah Archives
   Intelligence Files
   Pundik Papers
Central Zionist Archives
   Files of the American Section, World Zionist Organization, New
      York
   Zionist Organization of Canada, Minutes and Correspondence
   Special File (K14A/110)

4. United Nations
United Nations Archives
  Mediators Files
5. United States
National Archives
  General Records of the Department of State
  Records of the Army General Staff, Plans and Operations Division

II Private Papers and Diaries
1. Canada
Canadian Jewish Congress Archives (Montreal)
  Caiserman Papers
  Palestine Collection
Ottawa Jewish Historical Society
  Harold Shaffer Collection
Provincial Archives of Manitoba
  Jewish Historical Society of Western Canada Collection
Public Archives of Canada
  Joseph N. Frank Papers
  Samuel J. Zacks Papers
  Zionist Organization of Canada Papers
Privately Held
  Sydney P. Cadloff, papers and letters
  Willliam H. Novick, letters
  Victory Equipment & Supply Co. Ltd., records
2. Israel
Haganah Archives
  Ben Gurion Diary
3. United States
Truman Library
  Clifford Papers
  Wolfsohn Papers
Privately Held
  Diary of the late "Locky" Fainman

III Interviews (conducted by the author)

1. Canada

Appel, Moe
Baumholz, Joe
Beck, Morris
Brown, Max
Cadloff, Sydney P.
Cappell, Murray
Chetner, Dov
Cooper, M.
Doyle, Jack
Drache, Sam
Druker, Lionel
Drutz, Dave
Frank, Joseph N.
Freeman, Harold
Frieman, Arnold
Gelmon, A. D.
Goldstein, Jack
Good, Phillip
Gross, Jerry
Hamovitch, Ralph
Heaps, Leo
Hurtig, Jack
Hyman, Len
Joffe, Yale
Kaplansky, Dave
Kaplansky, Irving
Kates, Harold
Kettner, Frank
Kogan, Bernard
Lennett, Harold
Levi, Norman
Levine, A.
Nemetz, D.
Novick, W. H.
Ocopnik, Ben
Orloff, Harold
Panar, Dave
Peck, W. H.

Reiter, W.
Rosenberg, S. G.
Ruvinsky, Art
Secter, John and Lee
Shulemson, Sydney
Siegel, A. J.
Sirlin, Harvey
Solsberg, A. (conducted by E. Silverman
Wasser, Sam
Wilson, C. D.

2. Israel

Aron, Wellesley
Cohen, Sydney
Cravitt, Danny
Cuburnek, Jules
Goldberg, Arthur
Harris, John
Harris, Lee
Kaplansky, Eddy
Katz, Bill
Kollek, Teddy
Laskov, Haim
Lewis, Sam
Marks, H. P.
Naturman, M.
Remez, Aharon
Rosin, Danny
Senior, Boris
Shamir, Shlomo
Simon, Harry (Smoky)
Skidel, Akiva
Yurman, Shlomo

3. United States

Chinsky, Eddy
Eisner, Harry
Geberer, Harlow
Waldman, Len
Weiner, Joe (conducted by S. Silverman)

IV Interview Transcripts (conducted c. 1968 by J. McGunigal)

Augarten, Rudy McElroy, J.
Doyle, Jack Miller, Stan
Goldstein, Hyman Nachman, Harvey
Kates, Harold Panar, Dave
Lichtman, Giddy

V Newspapers and Periodicals

The Congress Bulletin (Montreal) The Jerusalem Post
The Daily Express (London) L'Unita (Rome)
D'var Hashavua Ma'arachot (Tel Aviv)
Frontline (Tel Aviv) Maclean's Magazine (Toronto)
The Globe and Mail (Toronto) The Miami Pictorial
Ha Olam Ha'zeh (Tel Aviv) The Gazette (Montreal)
Haganah Speaks (New York) The Ottawa Journal
Il Messagero (Rome) The Times (London)
Inter Office Information
(Montreal, Canadian Jewish
Congress)

VI Books, Articles and Unpublished Manuscripts

Allon, Yigal. Shield of David: The Story of Israel's Armed Forces. New
   York: Random House, 1970.
Antonius, George. The Arab Awakening. New York: Capricorn Books,
   1965.
Avriel, Ehud. Open The Gates! The Dramatic Personal Story of 'Illegal'
   Immigration to Israel. London: Weidenfeld and Nicolson, 1975.
Ayalon, Avraham. Givati Brigade During the War of Independence. Tel
   Aviv: Ma'arachot, 1959. (Hebrew)
Ben David, Judah. Sword in Foreign Lands: The Haganah in Europe,
   1945-1948. Tel Aviv: Ma'arachot, 1978. (Hebrew)
Ben Gurion, David. The Restored State of Israel. Tel Aviv: Am-Oved
   Publishers, 1969. (Hebrew)
Bethell, Nicholas. The Palestine Triangle: The Struggle Between the
   British, the Jews and the Arabs, 1935-1948. London: Andre Deutsch,
   1979.
Canadian Jews in World War Two. 2 volumes. Montreal: Canadian
   Jewish Congress, 1947.
Carmel, Moshe. The Northern Campaigns. Tel Aviv: Ma'arachot, 1949.
   (Hebrew).

263

Collins, Larry, and Dominique Lapierre. *O Jerusalem*. New York: Pocket Books, 1973.

Davis, J. M, H. A. Martin, and J. A. Whittle. *The Curtiss C-46 Command*. Air Britain, 1978.

Dupuy, Trevor N. *Elusive Victory: The Arab Israeli Wars, 1947-1974*. New York: Harper & Row, 1978.

Elon, Amos. *Herzl*. New York: Holt Rinehart and Winston, 1975.

Encyclopedia Judaica. New York: Macmillan, 1972.

Eytan, Teddy. *Neguev - L'Héroique Naissance de l'Etat d'Israel*. Paris: 1949.

Hadar, M. and Y. Ofer, eds. *The Israeli Air Force*. Tel Aviv: Ministry of Defence, 1971. (Hebrew)

Heckelman, A. Joseph. *American Volunteers and Israel's War of Independence*. New York: Ktav Publishing House, 1974.

Israeli, Josef. *Security Mission*. Tel Aviv: Am-Oved Publishers, 1972. (Hebrew)

Jackson, Robert. *The Israeli Air Force Story: The Struggle for Middle East Aircraft Supremacy Since 1948*. London: Tandem, 1970.

Kagan, Benjamin. *The Secret Battle for Israel*. New York and Cleveland: World Publishing, 1966.

Katzew, Henry. *South Africa's 800: The Story of Volunteers in Israel's War of Birth*. Unpublished manuscript, n.d., n.p.

Kimche, Jon, and David Kimche. *Both Sides of the Hill: Britain and the Palestine War*. London: Secker and Warburg, 1960.

Kollek, Teddy, and Amos Kollek. *For Jerusalem: A Life by Teddy Kollek*. New York: Random House, 1978.

Krammer, Arnold. *The Forgotten Friendship: Israel and the Soviet Bloc, 1947-53*. Urbana: University of Illinois Press, 1974.

Kurtzman, Dan. *Genesis 1948: The First Arab-Israeli War*. New York: Signet, 1970.

Lorch, Netanel. *The Edge of the Sword: Israel's War of Independence, 1947-1949*. Jerusalem: Massada Press, 1961.

Luttwack, Edward, and Dan Horowitz. *The Israeli Army*. New York: Harper & Row, 1975.

Ma'arachot. June 1978.

Mahal Comes to Israel. Study prepared by Public Opinion Research Unit of the Psychological Research Unit, Mobilization Branch, IDF Headquarters in 3 parts (separate booklets): A) Research on acclimatization of Mahal to Israel and its people; B) Research on programs of those who intend to settle in Israel; C) Research on attitudes of Mahal to army life. (Hebrew)

Mallin, Jay, and Robert K. Brown. *Merc: American Soldiers of Fortune.* New York: Signet, 1979.

Mardor, Munya M. *Haganah (Strictly Illegal).* New York: New American Library, 1964.

Mardor, (Munya) Meir. *A Secret Mission: Special Operations in Haganah Campaigns.* Tel Aviv: Ma'arachot, 1965. (Hebrew)

Mason, Francis K. *Archive Bristol Beaufighter.* London: Container Publications, n.d.

Meir Pail. *The Emergence of Zahal (I.D.F.).* Tel Aviv: Zmora, Bitan, Modan, 1979. (Hebrew)

Minnich, Mike. "The Queen's Last Battle: The Story of Israel's Three Bomber, B-17 Air Force!" *Wings,* February 1981, pp. 20-23.

Pearlman, Moshe, and David Ben Gurion. *David Ben Gurion Looks Back in Talks with Moshe Pearlman.* London: Weidenfeld and Nicolson, 1965.

Persson, Sune O. *Mediation and Assassination: Count Bernadotte's Mission to Palestine in 1948.* London: Ithaca Press, 1979.

Rubenstein, Murray, and Richard Goldman. *Shield of David: An Illustrated History of the Israeli Air Force.* Englewood Cliffs, N.J.: Prentice-Hall, 1978.

Sachar, Howard M. *A History of Israel: From the Rise of Zionism to Our Time.* New York: Alfred Knopf, 1976.

Schiff, Z. *A History of the Israeli Army (1870-1974).* San Francisco: Straight Arrow Books, 1974.

Shahan, Avigdor. *The Wings of Victory.* Tel Aviv: Am Hassefer, 1966. (Hebrew)

Sharef, Zeef. *Three Days.* New York: Doubleday, 1962.

Shatkai, Adam. *The Life and Youth of Squadron A.* Tel Aviv: M. Newman, 1949. (Hebrew)

Silverberg, Robert. *If I Forget Thee O Jerusalem.* New York: Pyramid Books, 1972.

Slater, Leonard. *The Pledge.* New York: Pocket Books, 1972.

Slonim, Shlomo. "The 1948 American Embargo on Arms to Palestine". *Political Science Quarterly.* Vol. 94, No. 3, pp. 495-514.

Slutzki, Yehuda. *The History of the Haganah,* III, No. 2. Tel Aviv: Am-Oved Publications, 1973. (Hebrew)

St. John, Robert. *Shalom Means Peace.* New York: Doubleday, 1949.

Talmi, Efraim. *Israel's Campaigns*. Tel Aviv: Ami-Mai, 1972. (Hebrew)
Weizman, Ezar. *On Eagles' Wings: The Personal Story of the Leading Commander of the Israeli Air Force*. New York: Macmillan, 1976.
Wilson, Evan M. *Decision on Palestine*. Stanford: Hoover Institution Press, 1979.
Yahil, Leni. *The Rescue of Danish Jewry: Test of A Democracy*. Philadelphia: Jewish Publication Society, 1969.
Yizkor-In Memoriam: Comprising Biographies of the Fallen in the Israel War of Independence. Tel Aviv: Ministry of Defence, 1955. (Hebrew)

Index of Personal Names

Abdullah, King, 175, 192, 224
Abromovici, Robert Adam, 30
Adelman, Major Ben, 60, 61, 79
Agronsky, Danny, 89, 90, 112, 113, 133, 134
Alexander, A. V., 26, 181, 182
Allenby, General, 3
Allon, Yigal, 192, 207, 218, 219-20, 221, 231
Alon, Modi, 118, 123, 199, 200, 226
Ambrosini, Angelo, 83
Andrews, Stanley, 202, 225
Appel, Moe, 47
Arazi, Yehuda, 22-23, 34, 35, 37, 38, 39, 83, 133
Arias, Gilberto, 41
Aron, Major Wellesley, 36, 54-56, 57, 58
Attlee, Clement, 26, 129
Auerbach, Hal, 87, 96, 97, 121
Augarten, Rudy, 206
Austin, Senator Warren, 33, 127
Avidan, Shimon, 123
Avriel, Ehud, 23, 30-31, 75, 140

Balfour, Arthur, 3, 4
Balfour, Sir John, 127
Barker, Lieutenant-General Evelyn, 43
Bartz, Gideon, 147
Baumholz, Joe, 45-46, 47, 48
Beane, James B., 132, 133
Beeley, Harold, 127
Begin, Menachem, 9, 150

Bell, J. Bowyer, xviii
Bellefond, Martin B., 40-41
Ben Gurion, David, 10, 99, 145, 150, 153, 197
    organizes defence, 20-23, 30, 34, 36, 37, 44, 49
    proclaims creation of State of Israel, 108-109
    searches for foreign volunteers, 51, 52, 54, 185, 186
    strategy for war, 82, 126, 192-93, 204, 221
Bernadotte, Count Folke
    administers ceasefire (June 1948), 129, 136-37, 140, 152, 154
    arranges second truce (July 1948), 175-76, 178
    assassinated, 179, 196
    proposes peace plan (July 1948), 153, 156
    revises peace plan (Sept. 1948), 178-79
Bernstein, Nahum, 36, 38, 39, 87
Beurling, George F. "Buzz," 74-75, 113, 114, 226
Bevin, Ernest, 129, 180, 181, 182
Bidmead, A.J., 76
Blackwood, Jimmy, 189
Blank, Jack, 150, 151
Blau, Tuxie, 94, 95, 111, 112, 199
Brown, Max, 78, 98
Brunton, Ray, 142, 143
Bunche, Dr. Ralph, 223

267

268

Index of Subjects and Places

271

Aqir, 14, 24. *See also* Ekron.
Arab Higher Committee, 13
Arab Legion, 18-19, 25, 98, 135, 175, 180, 181, 192, 224, 229
   fighting around Jerusalem, 109-110, 125-26, 128, 130, 135, 156, 166
Arab Liberation Army, 17, 19, 33, 82, 110, 154, 155-56, 157, 160, 161, 164, 174, 177, 183, 191, 192, 210, 211, 212
Arabs of Palestine
   demands following W.W. II, 16
   military forces, 18, 19, 82
   reaction to Balfour Declaration, 4, 5
   refugees, 76, 92, 166-67, 178, 179
   uprisings (1920-47), 1-2, 5, 6, 7, 13
Argentina, volunters from, 69
l'Armée Juif, 69
Armoured cars: home-made "sandwich," 32, 160
Arms procurement, by Jews, xiii, xvi, xvii, xviii, 21-23, 49. *See also* Aircraft.
   from Canada, 44-48
   continues during truces, 137, 140, 179-80, 182
   from Czechoslovakia, *see* Czechoslovakia: arms from.
   from the U.S., 34-41
Army, Israeli, *see* Haganah; Irgun; Israel Defence Forces; Lehi; Palmach.
Ashdod bridge, air attack at, 118-19, 123
Aviron, 21, 23, 24

Bacher's Farm, 64-65, 68
Balak, Operation, 120-23, 134, 136, 190-91
Balfour Declaration (1917), xiv, 2, 3-4, 5, 6, 11
Barak, Operation, 102
Bash-shit (town), attack on, 102-106
Beersheba (town), 204, 206, 209, 219, 220
Berosh, Operation, 163
Bet Hanun, 205-206, 208
Bilu, Camp, 101, 103
"Bombchucking," 124, 130, 173, 206, 216
"Burma Road" into Jerusalem, 126, 135, 156

Cairo, bombing of, 171-72
Canada
   arms and equipment from 44-47, 48
   planes from, 47-48, 216
   volunteers from, *see* Canadian volunteers.
Canadian volunteers, 76-79, 98-99, 101
   in "Anglo-Saxon" (72nd) Battalion of Seventh Brigade, 148, 183
   attack on Bash-shit, 102-106
   "Canadian platoon" in Givati Brigade, 103-106, 148
   in Eighth Brigade, 165
   in Israeli Air Force, 188, 190
   internment in Lebanon of *Marine Carp* volunteers, 115-18
   morale problems among, 78-79, 101, 146-48, 196-97, 213, 215
   recruitment of, 60-64, 73-75, 77
   and sinking of *Altalena*, 150-52
Canadian War Assets Corporation, 46, 47
Carmeli Brigade, 101, 156, 157, 159, 163, 211
Castiglione del Lago airport, 83, 84, 85, 112
Catania airport, Sicily, 112, 113, 120
Ceasefire, *see* Truce.
"Commando Français, Le," 185, 209, 220
Committee for Overseas Mobilization, 53, 72
Costelumbra, Italy, 100
Cyprus detention camps, 28, 137, 138, 144, 145
Czechoslovakia
   arms from, xvi, 30-32, 75-76, 82, 136, 139, 140, 173-74, 190-91, 229, 230
   flight instruction in, 141-42
   planes from, xvii, 118-23, 136, 140, 174, 190, 197-200, 219

Damascus, bombing of, 130, 173
Dani, Operation, 165
Deir Yassin (village), 76
Dekel, Operation, 156, 157, 161-62
Denmark, volunteers from, 69

272

273

Radio Communications Engineering (company), 36, 37
Radio equipment from Canada, 48
Rafah (town), 221
Ramat David airfield, 172, 173, 186, 189, 202, 203, 216, 225
Ramle, 165, 166, 175, 179
  evacuation of Arabs from 166-67
Rappaport's Bottle and Supply Company, 48
Reconstruction Finance Corporation, 38, 39
Recruitment of foreign volunteers, xvi, xvii, xviii, 49, 51, 69, 72
  in Canada, 60-64, 73-75, 77
  guidelines for, 53
  in South Africa, 42-43, 64-69, 73
  during truce, 137-38
  in U.S., 51, 52, 55-59, 73
Refugees, Arab, 76, 92, 166-67, 178, 179
Refugees, Jewish, 14, 15, 34, 51, 70, 99, 100, 114, 148
  Arabs and, 16
  Great Britain and, 7, 9, 12, 28, 70-71
  immigrant ships, 79, 99
  in Jewish forces, see Gahal.
Revolt of Palestine Arabs (1936), 6, 7
Rhodes, 88, 89, 90, 200, 219
Riots in Palestine (1920-1947), 1-2, 5, 6, 7, 13
Roads
  "Burma Road" into Jerusalem, 126, 135
  Majdal-Hebron highway, 207
  road from Tel-Aviv to Jerusalem, 75-76, 82, 99, 175
Rome, Italy: Haganah air operations in, 89, 90, 91
Royal Air Force reconnaissance flights, 217-18, 222-23, 229-30
Royal Canadian Air Force, 168, 169, 170
Royal Canadian Legion, Jewish branches of, 62, 77
Royal Canadian Mounted Police, 64, 169

Safed, 82, 134, 210
Saffuriya (village), 158, 159
Sasa (town), 210, 211, 212
Schipol Airport, Holland, 91, 140
Sdom, 189-90, 200, 216
Service Airways, 36, 39-40, 41, 56, 57, 58, 82, 83-90, 95-98, 108, 112-13, 167
Seventh Brigade, 114, 125, 126, 156, 157-58
  "Anglo-Saxon" (72nd) Battalion, 148, 183, 184, 191-92, 196, 212-14, 228
  fighting at Nazareth, 155-56, 158-62
  fighting in Upper Galilee, 210-12, 231
  foreign volunteers in, xviii, 148, 153-54, 155-56, 158-62, 177, 195-96, 231. See also "Anglo-Saxon" (72nd) Battalion, above.
Shafa Amr (town), 158, 159
Sherut Avir, 23-24, 57, 82
Shvitzers, 148
Societa Aeronautica Italiana (SAI), 83
Somaco (Belgian company), 91, 113
Sonneborn Institute, 35-37, 49
South Africa
  aircraft from, 41-42, 43-44, 67, 82, 92-95, 111-12
  medical personnel from, 142-45, 166-67, 177
  pro-Zionist attitude of, 42, 65
  recruitment of volunteers from, 42-43, 64-69, 73
  volunteers from, 99-100, 141, 146, 171, 183, 188, 189, 196
South African Jewish Ex-Service League, 66
South African League for Haganah, 66, 67
South African Zionist Federation, 42, 43, 65, 66, 67, 68, 196
Soviet Union, 175
  attitude to Israel, xvi, 31, 198
Special Night Squads, 7
Stern Gang, see Lehi.
Supply convoys, 32-33, 82, 192
  airlifting supplies, 81-82, 91, 138, 189-90, 216

Operation Dust, 193-94, 200-201, 230
Sykes-Picot Agreement, 5
Syria, 5, 179
Syrian Army, 17-18, 19, 25
  fighting in Israel, 110, 128, 130, 134,
  156, 162-64, 174, 210

Tamra, 177, 192, 195
Tanks, 164-65, 182, 207
Tarshiba (town), 210, 211
Tel Aviv, 10, 80, 81, 82, 122, 134, 141, 142,
  148
  Egyptian bombers attack, 109, 112,
  123, 173
  Egyptian troop advance on, 109, 118,
  119, 123, 127, 130, 135
  fighting between Irgun and IDF at,
  151
  opening of Tel Aviv-Jerusalem Road,
  75-76, 82, 99
"Tel Aviv Spring Fair," 48
Tel Kissan, 157
Tel Litvinsky army camp, 99, 100-101,
  153, 165
Teti (ship), 77, 79, 99
Tiberias, 76, 82
Tocuman airfield, Panama, 41, 86, 87,
  95, 120
Toussus le Noble airport, France, 91
Transjordan, 18, 138, 178, 179, 205. See
  also Arab Legion.
  appeals to Britain for resumption of
  arms shipments, 180
  receives arms from Britain, 127
Transshipment of supplies, xvi, 32, 48,
  229
Tretz training camp, 78-79
Treviso "incident," 133-34, 138
Truce, June 11 - July 8 1948, 129, 134, 135
  internment camps for immigrants of
  military age, 152
  U.N. truce supervision force, 136-37,
  151-52
Truce, July 18 - Dec. 22 1948, 175-76,
  178-79
  fighting continues, 177, 191-92, 216

truce supervisory force, 178, 183
  violations of arms embargo, 179-80,
  182
Tulkarm, bombing of, 172
Turkey, 3, 5

United Nations, xiii, xiv, xv, xix, 128,
  208-209, 219, 230
  ceasefires arranged by, 129, 175-76,
  221, 223
  fails to interfere in Arab invasion of
  Israel, 111, 127
  Special Committee on Palestine
  (UNSCOP), 14, 16, 27, 28
  truce supervisory forces, 136-37, 151-52,
  178, 183
  U.S. recommends U.N. trusteeship for
  Palestine, 33, 106, 107
  vote for partition, 14, 17, 31
United States
  aircraft from, see Aircraft: from the
  U.S.
  embargo on arms sales to Middle
  East, xvi, 25-26, 27, 28, 29, 35, 229
  Jewish weapons-procurement efforts
  in, 34-41
  opposes resumption of arms
  shipments by Britain, 181-82
  protests activities of Air Transport
  Command, 190-91
  pushes for ceasefire at U.N., 111, 127
  reaction to Bernadotte's peace plan,
  179
  recommends U.N. trusteeship for
  Palestine, 33, 106, 107
  recruitment of volunteers in, 51, 52,
  55-59, 73
  supports truces, 137-40, 175, 178
  threatens to lift arms embargo, 128
United Zionist Council, 45
United Zionist Purchasing Commission,
  45, 46
Urbe airfield, Italy, 90, 113
Urim airstrip, 200

Vaad Leumi, 10

Victory Equipment & Supply
Company Limited, 37, 45, 46, 48
Volunteers, foreign
in Air Force, see Air Force, Jewish:
foreign volunteers in.
"Anglo-Saxon" Battalion, 148, 183,
184, 191-92, 196, 212-14, 228
arrival of first, 76-79, 98-101, 114
and attack on Egyptian armies, 220
attitude of Israelis toward, 147, 215,
227, 228-29
from Canada, see Canadian
volunteers.
and capture of Nazareth, 155-62
contributions to Israeli victory, xvii,
229-32, 233
deployment in Jewish forces, xviii, 61,
98-99, 100, 101, 146, 147
in Eighth Brigade, xviii, 164-66, 207
from France, 69, 184-85
internment in Lebanon of volunteers
from Marine Carp, 115-18
in Landshut's gun company, 153,
162-64
medical personnel, 142-45, 166-67
memorials of, 225-26
morale problems among, see Morale
problems: among foreign
volunteers.
motives for serving, 69-75, 146
in Palmach, 183-84, 185
recruitment of, see Recruitment of
foreign volunteers.
salaries of, 63, 72, 79, 196, 197
in Seventh Brigade, xviii, 148, 153-54,
155-56, 158-62, 177, 195-96, 231. See
also "Anglo-Saxon" Battalion,
above.
and sinking of Altalena, 150-52
from South Africa, see South Africa:
volunteers from; see also medical
personnel, above.
training of, 58-59, 64-65, 68, 78-79,
98, 99, 101, 141-42
travel to Palestine, 59, 77, 78, 79, 138,
148-49, 183
after the War of Independence,
226-27

War Assets Administration, 38
Weapons, xvi, xvii
British arms shipments to Arabs, xvi,
25, 26-27, 28, 29, 111, 127, 128,
229-30
British embargo on sale to Palestine,
xvi, 24-25, 229
embargo during truce (June-July
1948), 134, 137, 138-40
procurement by Jews, see Aircraft;
Arms procurement, by Jews.
U.S. embargo on arms shipments to
Middle East, xvi, 25-26, 27, 28, 29,
35, 128, 229
Wedgwood (ship), 150, 151
White Paper on Palestine (Great
Britain, 1939), 6-7, 9, 14, 16, 77
Women's International Zionist
Organization, 145
World Zionist Organization, 4, 10

Yad Mordechai kibbutz, 118, 127
Yanuach (village), 211
Yehiam kibbutz, 81, 82
Yiftah Brigade, 193
Yishuv, xiv, xv, 2, 6, 11, 20, 33, 108-109
growth in, 10, 12
and White Paper on Palestine, 7, 9
Yugoslavia, xvi, 32, 173-74, 198-99, 219,
229

Zahal, see Israel Defence Forces.
Zatec airfield, Czechoslovakia, 119, 120,
121, 122, 132, 133, 134, 140, 171, 173,
190, 191
Zionism, xiv, 2, 3, 5
Arab view of, 5
British attitudes to, 4, 6-7, 9
demands following W.W. II, 16
Jewish attitudes to, 11, 12
South African Zionist Federation, 42,
43, 65, 66, 67, 68
Zionist Organization of America, 55
Zionist Organization of Canada, 44,
47, 63

278